AFRICAN AMERICAN HISTORY AND CULTURE

edited by

GRAHAM RUSSELL HODGES
COLGATE UNIVERSITY

CONTEMPORARY AFRICAN AMERICAN THEATER

AFROCENTRICITY IN THE WORKS OF LARRY NEAL, AMIRI BARAKA, AND CHARLES FULLER

NILGUN ANADOLU-OKUR

GARLAND PUBLISHING, Inc.
NEW YORK & LONDON / 1997

Library of Congress Cataloging-in-Publication Data

Anadolu-Okur, Nilgun, 1956–
    Contemporary African American theater : Afrocentricity in
the works of Larry Neal, Amiri Baraka, and Charles Fuller /
Nilgun Anadolu-Okur.
            p.   cm. — (Studies in African American history and
culture)
    Includes bibliographical references and index.
    ISBN 0-8153-2872-9 (alk. paper)
    1. American drama—Afro-American authors—History and
criticism. 2. American drama—20th century—History and criticism. 3. Neal, Larry, 1937–   —Criticism and interpretation.
4. Baraka, Imamu Amiri, 1934–   —Criticism and interpretation.
5. Fuller, Charles—Criticism and interpretation. 6. American
drama—African influences. 7. Afro-Americans in literature.
I. Title. II. Series.
PS338.N4A45 1997
812'.5409896073—dc21
                                                            97-16545

Printed on acid-free, 250-year-life paper
Manufactured in the United States of America

Dedicated to the loving memory of my father, Sahap Anadolu,
and to my son, Ali Murat, who believed in Mom.

Contents

Preface

"They rarely study African American dramatists," an African American playwright once said to me in response to my observation that the emphatic themes of African American drama are much different from the themes of European American drama. Indeed, this playwright's comment has since been confirmed in that I have found little critical analysis of African American theater based on theoretical aspects of drama. My research in this area was furthered during the years I taught American drama, with the help of some exceptional students. Subsequently, in 1988 a Fulbright post-doctoral research award at Temple University's African American Studies Department provided me with the opportunity to consolidate my concepts of African American drama. In this environment I was able to explore and discover the roots of African American theater. This undertaking has been both challenging and empowering.

Perusal of the texts of the Black Arts movement alongside those of the Black Theater movement provided a backdrop for my understanding of an African-centered world view. This inquiry soon evolved into the development of a framework for the critique of contemporary African American drama. Through reading texts by Larry Neal, Amiri Baraka, and Charles Fuller, I have been able to delineate the characteristics of this particular drama with a concomitant heightened appreciation of its value. More specifically, I have devised nine steps for the analysis of African American drama. The research has been rooted in and made possible by numerous factors: the study of Molefi K. Asante's works; the attainment of a position in the Department of African American Studies at Temple University, with its research environment devoted to Africalogical paradigms; and the full-time teaching of a diverse student body who have impressed upon me daily the power of their self-expression, both written and oral. Furthermore, immersion in this environment has strengthened my faith in the merits of multiculturalism.

Initially, the writings of Baraka seemed to provide the bulk of the material necessary to my book. Further research revealed, however, that Baraka's dramatic works allow for neither easy categorization nor straightforward comparison to works by other major African American playwrights. To illustrate: Baraka's ideas are definitely larger than the Black Arts movement itself, yet some of his work is far too indoctrinated to fit into a multicultural spectrum; nor do all his writings yield to a strictly African-centered interpretation. Meanwhile, another leader of the Black Arts movement, Larry Neal, is renowned as the precursor of the proponents of the African-centered world view. Charles Fuller enters the scene as one who continues a long tradition enriched by the developments that took place during the sixties' Black Arts and Black Theater movements. As many critics have observed, particularly in the wake of his 1982 Pulitzer-Prize-winning *A Soldier's Play*, Fuller excels in his style, mastery of technique, and commitment to truth in his material. Most significantly, his work yields to a new formulation which acknowledges African-centeredness in every aspect of life as it relates to African people worldwide.

The lessons inherent in Fuller's faithfulness to the preeminence of Africanness in African matters, without the need to claim universality or superiority, have guided this analysis. Add to this a milieu in which the multicultural characteristics of this nation are increasingly discussed and debated, and the necessary analytical path becomes even clearer. Moreover, pluralism without hierarchy, the main tenet of an Africalogical approach, points ironically to a possible reconciliation between the general construct of European American theater and drama, and African American theater and drama.

In view of these premises, I propose, firstly, that it is critical to examine the roots of contemporary African American drama in a different, more illuminating light. Secondly, African American drama needs to be evaluated using its own aesthetic standards and critical judgments, rather than as a supplement or hybrid within the genre of American drama. It is only through these two steps that African American drama can truly be understood in all its richness and complexity.

Introduction

Good morning, Revolution:
You're the very best friend
I ever had.
We gonna pal around together from now on.

—Langston Hughes, "Good Morning, Revolution"

The drama of the African's presence in the United States is the fundamental backdrop for any discussion of the role and function of black theater in the history of American dramatic criticism. Each element in the creation of culture is represented in the larger context of kidnappings, beatings, riots, resistance movements, and deaths during the enslavement of Africans from 1619 to 1865. A concurrent dramatic development in social interactions can be seen in the forms of verbal styles and physical responses created to deal with the peculiarities of this overarching drama of millions of Africans held in bondage by whites in a land foreign to both. The mastery of cunning, verbal resistance, cleverness, deceit, laughter, mystery, joy, suspense, and challenge would become the calling card of the African American theater because behind this theater was always the larger American drama of a racial crisis.

Unsurprisingly, critical studies of American drama have almost always focused on the European American theatrical tradition, ignoring, in large part, African American drama. The prevailing attitude towards any genre of African American creative production has been one of condescension and negation. As Toni Morrison asserts in *Playing in the Dark: Whiteness and the Literary Imagination*: "The traditional, canonical, American literature is free of, uninformed and unshaped by the four-hundred-year-old presence of, first Africans and then African Americans in the United States." She later adds: "Black people signified little or nothing in the imagination of white American writers."[1] For generations to come within the mainstream of American literature, African American literature provided a sub-title; far from being recognized as an autonomous entity, it was referred to as a by-product of American literature until at least the 1960s. These were the conditions out of which black literature grew in this land. Of course, from literary hegemony and negation, we can also trace cultural and social hegemony, as well as negation.

Although I do not agree with all that Samuel P. Huntington says in his recent book, *The Clash of Civilizations and the Remaking of World Order*, he makes an interesting point when he remarks: "The West may be 'unique' but its values are not universal." He adds: "The West had better shed the hubristic notion that its civilization is destined to spread its values across the globe. . . . Universalism is just a leftover from imperialism."[2] Such resentment against the claims of universalism often motivated by colonial attitudes has led to more democratic pursuits, of which the Afrocentric idea is the latest.

Essential differences that exist between cultures reveal themselves most explicitly in their literary creations and artistic aspirations. For instance, Janheinz Jahn in *Muntu* asserts that in Western poetry the image precedes the word. "Images are *ideas* in the Platonic sense, they are given in advance, even for the surrealists, who wanted to press on to new and deeper images through the use of trance and automatic writing." In African poetry, Jahn contends, "the *word is there before the image*. It is the word, *Nommo*, that creates the image."[3] Jahn believes that in the word there is a procreative force that transforms the things—the *Kintu*—into an image. The word has to be invoked in order to accomplish its task, as Aime Cesaire attests: "I have nothing but my word . . . It is enough to *name* the thing, and the *sense* appears in the *sign*."[4] The word itself produces, commands, and conjures; moreover, it is imperative. It speaks of the times and conditions as the poet wants them to be; not necessarily just past and present, but future, too. It is *projecting* life from within, as the poet makes it happen. Continuous transformation is the word's inherent characteristic and it is full of infinite potential. In Africa, newborn children's names are spoken into their ears by the father; only then do they begin life. In this sense the poet, too, becomes the *transformer* who speaks into the word and transforms it into an image, bringing force into action by means of utterance.

In examining the transformative power of the *Nommo* in African culture, it becomes apparent that differences between literatures exist and one has to be aware of these differences while maintaining an unbiased attitude. The problem we face today in terms of the dearth of viable intellectual theories in literary criticism is partly due to a lack in understanding the differences. African and African American literatures have their own aesthetic components that need to be recognized; this is the fundamental task of any writer-critic before any assessment can be made. Moreover, as described by Toni Morrison in *Playing in the Dark* (1992) and by Henry Louis Gates Jr. in his essay titled "Criticism in the Jungle" (1984), contemporary and future readers or writers of American literature need to draw maps of cultural geography that delineate the language and culture of the text. Readers and writers must rid themselves of the stigma of a "universal" character that does not apply to the varied texts that comprise American literature—texts that depend not only upon the location but also the origin of a particular work. For instance, any downtown bookstore or library in our neighborhoods reserves different spaces for books written by Leslie Mormon Silko, Audre Lorde, Maxine Hong Kingston, Ernest Hemingway, or Tennessee Williams. Why not utilize that same varied categorization in literary criticism? Objective evaluation, fairness towards the text, and an open mind free from preconceived notions serve not only the text but its critic too.

Within the general void that nullifies productive literary criticism in every genre, African American drama also suffers from an inevitable stigma that treats it as an appendage of the poetics of Aristotle and the numerous interpretations that spring from this source. Indeed, Aristotle considered drama to be a branch of poesis and its subdivisions to be tragedy, comedy, and related genres such as melodrama. The overriding structure of drama, in the Aristotelian vision, was a linear progression with reference to plot, character, and language. However, in the African American dramatic tradition, as Paul Carter Harrison emphasizes in his introduction to *Kuntu Drama*, "the event" rather than the play itself is of primary importance. What he meant by "the event" is the total accumulated effort in staging the play, from blocking the script to actors, make-up, and costumes; in other words, all the rites and rituals that take place on and off the stage. Harrison further illustrates his point as follows:

The souls of black folks cannot be dredged with carefully chosen words alone. If the soul is to be quickened, the event must own the sensate power and vitality of experience witnessed in the store-front church where the sins of natural life are assigned mythic relationships and focused through a cosmic source of light, utilizing those powerful Kuntu forces—Song, Dance and Drum—to capture the rhythms of that life, committing the community to a form of total engagement of body/spirit, thereby testifying to our continuation as an African people on this continent, in this unnatural mode of primal chaos.[5]

At one level of discussion, it is still possible to understand African American drama as a form which interacts with the European-derived forms because it is fundamentally an art form that has developed within the geographical and cultural boundaries of the United States. Whatever Africanisms it has inherited and imparts have merged and alloyed significantly with the Europeanisms that have been imposed on African peoples, their culture, and their aesthetic values for over four hundred years. In other words, African American drama has achieved its unique features due to the American context into which it was born. However, even with this understanding it must be recognized that African American drama is markedly different from European drama and is also not primarily a derivative of American drama. As Carlton Molette and Barbara Molette argue in *Black Theater: Premise and Presentation*, black theater and drama, as an art form, has existed in the United States since the arrival of the first group of Africans. This recognition causes the Molettes to further observe that "performance was not exactly as it would have been had it taken place in Africa instead of the United States."[6] It becomes evident that African American drama and theater is a legitimate outcome and product of African American culture.

Literature, arts, and drama naturally reflect the values of the culture that gives birth to them. In America, the values, traditions, and energies of black people coalesced, allowing them to define their unique place in a ravaging society by giving expression to themselves and their experiences through theater. However, what it is imperative for contemporary readers and critics of drama to understand is that the texts produced by numerous African American dramatists, from William Wells Brown to Ntozake Shange, suggest that new and different elements must be employed in the analysis of African American drama. Thus it must be recognized that not only has African American theater history been ignored and misinterpreted for many years, but it has also been considered non-existent under the pressure and scrutiny of a foreign set of values and standards.

Kariamu Welsh-Asante, whose extensive work on the *Umfundalai* school of thought constitutes one of the primary paradigms of the Afrocentric discipline, asserts that it is through associative symbols that "new energies are created, both individual and collective." These energies, Welsh-Asante indicates, "can sustain and manifest artistic renditions."[7] Moreover, she observes the influence of *Umfundalai*—which literally means "the essential" in Kiswahili—in all aspects of African art forms. Thus, the importance of understanding the impact of the African aesthetic on African American aesthetic forms becomes a crucial step in any African-centered analysis. To complicate matters, the convergence of African and European aesthetics has given birth to new aesthetic forms that continue to evolve and metamorphose. Welsh-Asante's 1996 dance piece titled "Herrero Women" illustrates this premise quite well. In it, she presents the mix of African and European influence on a given culture, in this case the impact of German on Namibian culture.

Yet even as we recognize outside influences, it must be acknowledged that unadulterated African dramatic forms exist and have existed for eons. As the records of ancient Ethiopia and Egypt become more available we will be able to make the necessary connections to demonstrate that drama, in its ancient ritualistic form in the Nile Valley, may have been carried to West Africa by migrations occurring over thousands of years. As importantly, the West Africans themselves developed within their own context outstanding dramas around epics such as Ozidi, Sundiata, and Woyengi. Nevertheless, the richness of Egyptian rituals, mythology, and traditional celebrations far exceeds that of other areas of the continent. Therefore, the following section is devoted to an analysis of Egyptian rituals and their impact upon Greek festivals. It is these festivals which initiated the birth of dramatic events and competitions in Greece.

Oscar G. Brockett asserts in *History of the Theatre* that Egypt influenced Greece in a considerable manner, but "never developed theatrically beyond ritualized performances, repeating the same ceremonies year after year for centuries," and eventually Greece "took the decisive step toward an autonomous theatre."[8] However, one must examine the premises underlying the disparate directions in theatrical development. In Egyptian life, the primary concern was that of abiding by the guiding principles of Ma'at—that is, Truth, Justice, and Righteousness—with an accompanying emphasis on the value of traditions. Consequently, in traditional African societies performing the ritual well, rather than displaying a contest to proclaim winners and losers, was the primary motivation. In Greece, on the other hand, through annual competitions in which the highest value was placed on introducing new scripts rather than maintaining the old texts, a variety of secular themes with high public appeal dominated the scene and eventually initiated the development of a new theatrical construct.

The history of Egyptian theater can be understood by referring to Brockett's analysis. He mentions the existence of more than fifty "pyramid texts" dating from 2800 to 2400 B.C., concluding that they may indicate the existence of Egyptian theatrical performances which utilized these texts as dramatic scripts. Although critics do not agree on the validity of the "pyramid texts" as dramatic scripts, there were other texts which denote the existence of performances, albeit in the form of rituals, dating back to 2500 B.C. By the time these texts came to light they were considered to be "traditional," placing their origin another century earlier. For instance, the "Memphite Drama" that was performed on the first day of spring commemorated the unification of Lower and Upper Egypt by King Menes around 3200 B.C. The important role of King Menes in ancient Egyptian history could not have been more majestically celebrated than through such a text depicting the double crowns and coronation ceremonies in two palaces. In *From Fetish to God in Ancient Egypt*, E.A. Wallis Budge indicates that this piece was in reality "the libretto of a drama or stage play which was probably acted when certain important festivals were celebrated at Memphis."[9] As a cultural center of majestic grandeur and the one-time capital of Egypt, the city of Memphis naturally hosted numerous celebrations, festivals, public events, and even funerals throughout its historic past. It is believed that the "Memphite Drama," the most popular text, was composed on one of these occasions during the first dynasty. It was rewritten by Shabako about 700 B.C. on a stone, which is now housed in the British Museum.[10] Another illuminating text is the "Abydos Passion Play," probably deriving its name from the city of Abydos. Based upon the myth of Osiris and Horus, it depicts death and resurrection, and presumably became a precursor of Greek plays that later dealt with similar themes.

The controversy surrounding the acceptance of these texts as the "earliest recorded theatrical productions" still continues.[11] Brockett provides numerous sources in an attempt to establish the connection between these texts and Egyptian origins of early theatrical performances. For instance, he mentions that a relief sculpture from a tomb at Saqqara depicts individuals during the performance of a dance, with some shown engaged in clapping accompaniment.[12] Additionally, an Egyptian deity named Bes is often depicted as a short man with a beard performing in the capacity of both dancer and musician. This deity, associated with amulets and frescoes discovered in Deir-el Medina, was known as the god of fertility and was also connected with childbirth, dance, and music.[13] Given these associations, Bes is probably a more suitable archetype than Osiris as the beginnings of theatrical festivities. After all, Osiris represented the underworld and funerary rites, while Bes conjures images of dance, song, music, and fertility.

Nor were indications of ancient Egyptian live performances limited to paintings or relief sculptures. For example, in *Civilization or Barbarism: An Authentic Anthropology* Diop mentions that even the royal family was part of a dramatic performance at one time: "Up to the first Tanite dynasty, the royal family itself acted in Osiris' drama. . . . Then later, only the priests would act, before the royal family, in the passion of Osiris, the mystery of his death, and resurrection."[14]

Whether it was to praise or pledge, ritual and performance were intertwined in the daily lives of Egyptians because there were no distinctions between the secular and the religious. It was probably because of such flexibility and fluidity in their world view that Egyptians adopted the wisdom of Ma'at as their governing principle.[15]

The intricacy of certain Egyptian architectural designs and structures within or around temples and burial sites—a long-time mystery for historians and scholars—also indicates the possibility of large and small performance spaces. One such example is the Step

Pyramid at Saqqara, built by the genius architect Imhotep for King
Zoser around 2778 B.C. The vast rectangular enclosure surrounding
the pyramid is suspected to originally have been built to provide a
performance space for the ceremonies of death and resurrection
initiated by Zoser at that time. What better place for such ceremonies
than a step pyramid, a symbol of eternity built to reach the sky, clouds,
and stars?

The most detailed description of the enclosure surrounding the
Step Pyramid appeared in a book by Sir Banister Fletcher, *A History of
Architecture on the Comparative Method*, published in New York in
1963. In many respects, Fletcher's description is in congruence with
the Molettes' initial thesis on "stage scenery":

> Surrounding the pyramid was a vast rectangular
> enclosure, 1790 ft from north to south and 912 ft
> wide, with a massive Tura limestone wall, 35 ft high,
> indented in the manner of the earlier mastaba
> facades. Around the walls were bastions, fourteen in
> all, and each had *stone false doors.* The only
> entrance was in a broader bastion near the southern
> end of the eastern face. In the fact that there is a
> small offering chapel (with stelae, offering table and
> a statue of Zoser) and a well-developed mortuary
> temple, containing two courts, a maze of corridors
> and many rooms, the buildings inside the enclosure
> show some relation to earlier developments of the
> mastaba; but these two buildings about the north face
> of the pyramid, instead of the east as was to be the
> common practice, and all *the rest of the structures
> are quite exceptional and unique to this complex.
> They are dummy representations of the palace of
> Zoser and the buildings used in connection with the
> celebration of his jubilee in his lifetime. Most of
> them therefore are solid, or almost so, comprised of
> earth or debris faced with Tura limestone. . . .* Just
> inside the enclosure entrance a narrow corridor runs
> deviously northwards to the Heb-Sud Court, the
> principal scene of this festival lined with *sham
> chapels,* each with its small forecourt, those on the

western side representing the provinces or "nomes"
of Upper Egypt and those on the eastern, of Lower
Egypt. These *virtually solid structures* . . . might
have symbolized the two kingdoms.[16]

The Molettes further indicate that the existence of the "dummy
representations" revealed an intention on the part of the builders "to
evoke a sense of place or places for the performance that occurred in
this 'vast rectangular enclosure'. . . . Their purpose, in current
terminology, must have been that of stage scenery."[17] Asserting that
"the ancient Egyptians would not have built these structures unless
they served some purpose," the Molettes conclude that the "first stage
scenery" was designed and built by Imhotep in approximately 2778
B.C. in Saqqara, Egypt. Such use of space indicates the traditional
African value placed on art as a functional endeavor, rather than as a
mere aesthetic enterprise in Egyptian society.

Any argument built upon establishing Imhotep as the first
designer of stage scenery does not contribute much to the main
discussion in this section. Neither does it validate, by itself, the
existence of theater buildings in Egypt prior to their appearance in
ancient Greece or Western Asia Minor. However, what is critical for
the purposes of this study is to look beyond the mysteries of the Step
Pyramid, and examine the underlying influences of certain Egyptian
structures, or architectural forms, such as columns, light kiosks,
propylons, doorframes, arched ceilings, colonnaded halls, clerestory
windows, and the interior designs of sanctuaries and temples. Such
Egyptian-built structures may have inspired foreigners to borrow ideas
and adapt them to their particular geography and cultural landscapes,
both for secular and religious purposes.

A striking example of such an imitation or borrowing can be seen
in those Greek theatrical structures which actually contain a temple,
an altar, and a *vouleftirion*—meaning "council chamber"—within the
boundary of the theater building itself. The theater building at
Thorikos at the southeastern tip of Attica, built around the sixth
century B.C., constitutes one of the earliest examples of this kind. In
western Turkey the Temple of Serapis in Pergamon, which was built
by Hadrian around A.D. 117-138, is recognized by art historians as
one of the best examples of Egyptian influence on Greek temples.
Known as the "Red Court" due to the red bricks covering the outer

facade, this temple was consecrated to Egyptian gods. The temple has a square-shaped stage or platform on which stood a statue. It is believed that the priest reached the platform through an underground passage and announced sacred messages as if they were uttered by the ten-meter-high figure of the deity.[18]

In his book *The Earth, The Temple, and the Gods: Greek Sacred Architecture*, Vincent Scully alludes to the concept of Western borrowing. He states: "Greek temples and their sanctuaries in fact gave form to concepts more balanced and complete than western civilization has normally been able to grasp in any of its post-Greek phases. It was possible for them to do this because, intellectually uncompromising as they were, *they still embodied the oldest traditions of belief which had been handed down since the Stone Age*" (emphasis added).[19] Scully goes on to emphasize the wisdom employed by Greeks throughout their life span, accentuating the accumulated wealth of information they inherited from the past. He points out that the Greeks restored the idea of "contentment, gentleness, wise action, justice and calm," particularly in their sacred architecture. Although "the temples came late, . . . first as the Greeks knew, was the earth: well-founded Earth, mother of all, eldest of all human beings. . . . Mother of the gods, wife of starry Heaven."[20] As the author notes, it was primarily the holiness of the earth which concerned Greeks, and before them the Egyptians. Such concern is evident throughout both groups' architectural and sculptural works, from the temples to the Sphinxes.

On the other hand, with regard to the development of drama and theater as an art form, there is no record of a dramatic script written to be acted by Egyptians. However, two significant venues which corroborate Egyptians as contributors to the development of theater in general lie within the cosmological and epistemological arenas. Looking first at epistemology as it pertains to the era under discussion, "the Greeks saw Egypt, an African country, as the cradle of wisdom and knowledge. The most famous of the Hellenes crossed the sea to be initiated, if they could at the temples of Egypt."[21] As Asante remarks, not only Greeks, but Sicilians, Persians and others traveled to Egypt as the perceived center of information. Orpheus and Homer, Solon and Plato, Thales, Pythagoras, Oenopidus, and Eudoxus are among famous Greeks who crossed the Mediterranean to visit Egypt.[22] Strabo is known to have stated that Plato and Eudoxus went to live in Heliopolis, where Plato spent thirteen years studying geometry and theology with Egyptian priests. According to Diogenes Laerce who authored *Thales*, a work about the famed thinker and mathematician born in what is today Turkey, Thales learned his astronomy and geometry from the Egyptian priests.[23] Furthermore, Laerce contends that Eudoxus was instructed by Khonouphis the Memphite, Solon by Sochis the Saite, and Pythagoras by Ounouphis the Heliopolitan. It is also reported that Ptolemy the Third was a collector of manuscripts. He borrowed from Athenians an old copy of the works of Aeschylus, Sophocles, and Euripides, the famous tragedians, and promised to return it after he had made a transcript in the best possible style. Subsequently, Ptolemy decided to keep the original manuscript for his own use and sent the copy back to Athens.[24] Each of these examples corroborate the intellectual impact Ancient Egypt had on Western civilization, and by extension, on the more specific area of theater.

Moving from the epistemological leadership of Egypt in antiquity to its influence in the cosmological arena, we must first understand the relationship between cosmology and mythology. Asante explains: "The place of African culture in the myths, legends, literatures and oratures of African people constitutes, at the mythological level, the cosmological issue within the Afrocentric enterprise."[25] Indeed, Egyptian mythology offers a rich and complex range of examples which portray the harmonious interaction of both human and divine qualities in mythological figures. In this context, derived from the myth of Osiris, Osirian ritual drama was one of the most important rituals that was exercised by the ancient Egyptians. Budge explains that "mysteries of Osiris and Isis were a series of Miracle Plays . . . which were reproduced mimically. At Abydos these were directed by a chief priest who was, of course a learned man, and he was assisted by a number of priests. . . . In some of the acts the public were allowed to take part, and thus the performance of the Osiris cycle of the 'mysteries' tended to the edification of all classes."[26] J. Gwyn Griffiths states that the worship of Osiris was the dominant religion of the ancient Egyptians from approximately 3400 B.C. through the Ptolemaic era.[27]

At the same time, there is evidence that Osiris actually existed. For example, based on Plutarch's text, the Egyptologist Budge states in *Egyptian Religion* that Osiris was a human being who ruled in Ancient Egypt at one time in history.[28] The archaeologist Abbe Emile

Amelineau (1850-1916) is known to have discovered Osiris's burial place and tomb at Abydos, and his skull in the necropolis in a jar.[29]

In essence, then, Osiris, both as king and god, received the utmost worship. The festival that was initiated for him by Isis—which used the phallus as its symbol of resurrection to honor the deified King— came to be celebrated annually in Egypt. This festival most likely provided the model for Dionysian rites and festivals considered to be the ancient beginnings of theater. Herodotus gives evidence of the theatrical journey from Egypt to Greece in his text titled *Histories*. In this work he mentions that ancient Greeks learned the worship of Osiris, whom they called "Dionysus," from Melampus, a son of Amythaon: "For it is Melampus who was for the Greeks the expositor of Dionysus—of his name, his sacrifice, and the phallic procession; strictly speaking, he did not put it all together and manifest the whole story for them, for there were teachers afterwards who advanced it further."[30] And although constraints of space and subject matter do not allow for an in-depth analysis of either Osirian or Dionysian festivals, at this point Egyptian spirituality and its concomitant spheres must be briefly analyzed. Such an analysis will facilitate an understanding of their transference to other cultures and their continued existence in contemporary African American drama.

One important aspect of Egyptian spirituality is bipolarity, a fundamental concept in Egyptian thought. Pharaohs or rulers were not only worshipped as Gods, but were believed to have descended from gods and goddesses. The sun as a metaphor was so dominant in Egyptian life that they attributed sun-like characteristics to their pharaohs. Representing the Sun on earth, his palace was described as the horizon; it was believed that when he showed himself, he (the Sun) rose and when he died, he set. For instance, Thutmose III is spoken of as "appearing as king in the ship of millions of years as the occupant of the seat of Atum like Re."[31] The Sun god's ship or boat was also used by Greeks in the depiction of Zeus on many of their vase paintings.

In a similar fashion gods and goddesses were attributed human characteristics which allowed them to interact with humans, interfering with their daily lives and destinies. Most often the powerful beings anticipated obedience and respect from their lesser charges. As previously stated, Osiris—better known by his Greek name than by his Egyptian name, Ausar—was the great mythological king of Kemet. He was married to Isis, or Aset, and through this marriage fathered Heru, who was identified as Apollo in Greek mythology. Ausar's murder by his brother Set, who carved his body into fourteen pieces and scattered them around the land of Kemet; Aset's frenzied search for her husband's body, with the discovery of all but the last piece, which happened to be his manhood; her construction of an obelisk to replace the missing piece; Ausar's eventual resurrection from death: these details have preoccupied the imagination of artists, writers, and dramatists over the centuries, with less interest in the story exhibited by historians. Here one can see a conspicuous convergence of the religious and the secular, facilitating an interminable amalgamation of two spheres. It is through such fluidity that the Egyptian legacy has acquired a permanent quality, unyielding to easy interpretations while its influence transcends the boundaries of the native land which bore it. One of these indirect influences, in my opinion, can be observed in the similarities between rituals and festivals in Egypt and Greece.

To illustrate: in those countries where Greek culture flourished, Dionysus, an Olympian god, son of Zeus and Semele—a mortal—was believed to have been murdered, dismembered, and then resurrected. The myths surrounding his name came to be related to cycles of life and seasons, that is, birth, growth, decay, death, and rebirth; and spring, summer, fall, and winter. His worship was designed to ensure the return of spring and fertility and it was accompanied by the consumption of wine. Originally a god of vegetation, Dionysus was later conceived as god and giver of the grape and its wine. Subsequently he was worshipped with orgiastic rites and conceived as the patron of drama. At this point, his chief festivals in Attica were the *Dionysia, Lenaea, Oschophoria,* and *Anthesteria.* The *Dionysia of Attica,* in connection with which the Greek drama is believed to have developed, was comprised of two celebrations: the *Rural Dionysia,* held in late autumn when the wine was first tasted, and located where the drama is said to have originated; and the *Great,* or *City Dionysia,* held in the spring, at which plays were regularly given from the time of Pisistratus.[32] The central feature of the *Rural Dionysia* was a procession escorting a phallus held aloft. Needless to say, the procession was designed to promote or encourage the fertility of the autumn-sown seed, or of the earth in general, at a time when it seemed to be slumbering.[33] At Delphi, too, Dionysus was supreme during the winter months.

With reference to actual drama, Aristotle is known to have asserted that it arose out of improvisation with hymns, known as *dithyrambs,* and dances.[34] The first record of theatrical drama is from 534 B.C. in Greece. At that time, the festival known as *City Dionysia* was reorganized and a contest for the best tragedy instituted. Thespis, the first dramatist whose name has come down to us through the ages, is known to have won that first contest.

By the eighth and seventh centuries B.C. contests for choral dances were being held at festivals honoring Dionysus. Much later, Dionysus came to be recognized by Romans as Bacchus, whose festival was celebrated by the Romans every three years with an orgiastic procession at night. Due to the licentiousness to which it gave rise, it was prohibited in 186 B.C.[35]

Anteriorly, in Egypt similar processions were held for the god Amon around the reign of the 18th dynasty (1567-1320 B.C.), according to writings of the Greek historian Herodotus. One related festival was that of *Min-Khamutef.* This celebration fell at the beginning of the harvest season and lasted for twenty days, during which time the death and rebirth of the Pharaoh and the God whom he incarnates, Min-Khamutef, were celebrated. It is reported that the festival with all its splendor was depicted on the walls of the Temple of Ramses III from the 20th Dynasty (1200-1085 B.C.) at Medinet Habu. However, there exists even earlier depictions on the pylons of Amenophis III's (18th Dynasty) temple at Luxor, in the temple of Karnak.[36]

Unlike the *Min-Khamutef* festival, the *Sed* festival was not celebrated every year; it normally took place thirty years after the King's accession to the throne. Its beginning coincided with the first day of the first month of spring-tide, known as Piret, which heralded the season of Coming Forth. This season was marked by the falling of flood waters and the sowing of barley, wheat, and sorghum in the following month. The *Sed* festival was closely related to the earth, specifically harvests and the inundation of the river Nile. Given that too high or too low a tide indicated either flood or famine, rulers felt the need to reassert their dominance over the land in order to maintain the beneficent relations between heaven and earth. Obviously, for Egyptians the preservation of their harmonious connection with the earth and the Nile was of inimical value to their existence.

Besides the *Min-Khamutef* and *Sed* festivals, there were certain days in the Egyptian calendar during which ceremonies were held to honor deities. The high point of the year involved the annual convocation of the deities Amun and Mut at the Temple of Ipet Isut (Karnak). Priests from the Temple of Ipet Isut and from the Temple of Mut (Luxor) would jointly move the great deity Amun to the Temple of the goddess Mut for seven days of consorting with each other. Following the seventh day, the priests—purified and dressed in multicolored robes and fine jewelry—would take the deity Amun back to his temple in a large procession passing through the avenue of the sphinxes. While the common people watched in awe, the golden statue of Amun was brought out of the Temple of Mut and carried back to the Temple of Ipet Isut to rest until the following year. This ensured that all was in order, the world was at peace, and stability and abundance reigned in the land.[37] This ceremony, beyond the significance of its ritualistic ties, constituted drama of the highest order. Not only did the procession involve dramatic action, that is the carrying of representations of the deities from one location to another, but it also brought together a large congregation to participate in the observation of the event.

In Greece too, festivals were enacted to honor Dionysus which involved a similar procession of imagery. According to Herodotus this procession was instituted by Melampus. Eighteen-inch-high images controlled by strings were carried around the town by women. These statuettes had a penis of at least the length of the body, that could be made to nod. Indeed the similarities between the Egyptian and Greek celebrations were so obvious that Herodotus wrote: "For the rest of the festival in honor of Dionysus, except for the dance choruses, the Egyptians celebrate it almost in everything like the Greeks." Later on he concluded: "It was Melampus who instituted the phallic procession to Dionysus, and it was from him the Greeks learned to do what they do."[38] In light of these developments it becomes apparent that the evolution of theatrical forms borrowed a great deal from mythology, with ancient Egyptian theology playing an integral part in the transfer of this knowledge to ancient Greek culture.

In later decades, on the African continent griots and storytellers operating within the oral tradition traveled from town to town, enlarging the scope of theatrical activity in both traditional and Western styles. Wole Soyinka and Femi Osofisan from Nigeria, Efua

Sutherland and Ama Ata Aidoo from Ghana, and Mbongeni Ngema and Percy Mtwa from South Africa are well-known playwrights who continue the tradition of myth and ancestral memory. Derek Walcott who wrote and directed for a local theater workshop in Trinidad, and Abdias do Nascimento from Brazil who led the Black Theater movement of South America and founded the African-Brazilian Theater, are literary figures in their own spheres whose plays deal with African cosmology regardless of their diasporan location. And finally, Edgar White, born in the West Indies, is among the well-known contemporary playwrights whose plays are accessible to international audiences in New York and London.

In the American context we see the early emergence of ritual practices in the hush harbors where enslaved Africans would act out certain ritual performances during births, puberty, marriages, and deaths. A brief examination of the beginnings of African American drama will add to our understanding of the genre. Genevieve Fabre in *Drumbeats, Mask and Metaphor* says: "Black theatre was born of practices older than the presence of Africans on American soil. From the time they boarded ships for the passage to the New World, slaves provided shows for the entertainment of whites."[39] Fabre contends that the early performances on the plantations which seemed to praise whites were in reality satires used to express the dissatisfaction and unhappiness of the Africans without risking punishment. Moreover, the performances exemplified the ways in which Africanisms or African institutions survived in the New World because satire is used as a means of social control in African societies. In addition to satire, sarcasm and joking along with dance and mime also played an important role in these performances. Fabre mentions the emergence of libelists, lampoons, chants, music, costumed parades, and pageants. Additionally, enslaved Africans held celebrations on occasions such as election days, and secretly organized religious gatherings in the woods which dramatized various episodes in the form of "mysteries." The performances in their myriad forms "strongly influenced the development of contemporary black drama."[40]

In analyzing the performances in more detail, Fabre notes that as the spoken language became bolder, gestures grew more emphatic and emotions were released without fear. Performers—who felt more at ease as a result of the popular acceptance of their shows—mocked each other, assumed the role of director and playwright, conversed with the audience, and often portrayed a humorous sketch of human life. On the other hand, the Molettes assert that the original African American minstrel performances not only entertained but made life tolerable through the use of ridicule, double-meaning, and comic irony. They add: "The successful functioning of this type of African American theater was a significant factor in the mental health and physical survival of African-American people within the slave experience."[41]

Unfortunately, when some of these performances were recaptured by "Negro minstrel shows" throughout later decades, the first seeds of stereotypical images were sown. Black face minstrelsy initiated an increase in the number of stereotypical negative images which, says Fabre, "gradually set the pattern of relations between blacks and whites that would dominate the world of theatre." She continues:

> Material drawn from the first entertainments given
> by slaves was appropriated and vulgarized, and the
> theatre was stripped of its satirical effect and of its
> symbolic language. The black audience was
> systematically excluded and when blacks were
> finally admitted to the troupes they had to submit to
> the will of white producers and to the conventions of
> a genre that perpetuated negative racial stereotypes.
> But at the same time, black minstrel actors,
> recognized as artists, probably opened the door for
> the prominent black actors of the twentieth century.
> American theatre had discovered a profitable
> commodity.[42]

Bert Williams, for instance, who gained recognition through black face minstrelsy, became one of the most famous and wealthiest of African American actors. Yet discrimination and racial barriers would not allow this gifted actor to enter the Press Club for a drink without a white sponsor accompanying him.[43]

At the start of the nineteenth century there were several attempts by free African Americans to establish a theater tradition. The performances staged in Mr. Brown's tea garden in 1821 are one such attempt. Mr. Brown, a former ship steward, built a three-hundred-seat theater for the group which he organized under the name "African

Company." The former tea-garden, built at the corner of Mercer and Bleecker Streets in lower Manhattan, was known as the African Grove Theatre and soon attracted both black and white patrons—the former seated in a segregated balcony.[44] Two famous African American actors, Ira Aldridge and James Hewlett, both from New York, joined the African Company for some time. Yet both left in disappointment; of the two Aldridge set sail for England, only to attain great fame as a Shakespearean performer in Europe.[45]

What is most noteworthy about the African Company is their indirect yet courageous attack on enslavement through the agency of the stage. When the company staged a British melodrama in 1822 or 1823 called *Tom and Jerry, or Life in London* based on Pierce Egan's original script, they added an extra scene titled "On the Slave Market." Addressing the anti-slavery issue, the scene was of historical significance: it was probably the first attempt of its kind by an African American theater company. Later the play was adopted by other groups and the title was changed to *Life in Philadelphia or Life in New York*.

Another production of the African Company, whose script is no longer extant, was a play called *King Shotaway* or *The Drama of King Shotaway*. According to a playbill it was performed June 20 and 21, 1823, and portrayed an uprising on the island of St. Vincent. The playbill announced that Mr. Brown—the manager and the playwright—actually took part in such an uprising, which attracted more audiences to the show. However, as the Molettes indicate, the claim may have been simply a fabrication intended to increase ticket sales. In fact, this marketing technique may have been utilized by almost all theater companies.

The heart of the matter is African American theater was already in existence in the 1820s, addressing social and political themes of the time. It was grounded in the historical experiences of the people, and more importantly, demonstrated its allegiance to the African concept of "art for society's sake," rather than the Western concept of "art for art's sake." Furthermore, *King Shotaway* was distinguished from its predecessors in two ways. First, it marked a sharp break from the comic irony which audiences praised in previous shows. Secondly, through its bold attack on enslavement, *King Shotaway* took on a pioneering role in militancy and generated an interest in the transfer of similar themes onto the stage.

White critics completely ignored the play and the Company.[46] Moreover, the African Company and its players, free black actors, were continuously harassed by the New York City Police Department during their production of *King Shotaway*. They were finally left with no choice but to discontinue the performances indefinitely sometime around 1823.[47] The most important factor in the termination of both the group and the theater was the hostility aroused by their popularity, which exceeded that of the "white-run Park Theater nearby." The latter group "apparently conspired to foment disturbances by white rowdies at the African Grove Theatre."[48]

King Shotaway, the first known African American drama by an African American playwright, was not a typical protest play as compared to productions of the 1960s Black Arts and Black Power movements. However, it was significant in reflecting one of the major goals of theatre as the most social of the arts: that of consciousness-raising. Through this play, black and white audiences were able to recognize the impediments of enslavement, as well as the complexities inherent in the idea of escape and freedom. Numerous plays were to follow in the footsteps of *King Shotaway*. Williams Wells Brown, himself a runaway, revealed his innermost feelings about enslavement in *The Escape: or, A Leap for Freedom,* a play written and published in 1858. The play came to represent anti-slavery sentiment through the popular appeal of theater among white audiences. Besides William Wells Brown, who acted as well as wrote, Ira Aldridge from New York and Victor Sejour from New Orleans also deserve mention.

As we approach a new century the "secret" has been revealed, albeit hesitantly, that African culture and theater by way of Egypt may have preceded Greek culture. The Dionysian rites which are considered to be the seeds of drama were basically ancient Kemetic (Egyptian) rituals offered to the deities in the Nile Valley civilizations.[49] Furthermore, Egypt's impact upon the development of human civilization in general has recently become the topic of several books. Given this Egyptian—that is, African—influence, any investigation of African American theater must embrace new paradigms and definitions that are specifically derived from definitions of African American culture and heritage. Paul Carter Harrison calls for authors who can see beyond the descriptive, sociogrammatic character of oppression; for directors who have prepared themselves with the knowledge of corresponding African and African American mythologies, and who are able to discern the motivating responses of black people to certain rhythms; and for actors who can move freely and securely within the rhythms of the mode with natural grace and potency.[50]

With its emphasis on the event—that is, on song, dance, drum, music, and rhythm—African American drama is the prodigy of a unique entity that has developed its own value system. It is further set apart by its portrayal of black lives and the inherent lyricism in its language. Thus, this drama needs expositions which are capable of complete Afrocentric descriptions. Expositions of this type are the means by which critics can overcome inadequate, *ahistorical* criticisms. Such criticisms lack authenticity because they are based on claims of universalism by Euro-American drama and theater critics. In this work, I am beginning that journey through the portrayal of African American drama in a different light. I have evaluated the genre using its own standards, that is, through an Afrocentric critique, whose true origins lie in the 1960s Black Arts and Theater movement.

NOTES

[1] Toni Morrison, *Playing in the Dark: Whiteness and the Literary Imagination* (Boston: Harvard University Press, 1992), 4, 15.

[2] Samuel P. Huntington, "The Clash of Civilizations and the Remaking of World Order," *The New York Times Book Review* (December 1, 1996), 13.

[3] Janheinz Jahn, *Muntu: African Culture and the Western World* (New York: Grove Weidenfeld, 1961), 151.

[4] Ibid.

[5] Paul Carter Harrison, ed., *Kuntu Drama: Plays of the African Continuum* (New York: Grove Press, 1974), 7.

[6] Carlton Molette and Barbara Molette, *Black Theater: Premise and Presentation* (Bristol, Ind.: Wyndham Hall Press, 1986), 23.

[7] Kariamu Welsh-Asante, "The Aesthetic Conceptualization of Nzuri," in *The African Aesthetic: Keeper of the Traditions*, ed. Welsh-Asante (Westport, Conn.: Greenwood Press, 1993), 9.

[8] Oscar G. Brockett, *History of the Theatre* (Boston: Allyn and Bacon, 1991), 39.

[9] E.A. Wallis Budge, *From Fetish to God in Ancient Egypt* (New York: Dover, 1988), 263.

[10] Molette and Molette, *Black Theater*, 41.

[11] Ibid.

[12] Ibid., 42.

[13] Morris Bierbrier, *The Tomb-Builders of the Pharaohs* (Cairo, Egypt: American University in Cairo Press, 1992), 69, 91.

[14] Cheikh Anta Diop, *Civilization or Barbarism: An Authentic Anthropology*, trans. Yaa-Lengi Meema Ngemi, ed. Harold J. Salemson and Marjolijn de Jager (Brooklyn: Lawrence Hill Books, 1991), 337.

[15] For a more in-depth discussion of Ma'at as it relates to drama, see my essays titled "Ma'at, Afrocentricity and the Critique of African American Drama" in *Molefi Kete Asante and Afrocentricity: In Praise and Criticism*, ed. Dhyana Ziegler (Nashville, Tennessee: Winston Publishing Company, 1995); and "The Beginning Before the Beginning" in *International Journal of Black Drama* 2, no. 2 (1996).

[16]   Banister Fletcher, *A History of Architecture on the Comparative Method* (New York: Charles Scribner's Sons, 1963), 30, cited in Carlton Molette and Barbara Molette, *Black Theater: Premise and Presentation* (Bristol, Ind.: Wyndham Hall Press, 1986), 45-46.

[17]   Molette and Molette, *Black Theater*, 46.

[18]   Ilhan Aksit, *Ancient Treasures of Turkey,* (Istanbul, Turkey: Haset, 1985),144.

[19]   Vincent Scully, *The Earth, The Temple, and the Gods: Greek Sacred Architecture* (New Haven: Yale University Press, 1962), 7.

[20]   Ibid., 8

[21]   Molefi Kete Asante, *Kemet, Afrocentricity and Knowledge* (Trenton, N.J.: Africa World Press, 1990), 64.

[22]   Ibid., 64-65.

[23]   Ibid., 65.

[24]   Arthur Elam Haigh, *The Attic Theatre: A Description of the Stage and Theatre of the Athenians and of the Dramatic Performances at Athens*, 3rd ed., in part re-written by A.W. Pickard-Cambridge (Oxford: Clarendon Press, 1907), 74.

[25]   Asante, *Kemet*, 8

[26]   E.A. Wallis Budge, *From Fetish to God in Ancient Egypt* (New York:Dover, 1988), 25.

[27]   J. Gwyn Griffiths, *The Origin of Osiris and His Cult* (Leiden, Netherlands: E.J. Brill, 1980), 41-43.

[28]   E.A. Wallis Budge, *Egyptian Religion* (New York: Bell Publishing Company), 75.

[29]   Wayne Chandler, "Of Gods and Men: Egypt's Old Kingdom," in *Egypt Revisited,* ed. Ivan Van Sertima (New Brunswick, N.J.: Transaction Publishers, 1989), 126-31.

[30]   Herodotus, *Histories,* trans. David Green (Chicago: University of Chicago Press, 1987), 2.42, 2.48-49.

[31]   Eva L.R. Meyerowitz, *The Divine Kingship in Ghana and Ancient Egypt* (London: Faber and Faber, 1960), 94.

[32]   *Webster's New International Dictionary of the English Language* (Springfield, Mass.: G.C. Merriam Company, 1926), 627.

[33]   Arthur Wallace Pickard-Cambridge, *Dramatic Festivals of Athens* (London: Oxford University Press, 1968), 42.

[34]   Brockett, *History of the Theatre*, 82.

[35]   *Webster's Dictionary,* 166.

[36] Meyerowitz, *Divine Kingship*, 177.

[37] Bierbrier, *Tomb-Builders*, 96-97.

[38] Herodotus, *Histories*, 2.48-49

[39] Genevieve Fabre, *Drumbeats, Masks and Metaphor: Contemporary African American Theater* (Cambridge, Mass.: Harvard University Press, 1983), 4.

[40] Ibid.

[41] Molette and Molette, *Black Theater*, 65.

[42] Fabre, *Drumbeats*, 5-6.

[43] *Ethnic Notions*, prod. Marlon Riggs, 56 min. (San Francisco: California Newsreel, 1987), videocassette.

[44] William Branch, ed., *Crosswinds: An Anthology of Black Dramatists in the Diaspora* (Bloomington: Indiana University Press, 1993), xvi.

[45] Molette and Molette, *Black Theater*, 56.

[46] Ibid.

[47] Ibid., 58.

[48] Branch, *Crosswinds*, xvii.

[49] Martin Bernal, *Black Athena: The Afroasiatic Roots of Classical Civilization* (New Brunswick, N.J.: Rutgers University Press, 1987), 64-116.

[50] Harrison, *Kuntu Drama*, 8.

Acknowledgments

I would like to remember and thank my parents, my late father Sahap Anadolu who taught me humility, justice, and patience; and my mother, Nuran Anadolu, who taught me endurance. I want to thank the ancestors who protected me and ensured that I had great teachers to guide me with their insightful critiques and words of wisdom. My small circle of friends and family at our "home away from home" were invaluable—Yildiz Anadolu, Ahmet and Sinem Bayer, Betty Mae Wilson, Ruth Rineer, Hulya Polat, Sekai Tillman, Arax Suny; their warmth and genuine affection were my true sources of strength.

Sincere thanks to mentor and scholar Molefi Kete Asante, whose vision and caring surpass any words of gratitude; and to colleagues and dear friends Kariamu Welsh Asante, Abu Abarry, and Nana Abarry for their continued support and sustenance. My deepest gratitude goes to Zohrab Kazanjian who renewed my faith at every turn and never hesitated to tell the truth. Michelle M. Myers, a distinguished graduate student, provided valuable editing. My friend and colleague, Letetia Coleman, provided a plethora of editorial expertise. I am particularly indebted to Letetia's family, Kenn Perry and little Niara Perry, who were extremely patient during the final countdown.

Zizwe, Joe Borghi, and Antonio Sanchez provided the technical assistance for which I am much indebted. I would also like to recognize my son for his helpful computer proficiency. A special thank-you to Kristi Long, Assistant Editor of Garland Publishing, who believed in this book. And finally, my students at Temple University contributed immensely to the development of this project through discussions and presentations that enriched me over the years.

Thank you all.

Contemporary African American Theater

I

The Critical Tradition in Drama

I am so tired of waiting,
Aren't you,
For the world to become good
And beautiful and kind?

—Langston Hughes, "Tired"

An emerging theoretical approach in American literary and dramatic criticism which finds its origin in the African cultural context is Afrocentricity. As expounded in the works of Molefi Kete Asante and the Temple School, Afrocentric critical theory centers its argument on the perspective of the critic as well as the perspective of the playwright. Thus, to examine the text of a play it is necessary first to "locate" the playwright. In order to accomplish this task one has to look carefully into the resources and material utilized by the author, as well as the ways and methods employed. However, one cannot locate the playwright without first locating one's self. In other words, the critic who analyzes Ed Bullins's *Goin' Buffalo*, for example, must bring to the work an understanding of the dimensions of the critical method. To apply Eurocentric methods to the writings of Ed Bullins or Charles Fuller would be like trying to apply African percussive elements to Korean folk music. By the standards of African percussionists, one could wrongly determine that Korean music is underdeveloped rhythmically. By evaluating Korean folk music using the standards and objectives of Korean instrumental and storytelling

3

elements, however, one would succeed in making a proper assessment of the music.

Whatever "objective" or "universal" aspects exist in music are necessarily the result of the examination of numerous systems of aesthetics, rather than the application of one system to the musical creations of different countries and varied cultures. As in music, all literary genres need to be analyzed according to their own cultural contexts; this requires separate evaluative standards. African-centered theory assumes that critics who pass critical judgment on African American creative works have an understanding of the African American culture. How is one to assess a play where there is an entire room on the stage covered with kente if one does not understand kente or its royal heritage?

I do not argue that the various Eurocentric critical methods—particularly those which take Greece and Rome as anterior cultures—are totally useless in understanding African American drama. Moreover, I contend that European drama has left its mark upon American drama, which from time to time has affected African American drama as well. However, the truth of the matter is European drama tradition and its theoretical construct fail to deal with the collective interaction of the exigencies found in African American culture. Therefore, a critical method that is akin to the culture itself can provide a more valuable platform for the evaluation and understanding of African American drama.

Beyond establishing a theoretical methodology for African American drama, such a method also speaks to the question of values in relation to African American historical consciousness. Accordingly, the theory suggests that if a playwright centers herself or himself in the motifs, images, and icons (concrete and abstract) of the African culture, the product will most likely be an agent for a holistic approach to the issues of self-esteem, confidence, and cultural appreciation. In this instance, then, drama expands beyond the concept of "drama for art's sake," and evolves into a new entity centered around "drama for the sake of community consciousness." Amiri Baraka and Charles Fuller (as playwrights) and Larry Neal, Maulana Karenga, and Molefi Kete Asante (as theoreticians), maintain the same position; that is, they call for *defining* black experience rather than allowing it to be defined by others. Thus, consciousness-raising remains a vital force in their writings, correlating to the didacticism found in the Black Arts movement. To explain the relationship between art and people, in his essay titled "Black Cultural Nationalism" Maulana Karenga said: "For no one is any more than the context to which he owes his existence, and if an artist owes his existence to the Afroamerican context, then he also owes his art to that context and therefore must be held accountable to the people of that context."[1]

Lately most intellectual and scholarly debates in the arena of African American studies center around arguments for and against the cogency of African agency as maintained by Afrocentrists. Naturally, the discussion has now been extended to all spheres of African American experience, including the artistic and aesthetic disciplines. In this milieu, drama and theater play a critical role in the assessment of the impact and influence of the Black Arts movement on the development of an African-centered idea. I submit that a framework should be erected for examining the extent to which the Black Arts movement of the sixties and seventies, and to a larger extent Africological approaches in the eighties and nineties, assisted the major playwrights in evoking new elements in African American drama. These major playwrights included the two lead theoreticians of the Black Arts movement: Neal in Philadelphia and Baraka in Newark and Harlem. Another Philadelphia native, Charles Fuller, must also be acknowledged as a forerunner of the African-centered approach to drama.

Interestingly, the Afrocentric idea came into prominence long after the Black Arts and Black Power movements, having followed the Ronald Reagan and George Bush eras. During this later period the majority of African Americans were in pursuit of a democratic spirit that would renew their faith and improve their status in society, a status worsened in many respects since the civil rights era. The interesting question is whether writers of this era were paving the way for the development of a new theory in the form of an African-centered approach to the arts and aesthetics. This approach was the fundamental base in the 1990s for the advancement of an explicitly workable theory towards what Neal, Baraka, and Fuller individually attempted to portray in their original creations during the early 1970s and 1980s.

The roots of the critical tradition probably go back to the mid-1600s when enslaved Africans in America first attempted to preserve their drums and other artistic/cultural artifacts despite being under attack and continuous scrutiny. Although Egyptian beginnings, as explained previously, are to be considered the ancestral origins of African American drama, for purposes of clarity and due to limitations of space I have chosen to examine more contemporary texts for analytical illumination on the works of individual playwrights.

Despite setbacks, severe impediments, lack of recognition, and discrimination against African American writers, these writers demonstrated unending resilience, vitality, and productivity throughout the centuries, even during the miasma of captivity. Alongside the over-arching "master narrative" of American literature, African American literature grew over the years in myriad forms and genres, reaching a stage whose impact surpasses in thematic scope most literatures of the world. In particular, it compares closely with those whose radical stance can be categorized as "leftist" or "protest" and that concentrate on a specific people's resistance to oppression, such as Argentinean, Algerian, and Turkish literatures. The Black Power movement of the sixties brought forth the archetypal paradigm for cultural nationalism and a kindling of black self-consciousness unmatched in energy by any development in African American socio-cultural history. Its impact on literature, art, and drama of the period is discussed in upcoming chapters.

In Chicago, Detroit, Los Angeles, Philadelphia, New York, and Atlanta, original voices and actions of resistance, definition, and reconstruction introduced a new impetus for reevaluation and redirection in the literary and artistic fields. Yet nowhere was the movement more profound in its call for authenticity than in Philadelphia. The city already lay on sacred ground, having been a historical site for the abolitionist movement, anti-slavery activities, and Underground Railroad operations. During the sixties, Philadelphia grew to embrace several charismatic men and women, among whom Neal reached prominence within the scope of the literary matrix developing at the time. Moreover, Neal is considered today as the direct precursor of African-centered perspectives—especially in relation to art, literature, and drama.

I am particularly concerned with the impact of the Black Arts movement on the development of African American drama and theater throughout the past thirty years. While giving due respect to the historical roots and trends which preceded the Black Arts movement of the sixties, it is my conviction that the avalanching force that gave birth to new ideas and trends in African American drama is the Black Arts movement as it was spearheaded by Neal and Baraka (then known as LeRoi Jones). As a matter of fact, the conceptual impact created by the Black Arts movement has rapidly moved beyond the local peripheries of theater, drama, literature, and aesthetics. It has resulted in a proliferation of works in the 1990s which incorporate almost all areas of media industries, that is, visual and performing arts, fashion, music, philosophical theory, sociological method, literary criticism, and historical analysis. Moreover, the inclusion of Afrocentric terminology in rhetorical and communicative studies, and its popularity among some African Americans, has added a new dimension to the contemporary study of African American drama.

This study aims to explore the transition from the Black Arts movement to African-centered ideology. Simultaneously it examines the aggregate influence of both stances on contemporary African American theater. To this effect, the first part of this treatise defines the basic premises of the two movements and their precursors as they relate to the genre. The succeeding chapters are devoted to the African American dramatic tradition, individual playwrights, and their fundamental works as representative outposts of contemporary African American theater. In chapter four, which focuses mainly on Charles Fuller, the African-centered ideology and the possibility of developing an analytical framework for the evaluation of African American drama are discussed in-depth.

THE BLACK ARTIST AND
BLACK ARTS/BLACK THEATER MOVEMENTS

In her volume titled *In Search of Our Mothers' Gardens*, Alice Walker relates the story of an old woman in Mississippi—a freedom fighter—who was arrested and suffered injuries to her leg as a result of police brutality. Upon being told that the "Movement is dead," she replied, "Like me, if it's dead, it shore ain't ready to lay down." Walker adds, "Man only truly lives by knowing. . . . It is knowing the words of James Weldon Johnson's 'Negro National Anthem' and even remembering the tune. . . . The dull, frustrating work with our people is the work of the black revolutionary artist. It means, most of all,

staying close enough to them to be there whenever they need you."[2]
Indeed, as the above anecdote reveals, Walker attributes a most
important task to the black revolutionary artist and asserts that he or
she must be a walking filing cabinet of poems and songs and stories, of
people, of places, of deeds and misdeeds. She concludes her article by
reaffirming her role as a writer: "The artist then is the voice of the
people, but she is also The People."[3]

Walker is not alone in her assertion that the artist is both the voice
of the people and The People. Many black artists, writers, poets,
critics, and musicians of the sixties era were voluntarily engaged in a
struggle with the American nation that would determine the future of
black arts and aesthetics. Those who believed in the shaman[4] role of
the artist voiced their opinions, and these writings came to be collected
in two seminal anthologies, namely *The Black Aesthetic* and *Black
Fire*; these served as *the* inspirational manifestoes of their time. The
following artists contributed to *The Black Aesthetic* in various ways.
Hoyt Fuller, Julian Mayfield, Maulana Karenga,[5] Addison Gayle Jr.,
John O'Neal, and Darwin T. Turner wrote theoretical essays that
explained the thrust of the Black Arts movement. Karenga introduced
his Kawaida theory concurrent with the publication of the above-
mentioned volumes. Due to its introduction and emphasis on the seven
principles of *Nguzo Saba*, Kawaida came to be recognized as an
influential theory providing spiritual concepts relevant to the needs of
hundreds of followers. Meanwhile, Jimmy Stewart, J.A. Rogers,
Baraka, and Ron Wellburn contributed through their writings to the
development of a music theory. In a later work, *Blues People*, Baraka
would further explore the impact of African aesthetics on the
development of the blues in America. Through their illuminating
writing, poets Haki Madhubuti (formerly Don L. Lee), Sarah Webster
Fabio, James A. Emanuel, and Dudley Randall; and dramatists Neal,
Ronald Milner, Loften Mitchell, Clayton Riley, and Baraka, had an
enormous impact upon the readers. In fiction, John Oliver Killens,
Adam David Miller, and Ishmael Reed were some of the young voices
who contributed articles to *The Black Aesthetic*. The old masters
contributed to this spirit as well; essays denoting the continuity of the
black aesthetic include Alain Locke's "Negro Youth Speaks" and "The
Negro and the American Theater"; W.E.B. Du Bois's "Of the Sorrow
Songs"; Langston Hughes's "The Negro Artist and the Racial

Mountain"; and Richard Wright's "Introduction: Blueprint for Negro Writing."

Black Fire, out-of-print since its second printing in the 1970s, offered a wider range of essays, poetry, fiction, and drama. The book included a foreword by Baraka and an afterword by Neal which symbolically reflected the editors' collective vision of an anthology intended to stand as the *password* for sixties' writing. James Stewart, John Henrik Clarke, Harold Cruse, Stokely Carmichael, A.B. Spellman, Sun-Ra, David Henderson, Sonia Sanchez, Clarence Reed, Lorenzo Thomas, Henry Dumas, Charlie Cobb, Julia Fields, Charles Patterson, Ronald Drayton, Marvin E. Jackmon, Ben Caldwell, Ed Bullins, Joseph White, Charles H. Fuller, and Jimmy Garrett were only some of the ninety artists and writers whose writings comprised *Black Fire*. It soon became—and still is—the most illuminating and encompassing anthology representative of the sixties' spirit.

But what was the "sixties spirit" really? Was it about anger and frustration, black rage and black pride, graffiti on inner city walls and a sense of abandonment? Was it about feelings, merely? Or was it about an aesthetic blossoming fostered by numerous socio-economic and historic agents such as the Civil Rights, Black Power, and Black Nationalism movements? All of the above-mentioned names represent small rivulets merging into a huge stream which we call the Black Arts movement. However, by the time it came to be recognized as a major artistic upheaval it had reached the intellectual vigor of a *matrix*. The most sweeping definition of a matrix that corresponds with the Black Arts movement has come from Houston A. Baker Jr. in reference to the blues. Baker observed that blues is a script in which African American cultural discourse is inscribed: "A matrix is a womb, a network, a fossil-bearing rock, a rocky trace of a gemstone's removal, a principal metal in an alloy, a mat or plate for reproducing print or phonograph records. The matrix is a point of ceaseless input and output, a web of intersecting, crisscrossing impulses always in productive transit."[6]

The Black Arts movement is the womb that bore a long-awaited generation of writers, artists, musicians, and critics; the rock that became the symbol of their endurance and strength; the ore which they believe, once dug up, would replenish the "Power to the People"; the plate on which they poured their creations to be *re-defined*, *re-illustrated* and *re-formed*. It was a reorganization of what was already there; the crossroads where the old met with the new and formed the mainstream; the overflow of thoughts into one large reservoir before they reached the size of a mighty falls.

Larry Neal heralded the arrival of the Black Arts movement in a historic essay which appeared in the *Liberator* in June 1965. Passages that are especially pertinent to this study are as follows:

> The Black Arts officially opened their school on April 30th with an explosive evening of good poetry. . . . The idea behind . . . this event . . . is to open a dialogue between the artist and his people, rather than between the artist and the dominant white society which is responsible for his alienation in the first place.
>
> . . . I believe that the highlight of the Black Arts weekend was the short parade which it held on Saturday morning in Harlem. Imagine jazz musicians, African dancing, and a group of groovy black people swinging down Lenox Avenue; while every body freely plays their instruments, and fine black girls give out bright yellow circulars that say: THE BLACK ARTS IS COMING! It was Garvey all over again. It was informal and spontaneous and should illustrate something of the potential for creative encounter existing in our community.[7]

Although no writer or historian of the era has yet made an assessment of the exact date, year, and place that mark the beginning of the Black Arts movement, Neal's observation is self-explanatory. Moreover, in *The Autobiography of LeRoi Jones/Amiri Baraka*, Baraka reminiscences about the start of the Black Arts Repertory Theater/School.[8] He reflects on the old brownstone building on 130th Street on which he had a mortgage of $100 a month, which he intended to pay through his plays that were then running at the St. Marks Theater. Baraka recalls: "We set up shop and cleaned and swept and painted. We got a flag, White designed, the 'Greek' theater masks of comedy and tragedy, rendered Afro style, like a shield, with spear behind, all in black and gold. The Black Arts Repertory Theater/School."[9] The parade in which Neal also participated was their first official activity across 125th Street. It was about arts, politics, and black revolution. As Baraka reveals:

> With Sun Ra and his Myth-Science Arkestra leading it, Albert and his brother Don blowing and Milford wailing his drums, the core of us, as it had grown, some other black artists from downtown and those in Harlem who'd now begun to come in, plus Baba Oserjeman and his Yoruba Temple. We marched down the street holding William White's newly designed Black Arts flag. I've seen one photo that survives of this (in a magazine put out by Asian activist, Yuri Kuchiyama, *North Star*). A small group of sometimes comically arrogant black people daring to raise the question of art and politics and revolution, black revolution![10]

The art that they envisioned would be able to reach the people; in Baraka's words it "would take them higher, ready them for war and victory, as popular as the Impressions or the Miracles or Marvin Gaye." He said: "That was our vision and its image kept us stepping, heads high and backs straight."[11] Throughout its duration, Black Arts endorsed the notion of the inextricability of ethics and aesthetics, art and life. It developed its own referential parameters that encompassed all genres of the African American literary ethos. Black theater, probably the most effective among its forms and genres because it is the most social of all arts, illuminated the role of art in human life— particularly black life.

The Black Theater movement of the 1960s and 1970s was populist in nature and aligned with the Civil Rights and Black Power movements. It was different from previous attempts in the sense that its playwrights were writing with a temperament contrary to so-called "traditional" attitudes in black theater. It was a movement which aggressively asserted a black identity founded upon an African American-centered consciousness, political activism, and a dynamic philosophy. Unlike some critics who have identified a French author's play—*Blacks* by Jean Genet in 1959—as the beginning of the 1960's Black Theater movement, I contend it was Baraka's play *Dutchman* (1964) which initiated the movement. The real forces that propelled the Black Theater movement were beyond the grasp of a French playwright who had spent most of his life outside the United States and whose knowledge in race relations was formed within a European context. Although *Blacks* might have been instrumental in initiating consciousness among white audiences, real credit is due to *Dutchman*, more than any other play, for heightening black consciousness and promoting the Black Arts movement. Baraka's unique contribution was the advocacy of an end to the centuries-old dream of integration. He presented us with an alternative—a slice of harsh, revolutionary reality whether black or white audience members and readers liked it or not. The direction among black playwrights from then on, and a justified one, was to follow separate paths from the American mainstream in art, aesthetics, and drama, establishing an uncompromising, liberated, powerful stance for the African American. This was the beginning of the revolution that gave birth to the Black Theater movement.

Although the Black Theater movement started in the North there were simultaneous movements all around the country which identified themselves with the roles played by New York and Harlem groups. In the South, the Free Southern Theater was organized in New Orleans in 1964. The Student Nonviolent Coordinating Committee (SNCC) led by Stokely Carmichael (later known as Kwame Toure) spearheaded the effort. For African Americans in the deep South, theater was probably the last concern in terms of the struggle for equal rights. Nevertheless in Jackson, Mississippi, members of SNCC proposed that a black theater is a necessary step in the liberation movement. Based on this premise they decided to tour remote towns in the South to present plays in poor communities.

In the same period, in New York the Negro Ensemble Company (NEC) began to stage plays in 1967 that addressed black issues from a centered perspective. Its goal was to avoid exclusion and mistreatment from mainstream theater establishments by creating and producing its own black theater with black playwrights, directors, actors, and staff, staging performances for a predominantly black audience. The National Black Theater (NBT) was established in Harlem by Barbara Ann Teer who had grown tired of the stereotypical images blacks were forced to portray for white theater productions. Rejecting the Western standards for theater, beginning in 1968 Teer's group became renowned for their "ritualistic revivals" which aimed to bridge the gap between the performer and the audience as well as the performance and reality. The New Lafayette Theatre (NLT), too, grew out of Harlem. In 1966 the NLT initiated a vision to carry on Harlem's old Lafayette Theatre. They offered free acting lessons for children and distributed free tickets for their performances. In their efforts to depict problems and propose solutions, the NLT created successful productions, but still came under attack by Neal. He criticized NLT's use of rituals, finding them both pretentious and a waste of "creative and artistic energy." However, by the time NLT closed its doors after six years in operation, New York and Harlem audiences had been familiarized with the concepts fostered by the Black Theater movement. The movement had failed to reach its ultimate goal, but had nevertheless initiated a widespread acceptance and awakening in terms of art's collective, functional, and committed ends.

NOMMO: TRANSFORMATIVE POWER OF THE WORD

The role of the artist, in a traditional African context, is not much different from that defined in the sixties by prophets of the Black Arts movement. The concepts that were most widely discussed during the Black Arts movement had their origins in traditional African concepts of art, concepts that defined the function of art and the artist. Through the Negritude movement and poets such as Aime Cesaire and Leopold Senghor, these concepts were passed on to the sixties' writers and poets. Thus, Baraka's and Neal's works became conduits for the expression of a new spirituality centered around *Nommo*. Moreover, these writers called for a negation of the Eurocentric values practiced by black artists adhering to Western models. In its place they proposed a critical methodology relevant to the black community that would "aid men in becoming better than they are."[12] The critical canons from Aristotelian Critics to the New Critics lacked this element. In other words, previous critical theories focused on an evaluation of art in terms of its beauty, and not in terms of the *transformation* from ugliness to beauty that the work of art, in an African sensibility, demands from its audience.[13] In contrast, writers of the Black Arts movement insisted that the change brought forth by the transformative power of the word be considered: "The question for the black critic today is not how beautiful is a melody, a play, a poem, or a novel, but how much more beautiful has the poem, melody, play or novel made the life of a single black man? How far has the work gone in transforming an American Negro into an African American or black man?"[14]

"All magic is word magic," says Janheinz Jahn in his book *Muntu: African Culture and the Western World* (1961). In this major work Jahn focuses on the concepts of the Bantu scholar Alexis Kagame, and identifies four categories and two principles of basic African ontology. The ontological categories Jahn elucidates using Bantu words are as follows: *Muntu* (human being; plural: *Bantu*); *Kintu* (thing, object, animate, and inanimate; plural: *Bintu*); *Hantu* (place and time); *Kuntu* (modality, quality, style, rhythm, and beauty). The two principles are *NTU* and *Nommo*.[15] While *NTU* is the principle of essential coherence and compatibility among all things or among all the disciplines, *Nommo* is "the driving power . . . that gives life and efficacy to all things."[16] *Nommo* is exclusively the property of *Muntu*, the human being, which is the only force that is capable of possessing the magic and power of *Nommo*. All forces would be frozen if there were no *Nommo*, because it is the "magical force that activates and enlivens all other forces."[17] Furthermore, according to African philosophy, by the force of his word man can change things, make them work for him, and command them.[18] Thus, in African art there is no irresponsibility; it is never *l'art pour l'art*, for when the artist initiates the word, he enforces a change. "There is no 'harmless,' noncommittal word; every word has consequences. Therefore the word binds the muntu. And the muntu is responsible for his word."[19] In this sense, the anticipated change that artists, poets, and philosophers of the Black Arts movement targeted coincided with their struggle to revolutionize the psyche in order to liberate black minds from Western lexicon, metonymy, and configuration. Their aim was to reestablish an African sensibility that would reclaim their knowledge and ensure their continuity in the future.

During the sixties, Black Arts movement writers relied heavily on the power of *Nommo*. They knew that it would be possible to influence the masses through the magic of the word, thus bringing about the change they had envisioned arising from the political struggle of the civil rights era. It is interesting to note that Calvin C. Hernton, who wrote the introduction for Jahn's book, asserts that "a powerful Muntu such as a griot or shaman, may be capable through Nommo-power of effecting anything."[20] With this statement Hernton attributes great trust and skill to the griot role of the writer. Fittingly, when talking about the influence of Neal on the artists and writers who identified themselves with the Black Arts movement, Eleanor W. Traylor has referred to Neal as "the shaman."

Under Neal's and Baraka's leadership the movement attempted to revive the African tradition and combine it with the new reality of the African American. Literature, in the form of the written and spoken word, constituted their main area of operation, specifically as it expressed their innermost sentiments against mainstream values and the acceptance of Western concepts as universal. Protest, therefore, became one of this literature's main themes and was the initial response to any potential hindrances to their freedom of expression.

These artists assumed a remarkable reverence for the power of the spoken word, the *Nommo,* and they maintained that it is the force that creates the artist and transforms the poet. "The magic of metamorphosis never stops," asserts Jahn.[21] For instance, in Aime Cesaire's revolutionary art—which was frequently quoted by young poets during the sixties—one is able to observe such transformation, even of one's self: "The weakness of many men is that they do not know how to become a stone or a tree. As for me I sometimes put lighters between my fingers, in order to have the pleasure of setting myself afire all evening in fresh poinsettia leaves."[22]

Change is revealed through the flowing of forces; *Nommo* is the essence of the fluidity. It contains the idea of revolution that the young poets, writers, playwrights, and musicians invoked in their work. In accordance with *Nommo,* they created the event first in their vision, with stanzas, texts, and lyrics commanding the future; they believed in their ability to change, transform, improve, and rebuild. Incantation— the utterance of the word—became at the same time transformation itself.

With the help of *Nommo,* one can put change into action because the word makes concrete reality of the vision, and the tension created by the utterance brings other forces it has produced into the relationship. Cesaire describes the experience thus: "Oh I listen through the cracks of my skull. It rises, it rises, the black flood rises. It rises out of the depths of the earth. Waves I hear of shrieking, swamps

I smell of animal odors, and storm foams from naked feet. And there is a swarm of ever new feet climbing from the mountains."[23] The transformation is fostered through a sequence of images: cracks in Cesaire's own skull, as if he has put his ear to the cracks of a rock; listening to a black flood rise in waves, shrieking waves; swamps, odors, storm foams, and the sound of the "new feet" climbing from the mountains. Rarely does one find such a vivid description of the change that takes place, first in the poet's vision and later as mass action manifested in revolution. However, revolution does not necessarily sanctify armed action; it may simply relish the ecstasy of freedom. Thus the poem itself becomes functional above all else, and it is invoked through the power of *Nommo*. Jahn states: "Since Nommo, the procreative word, represents the form-giving principle as such, every taking on of form *is* expression."[24]

Nommo's transformative power is *functional, collective,* and *committed.* The artist or the poet speaks *to* the community and *for* the community; his/her art is therefore functional, responsible, and collective. Collectivity is not meant to be anti-individualistic; it is, rather, the ability to reach the collective consciousness of the people. At the onset of the Black Arts movement, Maulana Karenga (then Ron Karenga) defined revolutionary art as "collective, functional and committing."[25] What Karenga and other black artists meant by revolutionary art was an art which was anti-racist, anti-capitalist, and anti-imperialist.[26] Baraka, who skillfully combined his paradigm for a revolutionary black art with a Marxist canon, continued to popularize basic concepts of the Black Arts movement as in the following definitive statements: "Collective, in that it had to express a whole people, that it had to come from a whole people, that it had to speak to a whole people. Functional, in that it had a use, it was specific; a specific use in the struggle to liberate ourselves. Committing, in that it committed us to a struggle; it committed us specifically to the struggle."[27] Furthermore, as Leopold Senghor writes: "Every artistic manifestation is collective, created for all and shared by all. Because they are functional and collective, Negro-African literature and art are committed. They commit the person, and not merely the individual."[28]

The word, *Nommo,* whose transformative power has always been revered and valued in African and African American aesthetics, is the key to change. One cannot do without it, as drama is about the spoken word and the change that comes with it. Transformation begins when the first word is uttered on the stage by an actor; what follows is a new awareness, an awakening into a new reality. As the Dogon sage Ogotommeli says: "All change reveals the flowing of forces; Nommo, the word itself is moisture, fluidity; word and seed and blood and water."[29] The poets, writers, and artists of the sixties were aware of this power, particularly as it related to their people. As Jahn remarked: "His word is the more powerful the more he speaks in the name of his people, living as well as dead. As a poet he is the representative of all, and as representative he is a poet. And in order to achieve his goal, namely freedom, he makes use of all the powers at his command."[30] Baraka's poems titled "SOS," "Black People!," and "Black Art"; and Neal's "Kuntu" and "Rhythm Is a Groove #2" best exemplify Jahn's preceding statement.[31]

In "SOS" Baraka exclaims:

> Calling black people
> Calling all black people, man woman child
> Wherever you are, calling you, urgent, come in
> Black People, come in, wherever you are, urgent,
>   calling
> you, calling all black people
> calling all black people, come in, black people, come
> on in.[32]

In "Black Art" Baraka consistently urges that the black man take a firm moral position: "We want poems / like fists / . . . We want 'poems that kill.' / Assassin poems, Poems that shoot guns."[33] He concludes the poem on the following note which sums up his aesthetic lineage, one that arises from the Black Power concept he embraced during his Black Nationalist period:

> We want a black poem. And a
> Black World.
> Let the world be a Black Poem
> And Let All Black People Speak This Poem
> Silently
> or LOUD[34]

What is more striking, however, is Baraka's invocation of the power of the word that will bring change to the world. While the poem affirms the integral relationship between black people and black art, through the power of *Nommo* the poet sees himself ordained with the wherewithal to change the world, that is, initiate a literary revolution. Capitalization, rhythm, and typography all contribute to the elevation of excitement in anticipation of a revolution, with recognizable implications for the birth of the Black Arts movement. Neal's comments on Baraka's "Black Art" shed more light on the constructive energy of *Nommo*, as it relates to the people through the functionality inherent in the poem: "Poetry is a concrete function, an action. No more abstractions. Poems are physical entities: fists, daggers, airplane poems, and poems that shoot guns. Poems are transformed from physical object into personal forces."[35]

In "Black People!" Baraka is speaking of total conversion, not through poems or incantation of words but through real action. If one does not object to the call for conspicuous disturbance in the poem—which is really about rioting in the streets of Newark, robbery, looting, and possible shoot-outs—then the gist of the poem is the transference of *Nommo* to the people: "We must make our own World, man, our own world, and we can not do this unless the white man is dead."[36] As Lee A. Jacobus asserts: "'Black People!' is a poem of finality; there are no alternatives, no ambiguities. The call is to magic, the black magic of the title; the dance is magic dance; the acts magic acts; the words magic words. In all there is no tinge of the white God, the white values: all is expunged."[37] The poem ends in an assertion grounded in both the Black Arts movement and the Black Power movement.

Neal's poem "Kuntu," which he wrote in 1966, is a self-explanatory testament to the power of the word. In this piece Neal affirms his allegiance to his roots and ancestors, to African cosmology and epistemology, wherein song, dance, drum, and *Nommo* are the primary motifs which construct and renew the incorruptible relationship between man and his universe:

> In Olorun, the Universe, I formed
> the Word and the Earth and linked
>   them in the dance
> the first form was formless sound
>   the first Word was Drum's Word

I am descended from Drum
Drum's words informed us, giving us flesh
and flesh shaped the Word.
    I say, and flesh shaped the Word
linked the song
    linked earth to sky.[38]

In "Rhythm is a Groove #2," which Neal wrote during the summer of 1968, the prophet of the Black Arts movement was initializing an incantation to the spirit of the sixties, in a fashion that derives its rhythm from African ritual orientation and its symbols. It is an afternoon at Mt. Morris Park, the sun is hot, people are packed and sweating. The poet/griot addresses the crowd, utilizing the power of *Nommo* that makes drums, the skins, and the beat "speak":

do the foot shuffle / the colors /
shuffle the beat / and the skins speak

Sun come black, juju wonder song.
Sun come black, juju wonder song.
Drum sing / speak black / black skin skin
shuffle the beat / shuffle the color / the beat speaks
color the shuffle / black brother brother
brother / brother / hurl drum into sky
make Sun come, hot pulse flaming
YEAH! ! ![39]

In addition to the above-cited poems by Baraka and Neal, one could refer to numerous poems by other poets writing during the height of the Black Arts era which depict the interrelationship of the black artist and his community. When one looks at history through the windows of the present, what manifests itself is a remarkable parallelism between the political and artistic concerns of the Negritude and the Black Arts movements. Senghor, Cesaire, and other poets of the Negritude movement sowed the seeds for the artistic and literary transformation that brought forth the works of Neal, Baraka, and Karenga in the sixties and seventies. Likewise, the latter group oversaw the germination of a new idea which expressed itself most succinctly in Asante's African-centered thesis during the late eighties.

A similar pattern is also evident in the development of African American drama.

The aesthetic values promoted during the Black Arts movement proposed a separate terminology, symbolism, mythology, iconology, and methods of critique, inaugurating a cultural revolution in art and ideas. Most often these poets used the transformative power of the word, *Nommo*, to express not only their genuine commitment to the cultural revolution that they were about to initiate, but also as a literary vehicle serving as a spawning ground for the new doctrine of change found in their poetry. However, it was through the medium of drama and its capacity to evoke cathartic effects by delineating myriad forms of human emotions, passions, and flaws that the essence of the word came to be recognized as a transformative agent, particularly with reference to the exposition of the African Americans' struggle for civil rights in the United States. In the next chapter, I explore this premise through an examination of the works and mission of Larry Neal.

NOTES

[1] Maulana Karenga, "Black Cultural Nationalism," in *The Black Aesthetic*, ed. Addison Gayle Jr. (Garden City, N.Y.: Doubleday and Company, 1971), 33.

[2] Alice Walker, *In Search of Our Mothers' Gardens: Womanist Prose* (San Diego, Calif.: Harcourt Brace Jovanovich, 1983), 120, 135.

[3] Ibid., 138.

[4] Shamanism is primarily the religion of the Ural-Altaic peoples of Northern Asia and Europe, in which the unseen world of gods, demons and ancestral spirits is conceived to be responsive only to the shamans, mediumistic magicians, or the medicine men. In similar religions or cultures, especially that of some American Indians, the medicine man performs much the same function as the shaman. (*Webster's Dictionary.*)

[5] For a better understanding of the Black Theater movement see Mance Williams, *Black Theater in the 1960s and 1970s: A Historical-Critical Analysis of the Movement* (Westport, Conn.: Greenwood Press, 1985), 11-19, 50-65.

[6] Houston A. Baker Jr., *Blues, Ideology and Afro-American Literature: A Vernacular Theory* (Chicago: University of Chicago Press, 1984), 3.

[7] Eleanor W. Traylor, "And the Resurrection, Let It Be Complete: The Achievement of Larry Neal (A Biobibliography of a Critical Imagination)," *Callaloo #23*, 8, no. 1: 49-50.

[8] Amiri Baraka, *The Autobiography of LeRoi Jones/Amiri Baraka* (New York: Freundlich Books, 1984), 205.

[9] Ibid., 202.

[10] Ibid., 205.

[11] Ibid., 204.

[12] Addison Gayle Jr, ed., "Introduction," *The Black Aesthetic* (New York: Doubleday and Company, 1971), xxii.

[13] Ibid.

[14] Ibid.

[15] Janheinz Jahn, *Muntu: African Culture and the Western World* (New York: Grove Weidenfeld, 1961), xx.

16   Ibid., xx, xxi.
17   Ibid., xxi.
18   Ibid., 135.
19   Ibid., 133.
20   Ibid., xxii.
21   Ibid., 138.
22   Ibid.
23   Ibid., 137.
24   Jahn, *Muntu*, 148.
25   Amiri Baraka, "Black Art," *Black Scholar* (January/February 1987): 24.
26   Ibid.
27   Ibid.
28   Jahn, *Muntu*, 149.
29   Ibid., 139.
30   Ibid., 143.
31   For a complete citation of Baraka's poems see William J. Harris, ed., *The LeRoi Jones/Amiri Baraka Reader* (New York: Thunder's Mouth Press, 1991), 218-19, 224; and Larry Neal, *Hoodoo Hollerin' Bebop Ghosts* (Washington D.C.: Howard University Press, 1974), 54, 74.
32   William J. Harris, ed., *The LeRoi Jones/Amiri Baraka Reader* (New York: Thunder's Mouth Press, 1991), 218.
33   Ibid., 219.
34   Ibid., 220.
35   Larry Neal, "The Black Arts Movement," in *Visions of a Liberated Future: Black Arts Movement Writings* (New York: Thunder's Mouth Press, 1989), 66.
36   Harris, *LeRoi Jones*, 224.
37   Lee A. Jacobus, "Imamu Amiri Baraka: The Quest for Moral Order," in *Modern Black Poets*, ed. Donald B. Gibson (Englewood Cliffs, N.J.: Prentice Hall, 1973), 123-24.
38   Neal, "Kuntu," in *Visions*, 218.
39   Larry Neal, "Rhythm is a Groove, #2," in *Hoodoo Hollerin' Bebop Ghosts* (Washington, D.C.: Howard University Press, 1974), 56.

II

Larry Neal

Stiff old Philly saints dripped gold
into the arms of Georgia Queens;
Columbia Avenue was snake eyes and
the hussy in red . . .

Can I tell you this story. . . ?

—Neal, "Can I Tell You This Story, Or Will You
Send Me Through All Kinds of Changes?"

THE WINTER OF DESPAIR/
THE SPRING OF HOPE

In 1952, when Larry Neal was fifteen years old, the Tuskegee
Institute reported that for the first time in seventy years of racial
turbulence no lynchings had taken place in the United States. Two
years later in 1954, the Supreme Court concluded that in the field of
public education the "doctrine of separate but equal" had no place. The
following year, the Court ordered public school desegregation with all
deliberate speed. The nation was geared towards civil rights battles,
and these were just a few steps on the long way to liberty, equality, and
pursuit of happiness. No teenager could have watched the pitched
battles for integration with more interest than the young Neal.

The sixties, in the memory of the nation, serves as the catalyst that
helped form in the American public's mind a further crystallization of

concepts such as "civil rights," "school desegregation," "equality," "brotherhood," "freedom of speech," and "equal opportunity." Although these inalienable rights were not won all at once, the fortitude that was manifested through the mutual efforts of African Americans and those who believed in these rights has left its indelible mark on the majority of American minds.

From the Montgomery bus boycott of December 1, 1955 to the Black Panthers' march on the Capitol in Sacramento in protest of a gun-control bill on May 2, 1972, the sixties witnessed a plethora of incidents, movements, and trends. Yet from nonviolent direct action to marches, mass demonstrations, sit-ins, kneel-ins, freedom rides, student movements, and self-defense tactics throughout the era, the key concept was always "self-determination." During this period the philosopher Maulana Karenga who founded Kwanzaa would popularize the Kiswahili word for self determination—*kujichagulia*—and it would become a regularly used term in the African American community. Protesters and activists asserted that freedom was anyone's natural right, and in itself was enough reason to protest against oppression. Sentiments were high; pride was in the air, Wasn't it, after all, the "spring of hope"?

However, with the assassinations of national and international leaders rapidly mounting—the Congolese Prime Minister Patrice Lumumba in 1961; Medgar Evers, June 1963; President John F. Kennedy, November 1963; Minister Malcolm X, February 1965; Dr. Martin Luther King Jr., April 1968; Senator Robert F. Kennedy, June 1968; and Kenyan Freedom Fighter Tom Mboya in 1969—as well as the murders of three freedom fighters in Mississippi, four young girls in Birmingham, and 16-year-old Emmett Till in 1955, juxtaposed with hundreds of random lynchings in the South, the optimism in the air was in fast decline. In the aftermath of fatal church bombings, widespread race riots, bus burnings, and protest marches both in the North and the South, the ill-fated decade left the nation in grief and mourning. Wasn't it, also, the "winter of despair"?

While violent clashes between the two races dominated the socio-political arena in the arts and literature, new moorings and props were activating the imaginative recollection and the historical consciousness of African American artists working mainly in urban centers such as New York, Newark, Philadelphia, Pittsburgh, Chicago, and Los Angeles. Poetry, prose, and drama with themes, narrative styles, and tones passionately wrought within the social and political climate of the decade were pouring out in large numbers. The sense of urgency that was put forth through these works still constitutes the most prominent characteristic of sixties' writing. It was followed by a widespread insistence upon the retrieval of genuine value systems that would enable a thorough understanding of African culture and its specific features as they impact African American life. Moreover, the artists and spokesmen of the sixties believed that works of verbal and expressive art have direct effects on the solution of social problems, as well as help raise and shape the social consciousness. Henceforth, it was this sense of immediacy and the urge to develop a separate system of agency that would deliver functional, realistic, and holistic images. Through the use of such images, the Black Arts movement became an instrument that projected the African American creative impetus.

The makers of this second renaissance were all independent artists who demanded the right to think for themselves and forcefully attained that right through *kujichagulia*. While engaged in their individual protests, these artists were also united in their radical attack against Eurocentric negations. Chief among the artists in this movement were Larry Neal, Amiri Baraka, and Charles Fuller. Their works emerge as relevant points of interest for a discourse on contemporary African American theater. Since Neal evolved as the precedent voice that gave direction to other artists, I will now turn to a discussion of his works.

THE MAN IN THE LEATHER CAP

It was during the late hours of a cold winter evening in 1980 when the man wearing a brown tweed jacket, leather cap, and purple scarf around his neck knocked on the front door of the three-story brick row house in North Philadelphia. The tall, ebony-complexioned man who opened the door welcomed the guest. "It's cold Charlie," said the visitor. They sat down, drank wine, and talked into the early hours of the morning until it was time for the caller to hit the New Jersey turnpike before the rush hour traffic.

Larry Neal had stopped to see Charles Fuller, who had been his friend for over thirty years. They enjoyed talking, debating, and testing their ideas on each other. Moreover, they were determined to pour out what they had in their minds and hearts into poems, essays, plays, and human sketches, as dictated by the generative spirit of *Nommo* and their long-continuing discourse in that arena. Their friendship as well as their common boyhood roots in the same depressed North Philadelphia neighborhood provided a linkage and an energizing capacity for the developing matrix. Both were apprehensive, artistic, and committed to African American culture, and had been so since they were quite young. Concomitantly the season was ripe for the growth they were to initiate.

Neal was born in Atlanta, Georgia on September 5, 1937. His mother worked as a domestic servant and was talented in music and storytelling; his father was a railroad worker. He was named Lawrence Paul, signifying his parents' desire to carry on the beloved poet Paul Laurence Dunbar's heritage, but it was more than the invocation of Dunbar's name which made him study literature, history, language, and political science in his future years.

When Neal was six, the family moved to Philadelphia where he grew up in the James Weldon Johnson Housing Project. In this neighborhood, Neal developed life-long friendships with Verta Mae Grosvenor, Jimmy Stewart, Charles Fuller, and many other Philadelphia artists. Growing up in a race-conscious family where much of the talk was about black history, aside from his studies, Neal spent his time visiting the barbershops along Ridge Avenue in North Philadelphia, talking and listening to old people. On the threshold of adolescence he became a member of a black Marxist organization known as Organization Alert. Meanwhile he worked at a bookstore, reading Marxist literature which helped form the fundamentals of his political education.

Following his graduation from Lincoln University, he received his M.A. from the University of Pennsylvania. In the stormy days of the late sixties, Neal was already recognized as a poet, orator, critic, and essayist who devoted his energy to define and advance the teachings of the Black Arts and Black Aesthetics movements. Frequently he was invited to college campuses to lecture and read his poetry, enchanting the audience with his charismatic style. Remembering one of Neal's public lectures at Yale University, Houston A. Baker Jr. writes:

> I remember your strut.
> Disguised as Garvey's ghost,

You entered the room.
Your plumed stride and narrow eyes
Matched the peacock's radiant glory.
You gave the shout of Shine,
Bellowed like James Brown,
Swam miraculously against white currents.[1]

In 1966 when Kwame Toure (then Stokely Carmichael) coined the term "Black Power," Toure urged everyone to join a united front for Black Power. Neal was among those leading the masses in urban centers like Philadelphia and Newark towards a major breakthrough in black art and aesthetics. For Neal the two were inseparable; art was the "aesthetic and spiritual sister of the Black Power concept," and it spoke "directly to the needs and aspirations of Black America."[2] Often emphatic on the unbridgeable dichotomy between ethics and aesthetics in Western art, Neal insisted that art would always be directed to and for the spiritual needs of African American people.[3]

He continued his consciousness-raising efforts by founding, editing, and publishing several magazines and journals simultaneously. *Liberator* magazine, *The Cricket, The Journal of Black Poetry, Soulbook,* and *Black Theater* are just a few of them. In 1968, a year plagued by political and social crises, literary artists seemed to arise from the chaos with vigor and power. During that year Neal co-edited with Amiri Baraka the renowned anthology *Black Fire: An Anthology of Afro-American Writing.* Meanwhile, he was pursuing a multi-faceted career as an English professor at City College of New York (1968-69); writer-in-residence at Wesleyan University in Middletown, Connecticut (1969-70); and Fellow at Yale University (1970-75). In addition to his teaching schedule, he also worked as Minister of Education in the Black Panther Party for a brief period. Neal was himself the embodiment of the consciousness which he articulated.

This talented man undoubtedly greatly inspired many of his contemporaries, yet his greatest impact was felt most significantly upon the next generation. Kimberly W. Benston, for whom Neal served as senior advisor at Yale University, reminiscences about him in the 1985 special issue of *Callaloo* dedicated to Neal and his work:

> For a whole generation, it must be said, Larry Neal
> was an intellectual hero. He was the greatest moral
> force in radical Afro-American letters during the
> past two decades: learned, fiercely independent,
> sometimes impulsive, but an utterly free man. His
> essays, letters, and poems chart a gradual
> redefinition of the past's specific role in shaping a
> new aesthetic moment . . . the eighties would have
> been *his* decade: more than ever, his enduring
> qualities of integrity, clarity, suppleness, dignity and
> discipline have entered what he called the "spirit-
> force" of Afro-American culture. For us he was an
> exemplary figure, and through him in great measure
> we have become a *community*.[4]

If it were not for his sudden death on January 7, 1981, Neal would
have continued his exciting odyssey; when he died he was only 44.
However, his legacy was honored in 1984 with a series of conferences,
lectures, and workshops commenced by the African American History
Museum of Philadelphia under the leadership of Eleanor W. Traylor,
the then literary consultant and program officer for the Museum. The
already mentioned special *Callaloo* issue, its twenty-third, also
celebrated Neal's achievement in a jubilant compilation of essays by
those who admired his work. Contributors included Houston A. Baker
Jr., Paul Carter Harrison, Mae G. Henderson, Ishmael Reed, and
Traylor. Sadly, though, this was the one and only collective
recognition given to Neal's entire career. Thus, in treating Neal in the
context of African American theater in this book I am continuing what
I believe will be a long tradition of literary criticism and insight into
the writings, influences, and mission of Neal.

But what was the unique achievement of Neal that distinguished
him from his predecessors? What were his ideas and feelings on the
literature, drama, poetry, and art of the African American ethos that
inspired others? These questions lead one closer to an understanding
of the intellectual groundwork of the African American dramatic
imagination, particularly since Neal was not the most prolific of the
African American literary figures or dramatists. Ed Bullins, for
example, offers us more substantive moments of theater, yet it is Neal
who defines the scope and tenor of the dramatic moment because of

his numerous publications on the aesthetic question, literary history, theory, and criticism.

To begin with it has to be recognized that Neal was one of those few gifted people who was able to unite action with thought during his brief lifetime. He was writing, publishing, conversing, lecturing, and discussing the necessity for a fundamental change in people's outlook on black arts and aesthetics, while at the same time actively engaged in the activities of the Revolutionary Action Movement of Philadelphia (RAM) during the early sixties. Known as an underground organization, RAM was committed to Afro-American liberation, African culture, and African perceptions. Such affiliations and interests equipped Neal with a strong sense of connection to the masses for whom he was soon to become a literary prophet.

Black Boogaloo: Notes on Black Liberation, his first volume of poetry, was published in 1969 by the Journal of Black Poetry Press. These early poems comprised the most fundamental reflections upon his revolutionary stance. For instance, in poems such as "The Slave"— which he dedicated to Baraka (then LeRoi Jones), "Oath," "The Narrative of the Black Magicians," "Can You Dig It?," "Cross Riff," and "Morning Saga for Malcolm," Neal emerges as a dynamic revolutionary poet whose spiritual strivings for the liberation of his people disavow simplistic explanations and easy interpretations. These poems, when first published, served a multiplicity of ends. Besides announcing Neal's aesthetic aspirations, they kindled the spirit of brotherhood, communal awareness, and unity. Additionally, the poems exemplified for his readers a high-pitched resonance with key concepts such as Pan-Africanism, reminiscent of Marcus Garvey's determination and W.E.B. Du Bois's resolute sensibility. Commitment to the cause was the *piece de resistance* in Neal's aesthetic consciousness: "We were very much committed to African ideas and to African liberation and to African culture and African perceptions. . . . We were looking for a big feeling; we were really trying to connect. I was aware of a whole kind of cosmology of love that I had never dealt with before, and I was aware of it. I was trying to sing to all of that."[5]

His second volume of poetry, *Hoodoo Hollerin' Bebop Ghosts,* was published by Howard University Press in 1974 and contained new poems in addition to those revised since the publication of the previous volume. In subsequent years Neal's poems appeared in numerous anthologies, including *American Negro Poetry* (revised edition 1974), edited by Arna Bontemps; *Black Spirits* (1972), edited by Woodie King; *The New Black Poetry* (1969), edited by Clarence Major; *The Black Poets* (1971), edited by Dudley Randall; *New Black Voices* (1971), edited by Abraham Chapman; *Black Literature in America* (1971), edited by Houston A. Baker Jr.; and *Cavalcade* (1971), edited by Arthur P. Davis and Saunders Redding. His short fiction titled "Sinner Man Where You Gonna Run To?" appeared in *Black Fire* (1968), along with some of his poems.

Music—especially jazz—combined with an emphasis on rhythm, melody, and tone, constituted the backdrop for Neal's literary frame of reference. Growing up in Philadelphia "with the Bebop sound" in the background, where the "hurly burly" of the streets never quieted down, where Broad and Girard met to acclaim the lonely guitar's growling vamp or the saxophone's sardonic boast, Neal developed an exquisite taste for music. At one time, he even started to write a play about a musician going to Philadelphia in 1945. Musicians, after all, had been his favorite heroes since his early days. "I think of us as being an essentially lyric people. . . . We had great singers with us like Smokey Robinson, Stevie Wonder, Marvin Gaye . . . and we had the great oratorical tradition of Martin Luther King . . . and poetry lends itself to oratory. So you've got great oratorical poets like Margaret Walker. The lyricism in Gwendolyn Brooks . . . and Langston Hughes, the kind of blues thing, David Henderson who's into the rhythm and blues feeling."[6]

The African American poetic tradition and the lyricism that it conveys were celebratory achievements in Neal's aesthetic vision. Yet when it comes to drama, Neal could not maintain the same optimism, particularly when he compared the energy and commitment of the sixties with that of the dawning seventies. Being a perfectionist, he was expecting brilliant plays that would aesthetically incorporate the message and the style that he had envisioned. "The area black people have trouble with is the theater; theater needs crafting and it demands a certain kind of technical thing. Very often we haven't had the time to get the technical thing together."[7] In the sixties, however, Neal asserted that developments in drama and theater had reached a high-tide mark: "In the 1960's black drama was flowering forth in its fantastic ferment of revolutionary ideas and social activism . . . [it] was a very engaged theater. This is a theater that consciously—more than any other time in history, and this is one of the things the 1960s is most important for, for all its ranting and raving and bullshit—forced black artists to look at black people, to address their art to black people, which to me is absolutely necessary in order to get a focus."[8] The real "low-tide" of African American drama, as Neal pointed out, came during the 1920s when black drama was mostly represented by musical comedy, burlesque, and dance. Lacking a serious social content and focus, and unable to dispel the popular stereotypical images or misguided remnants of the minstrel tradition, African American drama, at that time, could not completely overcome the prevailing disorientation among African American dramatists. However, in the sixties, through committed audiences and prophetic playwrights, the promise was renewed. After all, it aspired to be an art form *for the people from the very heart of the people*! Who could possibly express the transcendence of the sense of functionality heretofore attached to art more emphatically than Baraka?

> We are unfair
> And unfair
> We are black magicians
> Black arts we make in black labs of the heart
> The fair are fair and deathly white
> The day will not save them
> And we own the night.[9]

Baraka's friendship with Neal goes back to the roaring dawn of the Black Liberation movement. The two were the representatives of a new generation of intellectuals most clearly distinguished from their predecessors by their different philosophical and ideological stances with reference to the ideals of American egalitarianism. Neal and Baraka belonged to the emergent generation whose members were a dynamic, vibrant group of men and women, constituting the heart of Afro-America. The new poetics which emerged out of this ideological orientation expressed a clear imperative for African American society to focus its social efforts and political vision on its own self-interests rather than on that of others. It was in the context of this challenge that Neal and Baraka collaborated on many projects.

Throughout the urban uprisings of Harlem, Watts, and other communities it was clearly manifest that the previous decades' "integrationist" poetics would be replaced with black political and social sovereignty. This signaled the birth of a new ideology, one that originally received its name when Stokely Carmichael addressed the crowd in Mississippi during a protest march, in a call-and-response chant. The term later appeared in the volume *Black Power: The Politics of Liberation in America* written by Carmichael and Charles Hamilton, with the following designated goals: "[Black Power] is a call for black people in this country to unite, to recognize their heritage, to build a sense of community. It is a call for black people to begin to define their own goals, to lead their own organizations and to support those organizations. It is a call to reject the racist institutions and values of [American society]."[10] Carmichael and Hamilton entered the movement fully aware of the complementarity of the Black Arts and Black Power concepts, aiming for a "radical reordering of the western cultural aesthetic."[11] Their comradeship, which began on the streets of New York, led to numerous productive avenues over the years, such as the establishment of the Black Arts Repertory Theatre/School (BART/S) and publication of the anthology *Black Fire*. Baraka reflects on those days as follows:

> Larry was there. Young, hip, talking black revolution. Clean as, and like the rest of us, arrogant as, the afternoon sun. Hot and brightly shining. Full of life, energy and Black Fire! . . .
> I found out Larry was an artist, a poet, writer after our mutually expressed commitment to destroy white supremacy. . . .
> It was part of our commitment to the black revolutionary democratic struggle that we collaborated to create the Black Arts Repertory Theater School (BARTS) in Harlem. . . . The institution set a concrete example for the movement, it was part of—the Black Arts Movement![12]

The Black Arts movement inspired a reawakening in the new generation of black artists to launch a massive assault in art, literature, and drama—an assault directed at the struggle against oppression, stereotyping, and the smothering politics of racism that jeopardizes and limits free acts of creation *by and for the people*. It was characterized by a revolutionary dynamism which fiercely and effectively emphasized the education and unification of the black masses. Elevating black life and history, focusing on black heritage, and advocating the legacy of resistance required enormous discipline and serious commitment. Teaching through music, poetry, dance, drama, and other genres of black expression was considered the ultimate goal for an understanding of cultural aesthetics. In keeping with this premise, educational alternatives were frequently explored, and reverence for all heroes and heroines was included in the educational programs designed for the young ones.

One of the educational programs that stands out in this era is BART/S. Despite its short existence, BART/S was a successful model in the development of revolutionary arts education and performance, and Neal was definitely *the* inspirational source in its realization. Baraka recalls Neal's impact on BART/S: "We wanted a *mass art,* . . . what we wanted to create would be African American and Revolutionary. In fact it would be the real link to our history—part of the mainstream of black art through the century. . . . We wanted the oral tradition in our work, we wanted the sound, the pumping rhythm of black music. The signifying drawl of blues. Larry incorporated it all into his work. . . . High intelligence, revolutionary commitment, and great skill."[13] Later Baraka compares Neal's art to Mao Tse-Tung's idea of "mass line," where the aim of all art and life is to reach people as revealed in Mao's motto "from the people to the people." As a matter of fact, it was through communal activism and commitment that the Black Arts movement came to be recognized as a revolutionary movement, more forceful and assertive in scope than any of the previous aesthetic and literary endeavors engaged in by individual African American authors.

Although he was a preeminent theoretician, Neal was not the first man of letters in African American literature to talk about an art that is oriented towards the needs of the masses. Before him, W.E.B. Du Bois and playwrights Willis Richardson and William Wells Brown had expressed their concerns, particularly in relation to drama: All three men vehemently insisted on the necessity of establishing a focused national theater or touring companies which would take black plays by black playwrights to remote towns in order to inform the unknowing. Du Bois' establishment of the Krigwa Players, a comparatively long-lived theater company, and Willis Richardson's experimental essays on drama and theater that appeared in *Opportunity* and *Crisis* mark early endeavors and preoccupations in the same vein.

As previously stated, inspiration evoked by Neal's ideas combined with Baraka's call for black nationalism and his devotion to the continuance, development, and strengthening of aesthetic concepts fostered their collaboration in further projects. For instance, the launching of a music magazine, *Cricket*—which published merely three issues—demonstrated, as did other publications, that black expression, whether in art, aesthetics, drama, music, poetry, or education, entered a distinctly *nationalistic* phase in the mid-sixties. This phase had ramifications that have been felt in a variety of contexts in subsequent decades. The recent discussions on school curricula in and around the school district of central Philadelphia— where the majority of the students are people of color—are just one example of this influence. Current dialogue not only generates questions about the impact of Euro-American value systems in the curricula, but could benefit from a number of Neal's insights. On the pertinent issue of a waning Western influence, for example, Neal has stated:

> I recall once reading an article about a son of A.J. Sax, the Belgian instrument maker, who said something to the effect that he didn't believe his father intended for the instrument to be played the way jazz musicians were playing it. Yeah, you can take the other dude's instruments and play like your Uncle Rufus's hog callings. But there is another possibility also: *You could make your own instrument.* And if you can sing through that instrument, you can impose your voice on the world in a heretofore-unthought-of manner.[14]

Neal, considered a cultural prophet of his time, foresaw that respect for other cultures and recognition of differences are prerequisites of the democratization process around the world. Even before the Afrocentric movement was identified, Neal understood that Eurocentrism tended to be indifferent towards this premise, and therefore, African and Asian cultures needed to emphasize their respective identities and ensure their acceptance, particularly in matters of aesthetics, society, and education.

Neal perceived the Black Arts movement as a "corrective," that is, "as a means of assisting African American people out of the polluted mainstream of Americanism, an Americanism that was often anti-African." Furthermore, he was expert at offering logical, reasoned arguments as to why he should not desire to join the ranks of a Norman Mailer or a William Styron: "To be an American writer is to be an American, and, for black people, there should no longer be honor attached to either position."[15] Upon his entry into the literary field, Neal had joined hands with his predecessors—William Wells Brown, James Weldon Johnson, Paul Laurence Dunbar, W.E.B. Du Bois, Zora Neale Hurston, Langston Hughes, Sterling Brown, Richard Wright, Margaret Walker, James Baldwin, and Ralph Ellison—in harvesting the crops of a long-awaited germination. However, he was clearly adamant in distinguishing between his predecessors' integrationist politics which adhered to a single standard of criticism in art, literature, and aesthetic taste—the standard common during the twenties' Harlem Renaissance era—and that of the sixties' revolutionary Black Aesthetic paradigm. The latter had "distinctive perceptual and semantic ramifications . . . which changed the meaning of both 'black' and 'aesthetic' in the American literary-critical universe of discourse so that these terms could continue to make 'useful distinctions' in a world where works of Afro-American expressive art had come to be seen quite differently from the manner in which they were viewed by an older integrationist paradigm."[16]

Additionally, Neal aimed at synthesizing ethics and aesthetics in a revolutionary mode of expression, an expression based upon a binary vision proclaiming that ethics and aesthetics are inextricably intertwined. This premise would provide the essential structural base for the development of his critical methodology, for as he would later assert in the *Liberator* while reviewing Ellison's *Shadow and Act*: "It is ultimately the necessity of the writer to seek 'truth' to which all viewpoints, critical and social, must *eventually* pay homage."[17] In 1976, Neal would further elucidate on the task of the black writer: "The task of the contemporary Black writer, as of any serious writer, is to project the accumulated weight of the world's aesthetic, intellectual, and historical experience. To do so he must utilize his ability to the fullest, distilling his experience through the creative process into a form that best projects his personality and what he conceives to be the ethos of his national or ethnic group."[18]

However, among all his writings, it was Neal's 1968 essay "The Black Arts Movement" that generated an authoritative influence, mainly because it set the tone for a new policy and outlook on black art and aesthetics. Designed as a manifesto in its daring eruptions against what was considered elite and mainstream until then, Neal's essay suggested that art and politics are intertwined. Furthermore, it pronounced the necessity for an acrimonious separation from Western aesthetics: "The motive behind the Black aesthetic is the destruction of the White thing, the destruction of ideas, and white ways of looking at the world. The new aesthetic is mostly predicated on an Ethics which asks the question: whose vision of the world is finally more meaningful, ours or the white oppressor's? What is the truth? Or, more precisely, whose truth shall we express, that of the oppressed or of the oppressors?"[19]

Traylor, who was instrumental in popularizing Neal's lifetime commitment to African American letters, particularly after his death, often referred to him as a *shaman*. Indeed, as a spokesman for his community and as a healer whose spiritual guidance was sought in times of distress, Neal led an ideological movement which set out from the peripheries of dispossession and "landlessness,"[20] and moved towards repossession and ownership rights:

> We bear witness to a profound change in the way we now see ourselves and the world. And this has been an ongoing change. A steady, certain march toward a collective sense of who we are, and what we must now be about to liberate ourselves. Liberation is impossible if we fail to see ourselves in more positive terms. For without a change of vision, we are slaves to the oppressor's ideas and values—ideas and values that finally attack the very core of our existence. Therefore we must see the world in terms of our own realities.[21]

The landlessness that Neal speaks of represents a physical reality which resulted from the historical forces of oppression levied against the black man. But whereas Neal sees liberation in terms of a change of vision, Baraka demands a more assertive participation on behalf of the African American people in order to *bring forth* the change. "What the Black Man must do now is look down at the ground upon which he stands, and claim it as his own. It is not abstract. Look down! Pick up the earth, or jab your fingernails into the concrete. It is real and it is yours, if you want it."[22]

The culmination of Neal's ideas asserting a deliberate *change* in perspective toward self-realization and self-definition in life, in art, and in aesthetics appeared most clearly in two of his essays: "The Social Background of the Black Arts Movement" and the above-mentioned "The Black Arts Movement." In the former essay, which has been recognized as a manifesto since the day of its appearance, Neal discusses the landscape in which the Black Arts movement developed, how language gradually changed the definitions, the contributors, and the factors which produced the movement. In this essay Neal is convinced, as was Baraka, that black art is the only reality of black life and people.

A powerful argument that Neal put forth in "The Social Background of the Black Arts Movement" concerned language and its empowering quality in the reinforcement of a revolution. In his discussion of the Southern and the street corner oratory, Neal compared Martin Luther King Jr.'s and Malcolm X's respective oratory styles, concluding: "The folk rhythms of King are the Southern folk rhythms, the church rhythms of the gospel, whereas the urban rhythm is the urban blues and the root of that language is the toast of the dozens."[23] What Neal would see developing in the urban areas would be an aesthetic form devoid of much of the rhythms of the South. As Neal pointed out later in the essay, the predominant characteristic of the Black Arts movement was its interaction with the urban environment that bred it. The end result could have been much different and the movement less visible if it had not been produced in the heart of the city.

Clearly the dynamism, energy, and competence which became the definitive power of the literary works produced during the Black Arts era owed much to the cities, the street blocks, the masses of people who lived in close proximity to each other. In other words, the urban landscape which had inspired many artists since the days of the Industrial Revolution possessed a similar charisma during the sixties for urban black writers, poets, and activists who used the tonal qualities—the staccato rhythms of the mechanized city—to create new artistic forms. Its landmarks, such as 27 Cooper Square or the Black Arts Theater where poetry readings attracted a large audience; its music, which they called "loft jazz"; the publications that came out of the Grove Press, such as Frantz Fanon's *The Wretched of the Earth*, Janheinz Jahn's *Muntu*, and some of Baraka's early works—all pointed to a happening that would bring change in its full force. As Neal put it, it was "something that was really consuming in terms of your personality."[24] He also asserted: "This particular group of writers could never go for Martin Luther King. . . . We were urban. We had grown up in tough neighborhoods. There was no way we had the kind of fortitude that it would take to go anywhere and turn the other cheek."[25] Consequently, the polemic mode of their discourses—the politically geared subject-matters, the frequent quotations from Marxist philosophy and Fanon's *The Wretched Of the Earth*—greatly influenced the writing of the period and became the fighting words and the battle mottoes of the time. Neal said: "If you were supposed to be anything, black and intellectual, if you hadn't read Fanon, you were out of it." He added: "I had my Marxist vocabulary together. I was very righteous, you know."[26]

The increase in the number of people who read Lenin, Mao Tse-Tung, and particularly Fanon, signified a major shift in the course of race relations across the nation. Apparently the black community was turning its focus away from civil rights, integration, and assimilation, and was moving towards black nationalism. But it was the inspiration Fanon brought to the discussion of human interaction that underscored the commitment to an engagement with oppression. Fanon had shown that the Algerian people had used their power—intellectual and social—to turn Algiers into a living hell for the French occupiers. It was from this vantage point that the new radical blacks felt the necessity to appropriate Fanon for a vigorously new struggle on the American continent. Fanon was at once urban and revolutionary, and indeed, very black. During social gatherings or poetry readings the black artists consistently tried to ensure that the form they were evolving was a form that could include the people, the community.[27] This idea validates the source of the strength of the Black Arts movement and the richness of the material that followed it.

Music had been one of the major areas of interest throughout Neal's life; he had a natural affinity for that art form. Paul Carter

Harrison informs us that in 1974 Neal started taking took piano
lessons from Bill Dixson at Williams College and he was able to play
tunes from the songbooks of Bud Powell, Theolonius Monk, and
Horace Silver.[28] For Neal, music always played a central role,
especially during the height of the Black Arts movement, because he
believed the new music shaped the language of the movement. He
asserted that James Brown was "the big hero for the poet" and added:
"We all thought that James Brown was a magnificent poet and we all
envied him and wished that we could do what he did."[29] Besides James
Brown—who embodied the soul of a people in his electrifying
performances, who induced catharsis by his spontaneous invocations
of "I'm Black and I'm Proud"—there were others who came into
prominence with their emphasis on a high-powered, magnetic rhythm
that corresponded to the kinetic and explosive energy of the age. Their
emergence corresponded with the development of the Black Arts
movement in Harlem; as Harrison comments the majority of them
were "an underground movement of musicians [who] surfaced in
Greenwich Village."[30]

John Coltrane, Eric Dolphy, Charles Mingus, Oscar Brown Jr.,
Cecil Taylor, Albert Ayler, Archie Shepp, Ornette Coleman, and Sun
Ra were successful in expressing the transition of the mood from
smooth tunes of non-violent passive resistance to a more definite,
passionate sound which depicted the intensity of emotions shared by
the nation. Neal said: "We connected with the sound because . . . it
was sound and abstract. We laid on this sound a certain kind of
attitude and meaning. We said it was out of the African mode and it
was revolutionary. . . . It broke with all of the previous ways of
improvisation."[31] "Magicians," as he often called them, had deeply
impressed him with their "crafted, improvisational coherence."[32] Neal
felt that this new style, which brought forth a new sound that
"disavowed the categorical riffs of standard jazz,"[33] could establish the
true link between black folklore and the black theater. His speculation
gained additional ground when he observed a production of Baraka's
Slave Ship. About the play he said: "This work has special affinities
with the New Music of Sun Ra, John Coltrane, Albert Ayler, and
Ornette Coleman. Events are blurred, rising and falling in a stream of
sound. Almost cinematically, the images flicker and fade against a
heavy back-drop of rhythm. The language is spare, stripped to the
essential. It is a play which almost totally eliminates the need for a

text. It functions on the basis of movements and energy—the dramatic equivalent of the New Music."[34]

Neal's preoccupation with music and African American aesthetics eventually gave way to various scholarly and reputable essays. In "New Space: The Growth of Black Consciousness in the Sixties," first published in 1970 in *The Black Seventies*, Neal compares the African American experience to the blues matrix:

> The African past . . . is an archetypal memory. Unless that past can be shaped within the context of a living culture, it basically has no function. That is to say: we are *an* African people, but we are not Africans. We are slave ships, crammed together in putrid holds, the Mali dream, Dahomey magic transformed by the hougans of New Orleans. We are field hollering Buddy Bolden; the night's secret sermon; the memory of your own God and the transmutation of that God. You know cotton and lynching. You know cities of tenement cells. What we have got to do is to understand that there are no blues in Africa. That is to say, the world view that created the blues is not there. . . . Just as the blues confronts a specific emotional history, it is necessary, for us, to confront the folkloric as well as written past. . . . We need to shape, on the basis of our own historical imperatives, a life-centered concept of human existence that goes beyond the Western world view. . . .[35]

In his 1971 essay "The Ethos of the Blues," Neal once again tackles the origin and history of the blues and asserts: "The blues, with all of their contradictions, represent for better or for worse, the essential vector of the Afro-American sensibility and identity."[36] It is interesting to note that Neal attributes an important duty to the blues singer, who resembles an artist, or more likely a playwright: "Like any artist, the blues singer has the task of bringing order out of chaos. The songs he sings, whether his own creations or others', are reenactments of his life and the lives of his people . . . symbolic of the larger human dilemma."[37] On the other hand, besides his secular role, the blues singer has a ritualistic and spiritual message to deliver. Through his ritual role in the community, the blues singer is linked to the traditional priests and poets of Africa. Neal further asserts: "Let us keep in mind, therefore, that the blues are primarily folk expression. Consequently they are subject to the processes of myth and ritual out of which all folklore is derived."[38] "The Ethos of the Blues" makes frequent allusions to Baraka's *Blues People*, which still remains the most extensive study on the origin and evolution of the blues tradition. Neal's essay, though brief and compact, pays homage to blues masters like John Lee Hooker, W.C. Handy who popularized "Saint Louis Blues," and Hart Wand who published "Dallas Blues" in 1912. As he concludes his essay Neal says: "The ethos of the blues, then, is the musical manifestation of one's individual cultural experiences in Afro-America with which members of the black community can identify."[39] Neal's definition of the blues and black aesthetics are one in the sense that both dwell within a community-shared experience, a cultural framework which operates from the standpoint of epic memory and commonalties in that sphere. While his thesis is comparable to Karenga's definition of black art as collective, functional, and committing, the two men disagree on one aspect of the blues, which I would like to mention here.

In his 1968 essay "Black Cultural Nationalism" Karenga speaks about the revolutionary characteristic of black art, asserting that "all our art must contribute to revolutionary change and if it does not, it is invalid. . . . Therefore . . . the blues are invalid; for they teach resignation, in a word acceptance of reality—and we have come to change reality."[40] Later on Karenga explains that the blues are not invalid historically, and that "they will always represent a very beautiful, musical and psychological achievement" of the African American people; however, since they tend not to commit people to the struggle they are not functional.[41] In contrast Neal, who had always avowed the quiet wisdom resonating in the blues, says: "They do *not*, as Maulana Karenga said, *collectively* 'teach resignation.'" Neal continues: "The blues are basically defiant in their attitude toward life. They are about survival on the meanest, most gut level of human existence. They are, therefore, lyric responses to the facts of life. The essential motive behind the best blues song is the acquisition of insight, wisdom."[42]

While Karenga represented the revolutionary cultural ethics of the Black Arts movement, Neal was involved more with the definitions and re-definitions in arts and aesthetics, changes which came with the Black Arts, Black Power, and Black Theater concepts of the post-Civil Rights era. Neal's position was that the blues, with all their contradictions, represented an agency that was unique to the African American experience no matter what "mood" or "mode" they came to stand for. What was paramount in Neal's theoretical formulation was inclusion of the total experience of his people, engendered in the blues' concurrent rhythms. The blues in that respect constituted a cornerstone whose impact is evident in African American literature, arts, and drama.

Paul Carter Harrison asserts that Neal had turned his attention during the seventies to the observation and documentation of black cultural exercises which might lead to the concretization of black aesthetics.[43] He remarks:

> He [Neal] was convinced that the cluster of values that should be attended in the vision of Black theater could be found in the folkloric nuances of the Mississippi Delta, the secrets embedded in the red clay of Georgia Pines, the riddles of Double-Dutch, the enigmatic mask of jubilation on the face of sorrow, the scat-song of the urban story-tellers, the parabolic wisdom of Elders, the spiritual vectors that invoke *Hoodoo Hollerin' Bebop Ghosts.* Spirited by an unassuageable passion for Black Music, his search for *vision,* thus form, led to the inventions of contemporary "jazz" musicians who played the *New Thing.*[44]

Neal foresaw that African American literary criticism and theory could become more than a comment on literature and drama; indeed he believed it should become a commentary on every aspect of African American life. During the seventies, alongside *Slave Ship* many plays which stepped outside the conventional dramaturgical standards paraded on the stages amidst threatening criticisms of the mainstream establishment. Baraka's *A Recent Killing,* Charles Gordone's *No Place to Be Somebody,* Ntozake Shange's *for colored girls who have considered suicide when the rainbow is enuf,* Charles Fuller's *Zooman and the Sign,* and Bill Gunn's *Last Picture Show* are only a few of these plays. As Neal asserted, the new theater was "a theatre of the Spirit, confronting the Black man in his interaction with his brothers and with the white thing."[45] These plays displayed expressionistic styles, non-linear plots, forceful relationships among the characters, and a spontaneity in the language that sounded more like music than mere conversation. It was *"instant theatre"*[46] or total theater, the "event" that encompassed many forms and structures within its entity.

In addition to language and music, Neal articulated the composite media which comprised the Black Arts movement and explained how politics, social landscape, culture, aesthetics, and economic differences illuminated the direction that would be followed by the movement. He stressed, however, the significance of language and the medium produced through that agency that was shaped solely *by* and *about* the African American. Indeed, he was predominantly concerned about interference from the mainstream which had proved damaging in past eras: "We didn't want the white critics in there. I think the object was for black people to find out who they were without someone looking over their shoulder."[47] In some respects this foreshadowed the coming of the Afrocentrists who would claim that African agency must be allowed to operate on its own, free from the imposition of whites.

In the essay "The Black Arts Movement" which he wrote in 1968, Neal is more directly concerned with the future of the movement and the roles that need to be activated by black writers. He encapsulates his ultimate vision of black art and aesthetics as follows:

1. The artist must not alienate himself from the community;
2. The Black Art concept is akin to the Black Power concept;
3. The Black Artist must speak directly to the needs of Black America;
4. Western cultural aesthetics do not conform to the realities of Black aesthetics;
5. Black aesthetics need a separate symbolism, mythology, critique and iconology;
6. The Black Arts movement is nationalistic and revolutionary;

7. There is a need for a cultural revolution in art and ideas because without such a revolution the oppressed will continue to be in cultural bondage to their oppressors;
8. The Black Arts movement is an ethical movement and, in this context, it announces that ethics and aesthetics are one.

In order for black art and aesthetics to flourish in an environment free of oppression and manipulation, Neal suggests that the preliminary goal should be that of eliminating Eurocentric negations from the African American nexus. As he asserts: "Much of the oppression confronting the Third World and Black America is directly traceable to the Euro-American cultural sensibility. This sensibility, antihuman in nature, has until recently dominated the psyches of most black artists and intellectuals; it must be destroyed before the black creative artist can have a meaningful role in the transformation of society."[48]

During this period Neal authored other essays alongside "The Black Arts Movement" in which he further explored the possibility of creating an exodus-movement so as to explain the gist of black aesthetics and bond it with the traditional epistemology of the African American. For instance, his essay "Black Art and Black Liberation," which appeared in a special issue of *Ebony*, enforces the idea that black music represents the highest achievement of the African American because "blues tie the Black man to his past where art served to connect his ancestors with unknown psychic forces which they knew to exist in the universe."[49] In the essay Neal advances the idea that the blues plays an exemplary role in bonding the Black Arts movement with the black aesthetic because the blues is about survival, about people and their aspirations, past, present and future. Everything in African American culture could eventually lead back to the blues, according to Baker, Harrison, and Molefi K. Asante. These writers and theorists believe that the blues is at the heart of the African American soul, for it is in the blues that we find the incipient protest, the criticism of conditions, the nostalgia for a lost home, as well as the possibilities inherent in the future.

Somewhere in the soul of the African American the deepest expressions of survival and the most ardent feelings of victory come together in the elements of the blues. The solitary nature of the blues singer is reminiscent of the longing often found in the best of the spirituals when a singer, male or female, calls out to the spirit: "Sometimes I feel like a motherless child, a long ways from home." In the creative vocabulary of the blues singer—often alone, or at least singing alone—one finds the same insistence on overcoming the sense of loss.

But what is it that the African American has lost? I believe that Neal felt that the African American has lost cultural rootedness, a sense of location in time and space that is culturally solid. It was made real in the words of Malcolm X, El Hajj Malik Shabazz, who argued that the African in America who was disconnected from Africa had "lost his mind." But to lose one's mind is to lose the things that make one whole, and the African American's incompletion was the crux of the matter in Neal's terms. Yet he understood more than others that it was not solely the African who was responsible for this loss of mind; the conditions of oppression, enslavement, discrimination, and the active attempt to drive a wedge between the African and his or her culture were the culprits. Acquiescence in the activity contributed to the loss of mind; that is, when African Americans accepted the new definitions of themselves they fell into the trap of self-deprecation. Thus, this is not loss of mind based on the unwillingness of the African to know himself, it is loss of mind forced on the African and thus made concrete by the various attitudes of society. For instance, if the African spoke Ebonics, then Ebonics was automatically an inferior language. The blues, in its most authentic form, was a recognition of the solitary nature of the struggle against anonymity and nihilism.

Neal's most comprehensive ideas on art, aesthetic theory, poetry, drama, and literature in general appeared in his *Visions of a Liberated Future: Black Arts Movement Writings*, published after his death in 1989 by Thunder's Mouth Press. A compilation of numerous essays, poems, and a section of a play titled *The Glorious Monster in the Bell of the Horn* (1976), it included commentaries by Kimberly W. Benston, Amiri Baraka, Houston A. Baker Jr., Stephen E. Henderson, Stanley Crouch, Eleanor Traylor, Jayne Cortez, Paul Carter Harrison, and Charles Fuller. The volume charts the flow of expert intellectual and social thought in order to embark upon a social, cultural, and literary transformation. While it is true that similar types of collected writing are usually interpreted as "protest literature," such a premise would underestimate and oversimplify what Neal and his commentators put forth in their volume. More importantly, an amalgamation of nationalistic aspirations and the trust that emanates from sharing that experience are the issues that run through *Visions of a Liberated Future*. Fittingly, the title of the book springs from Neal's brilliant metaphorical style of narration in his description of black art: "An art that opens us up to the beauty and ugliness within us; that makes us understand our condition and each other in a more profound manner; that unites us, exposing us to our painful weaknesses and strengths; and finally, an art that posits for us the Vision of a Liberated Future."[50]

The imperatives of cultural and political self-determination, the principle of self-definition and personal self-determination, the will to adorn a *place* on earth and shape it in one's own vision is essential to Neal's strategy. According to Neal's assertions, there should be an end to cultural and conceptual "landlessness."[51] The diasporan Middle Passage had to be surmounted; African Americans could no longer be seen as vagabonds. Home is a relative concept; it is not just a space or taking back what used to be yours, it is more than that. It represents a sense of belonging and affiliation to a group. As Alice Walker said, without the people freely pacing its floor home is not truly home. In her book *In Search of Our Mothers' Gardens,* while reflecting on the impact of the sixties Walker looks into the importance of the concept of land as part of the common ancestral memory for African American people:

> The history of my family, like that of all black Southerners, is a history of dispossession. We loved the land and worked the land, but we never owned it; and even if we bought land, as my great-grandfather did after the Civil War, it was always in danger of being taken away, as his was, during the period following Reconstruction . . . black people— including my parents—had learned a long time ago that to stay willingly in a beloved but brutal place is to risk losing the love and being forced to acknowledge only the brutality.[52]

For Alice Walker, landlessness was an enigmatic experience which endangered not only the African American heritage but a healthy state of mind, too.

It was Martin Luther King Jr. in the sixties who brought substantial recovery from a sense of spiritual dispossession and landlessness. Of his struggle Walker said: "He gave us continuity of place, without which community is ephemeral. He gave us full-time use of our own woods, and restored our memories to those of us who were forced to run away, as realities we might each day enjoy and leave for our children."[53] For Neal, however, rather than Martin Luther King it was Malcolm X and his fierce energy that motivated the masses to claim ownership of what they used to have—African identity, heritage, or land—by whatever means necessary. In Neal's terms, it was the language and style of Malcolm X that would be the guiding post for the liberated literary leaders of the Black Arts movement. Still, it must be acknowledged that although the two leaders differed in language and strategies, they were united in their goal.

Throughout his writings Neal did not give "a definitive statement of the African aesthetic," but he found in the African context a philosophical connection useful for understanding a revolutionary art form.[54] He had a profound understanding of the function of the artist's work to speak *directly* to black people about the true nature of their oppressive conditions in the United States. A closer look at some of the essays in *Visions of a Liberated Future* definitely lets his *Nommo* speak for itself.

The next section explores certain themes that direct Neal's orature and is divided by headings that combine related articles under a particular theme. "The Resistant Spirit," for instance, dwells on an important essay: "And Shine Swam On." The section titled "Black Writer's Mission" focuses on a series of essays on African American authors, such as "The Black Writer's Role, I: Richard Wright," "The Black Writer's Role, II: Ellison's Zoot Suit," and "The Black Writer's Role, III: James Baldwin." Neal also wrote two plays: a three-act play, *The Glorious Monster in the Bell of the Horn*, which was produced by Woodie King at the New York Federal Theater on July 6, 1979; and *In An Upstate Motel: A Morality Play* in 1980. The latter was directed by Harrison and performed by the Negro Ensemble Company in April 1981. A brief review of both plays renders the opportunity to observe

Neal's dramatic imagination and his place in the development of contemporary African American theater.

THE RESISTANT SPIRIT

Just then the Captain said, "Shine, Shine, save poor me,
I'll give you more money than a nigger ever see."
Shine said to the Captain: "Money is good on land and on sea,
but the money on land is the money for me."
And Shine swam on . . .
—Neal, *Visions of a Liberated Future*

"And Shine Swam On" took its title from an urban "toast" called "The Titanic" whose numerous versions have appeared in various sources since the beginning of the century. In the early part of the twentieth century Shine represented the most resistant African spirit. Using the biggest news event of the era as a starting point, the sinking of the Titanic, African American folklorists created Shine as a heroic figure who was able to save himself despite the fact that he was only a furnace-man on the ship. It did not matter that the whites had more money and thought of themselves as superior; when it came to swimming to land, only Shine had the ability to make it to the United States. This story circulated throughout the Americas and became one of the best-known stories in the folk tradition. Shine was, indeed, an indestructible spirit obviously created as a metaphor for the many dreams and wishes of the African people in America.

As the opening essay of *Visions of a Liberated Future*, the story of Shine also sets the tone for the subsequent pieces, propelling Neal's definition of the Black Arts movement towards its ultimate destination. As Neal asserts: "Most of the book can be read as if it were a critical re-examination of Western political, social and artistic values . . . as a rejection of anything that we feel is detrimental to our people."[55] First published in 1968, Neal's essay compares the situation of black people in the United States to the below-deck furnace-men of the infamous Titanic which sank on its first voyage. In this context, Shine is recognized as the only survivor of the sinking ship which symbolically stands for America. Discrimination and racism have collaborated in pushing Shine to the lower decks of the social strata, but when real trouble appears Shine is ready to swim on, leaving the rest of the passengers begging for help and literally drowning. Shine represents strength, determination, self-capability, and self-discovery in the midst of chaos.[56] He is one of the most significant mythoforms which carries African American mythology into modern-day circumstances, and thus continues giving sustenance and hope. Meanwhile, Neal proposes the critical question as follows: "Shine is US. We have been below deck stoking the ship's furnaces. Now the ship is sinking, but where will we swim?"[57] His response reads throughout the text as a testimony to the development of the Black Arts movement as well as the historic struggle of black people in the diaspora.

Besides providing the basis for the resistant impulse against the suffocating impact of oppression, Neal's essay also delineates his pragmatic concern for "direction." This is not indicative that the black masses have not known where to go, but rather that the gates have always been blocked by Western literary, artistic, and aesthetic standards and values which have rendered African American standards and values peripheral. An understanding of the continuity of the resistant spirit in the African American experience is essential to any understanding of the route followed by the Black Arts movement, a route that led to such later developments as Afrocentricity.

In the lengthy essay "And Shine Swam On," one of the aspects that Neal explores is the impact of the past on future generations' lives; no one can deny the indelible mark of the past on a nation's destiny. Perseverance and the ability to sustain the nationhood springs, in Neal's view, from a variety of sources, including historical factors as well as exemplary acts set forth by that nation's ancestors. With reference to history's significant role in forging a nation's destiny, Neal's stance reveals a surprising duality. On the one hand he is sympathetic to Du Bois's historical argument on "double-consciousness"; on the other hand he praises Malcolm X, who aimed to destroy the spirit of double-consciousness. Meanwhile, his admiration for Malcolm X and the extensive praise he gave to the slain leader symbolically correspond with the title of the essay, because Shine as a cultural mythoform in African American literature represents hope and salvation in the midst of chaos. As the precursor to the idea of salvation, Shine is evident in Malcolm X's personality and has transferred to younger generations as the embodiment of strength, courage, and uncompromising nobility.

The way people see their history shapes the national character; it either builds their self-esteem or destroys it. Throughout his essay Neal asserts that there is a need to recognize the past, for the tension he sees within black America has its roots in the general history of the race. "The manner in which we see this history determines how we act. How should we see this history? What should we feel about it? This is important to know because the sense of how that history should be felt is what either unites or separates us."[58]

Neal believed that the lack of vision regarding how to proceed emanates from the tension created by what Du Bois called the double-consciousness. He therefore asserts that Frederick Douglass, Du Bois, Booker T. Washington, Marcus Garvey, and others struggled during their professional lives to render a viable meaning to the sense of double-consciousness, and somehow could not totally eliminate it from their struggle. Only in Malcolm X could the nation see a complete, systematic assault on Western values and society. "He was the conscience of Black America, setting out, like a warrior, to destroy the double-consciousness. He did not eschew dialogue. He attempted instead to make it more meaningful by infusing some truth into it."[59] When Malcolm X talked about brotherhood, nationhood, and developing strategies to cope with racism, he was, in reality, targeting a revolution of the psyche, a revolution about "how to see one's self in the world."[60] Towards the end of his life, Malcolm X spearheaded the movement which aimed to carry the civil rights issue in the United States to an international arena where human rights should supersede civil rights. In this context, he believed he could unite the struggle of African Americans with those of the so-called Third World people, thus encompassing and uniting all oppressed people throughout the world.

In the essay it is evident that Neal's prophetic vision derives its strength from African American literature—particularly that of his own times—which he saw as superior to and more dynamic than Euro-American literature. He said; "The white world—the West—is seen now as a dying creature, totally bereft of spirituality."[61] The only hope in Neal's view is "in psychic withdrawal from its values and assumptions." Neal further argues that the Western mindset is different from the rest of the world's; as the Western man possesses a different sense of meaning, his truths may not have relativity to everyone else's truths on earth. To this effect Neal comments: "Western mind construes reality differently from that of the rest of the world; an African sculpture in a Madison art gallery is disconnected from its creator as much as its roots or its ontology."[62] This is in contrast to its symbol in Africa as "the connection between man and his ancestors." Stolen or taken by force from its original location and placed in an alien space within an undefined time period, the African sculpture is probably longing for its own familiar setting. In the art gallery it is merely an object, a lonesome artifact cut off from its roots and its essential function. The aesthetic agency which rendered a basic function to the beautiful object created by the artist implies the golden premise regarding the unity of form and function in traditional African art.

Neal's essay "And Shine Swam On" explicates the direction to be followed in a varied assortment of ideas that coalesce around the mission of writing and the role of the black artist in the midst of chaos. Neal believes this chaos has been brought upon the world by the dying value system of the Western world. A change is needed which will encompass art, drama, and literature, but with new definitions adhered to the creative products. For instance, Neal asserts: "We will have to alter our concepts of what art is, of what it is supposed to 'do.' . . . We can learn more about what poetry is by listening to the cadences in Malcolm's speeches than from most of Western poetics."[63] Later on he continues to emphasize the importance of freedom, of liberating one's self from preconceived forms and judgments as one develops a new synthesis for literature, art, and aesthetics. The unshackling of the state of double-consciousness is fundamental; no wonder he claims "we must liberate ourselves, destroy the double-consciousness. We must integrate with ourselves, understand that we have within us a great vision, revolutionary and spiritual in nature."[64] In this regard he becomes a sort of Malcolm himself, an avatar against double-consciousness.

According to Neal, black literature should aspire to achieve what black music—"the most dominant manifestation of what we are and feel"[65]—has achieved. To accomplish this the poet has to assume a new identity; he must become a performer and take his work where his people are. Baraka, who changed his name and left Greenwich Village for Harlem and Newark, is one of the best examples of this creed. Neal also stressed the importance of linking one's work to the struggle for liberation nationwide because he believed the artist and the political activist are one in shaping the reality for today and tomorrow. What Neal saw as inactive and barren in Western literature was probably grounded in his reading of Existentialist writers and artists, mostly European, such as Sartre, Brecht, Camus, Albee, Burroughs, and Fellini. These writers displayed in their individual works an endless quest for meaning in humankind's relationships with the universe, yet often concluded with a deep nihilism, sense of alienation, and dislocation.

In contrast, black literature must take its cue from black music's representation of the collective psyche; it "must attempt to achieve that same sense of the collective ritual, but ritual directed at the destruction of useless, dead ideas."[66] For a poet or an author, "taking the work to where the people are"; linking the work to "all usable aspects of the music"—for Neal insists that poets must learn to sing, dance, and chant their works; and establishing the link between the work and the struggle for personal and collective liberation constitute the most fundamental steps for moving people towards a deeper understanding.[67] To accomplish this task the poet or the writer must act as "a priest, a black magician, working juju with the word on the world."[68] The primordial essence of the word, the *Nommo*, can be trusted to bring forth the unspoken and stand witness to its final deliverance of the change that will impart psychological liberation. Those who will embark upon the struggle for liberation are the poets and the activists because Neal is convinced that the "artist and the political activist are one. They are both shapers of the future reality."[69] Needed change will be generated by these two groups, for as Neal claims, "they are warriors, priests, lovers and destroyers."[70]

BLACK WRITER'S MISSION

As early as 1968, Neal was prophetically exhorting his fellow artists to first understand who they were and where they stood before addressing the world at large: "It is impossible for the Black artist to create anything that is finally meaningful to his people unless he has a sense of national consciousness and a sense of national purpose."[71]

The first duty of the Black Artist, according to Neal, was to "clarify the nature of the world from the point of view of his people."[72] In this respect, "to clarify" meant to set the standards of African American experience from a holistic perspective inclusive of the forced removal from the Motherland, the Middle Passage, slavery, and emancipation, with the superimposition of African philosophy over the entire range of experience. Neal also emphasized the urgent need to discard most Western critical assumptions because Western aesthetics separated art from life and rendered a single dimension to art. To this end, he wrote three essays collected under the title "Black Writer's Mission" which respectively focused on Richard Wright, Ralph Ellison, and James Baldwin. Before engaging in an analysis of these essays, however, it is relevant to explore Neal's ideas on art, aesthetics, and their functions with regard to aspects of black life.

Contrary to Eurocentric approaches, in African aesthetics the function of art is understood as not to entertain, but "to make man stronger, to make it more possible for man to understand the nature of the world he sees around him and finally to shape that world into a more meaningful entity."[73] As stated earlier in this study, African philosophy stresses the fact that "all that is beautiful is also functional." Out of this, a world view which harmoniously unites art and life would eventually come into being and be aptly adopted by black artists. Neal's vision advanced the consensus for building a new critical methodology by which to regard black art: "Since life is change, art must be change. . . . Most Western critical assumptions deny change. It is for this reason that we must discard them. *We must develop our own critical methodology,* one that is more nearly related to the condition in which we find ourselves. We must first understand and utilize our own culture as the basis for the creation of art. Otherwise, it will be impossible to add anything new to the concept of the universe."[74]

In his quest for a critical methodology pertinent to African American literature Neal focused on three authors: Wright, Ellison, and Baldwin. At the outset Neal establishes his premise that every black writer's work must teach responsibility and guidance. The black writer has to consider, at all times, the needs of his community and respond to them accordingly in order to enforce a change within the human condition as a whole. Neal looks at Wright's, Ellison's, and Baldwin's works with a critical insight and he finds them lacking, to some extent, in the fulfillment of the role he has envisioned for the black writer. Although his analysis does not encompass these authors in their whole capacity, it is reflective of Neal's unwavering preoccupation with the role of the artist and the functionality of art.

Neal asserts that Wright's novel *Native Son* (1940) "is considered throughout the world as one of America's greatest literary achievements."[75] As Neal sees it, Wright sought a reconciliation of the black man's "nationalism and his revolutionary aspirations" through the utilization of black tradition and culture, which developed from the black church and folklore.[76] Neal celebrates Wright's insight which emphasizes the predominance of black folklore as the source of the "most indigenous and complete expression" for the African American.[77] However, Neal is critical of Wright's inability to set forth a clearly defined nationalistic goal for the black writer. This inability arose indirectly from Wright's involvement in the Communist Party. As Neal observes, "the party had a policy of discouraging nationalism."[78] Wright did attempt to reconcile nationalism and communism in a 1937 essay titled "Blue Print for the Negro Writing." However, the impact of Wright's version of nationalism—one that was combined with American communism—proved to be "harmful and uncreative" with regard to the independent development of a united black front that would avoid the influence of mainstream politics.

In his criticism of Wright's work Neal seems to imply, rather than openly declare, that although Wright did manage to produce a timeless novel which realistically portrays American race relations and somewhat succeeded in dealing with the theme of "protest," he failed on numerous other fronts. For Neal, Wright's work did not fulfill the historical role it should have. Neal asserts: "The black writer's problem really grows out of a confusion about function, rather than a confusion about form."[79] The forms—particularly those that are concerned with aesthetic and literary excellence—that are forced upon the black writer by society are not his *own*; he needs to reject them in order to construct new ones. About *Native Son*, which is considered a classic of American literature, Neal asks the following questions before he ends his inquiry: "What did Wright feel was the role of the black writer? Was there a special role consigned to the black writer? . . . What about an Afro-American culture—an Afro-American tradition, do these have any bearing on the problems confronting black writers?"[80] In his final evaluation, Neal states that although Wright grappled with these questions early in his career he was unable to put them into practice, causing one to wonder if Wright himself was ever able to be "a part of the change" that was to transform society. [81]

For Neal, the responsibility of the black writer to transform society is vital as he insists that the writer "must be the conscience and spirit of that change."[82] Neal's basic principle in his approach to the role of the black writer relies heavily on his understanding of the critical relationship between the artist and his community. As he sees it, the black artist/writer needs to be a conduit for the aspirations of his/her people. In order to create an art that is consciously committed and addressed primarily to black and Third World people, the black artist/writer has to alienate him/herself from European forms, sensibilities, and expectations. He/she must "evolve . . . techniques and forms from the black community's needs. . . . The black writer must understand that his destiny as an artist is ultimately bound up with, and integral to all other aspects of the human condition."[83] Apparently Wright attempted to achieve this goal but succumbed to the dichotomy between nationalism and communism.

Neal continues to explore the role of the black artist in his examination of Ellison's and Baldwin's works. In "Ellison's Zoot Suit," Neal summarizes some of the reviews on the *Invisible Man* and reveals what critics said of Ellison's work in general. However, the essay focuses mainly on Ellison's relationship with the Communist Party and the leftists more than on the role of the black writer. I will concentrate on the section in which Neal presents a realistic critique of Ellison's work as he looks at it from the vantage point of the black writer's role and responsibility.

Neal finds Ellison to be strongly located in the African American folk tradition. He states that the novelist has welded into *Invisible Man* numerous scenes in which the blues acts as a central metaphor. Moreover, Neal asserts that most of Ellison's writing is valuable and centrally grounded in the African American experience. Yet what he does not agree with is "Ellison's tendency to imply that black writers should confine their range of cultural inquiry strictly to American and European subject matter."[84] On the other hand, Neal also disagrees with an attitude that limits a writer's range strictly to African and African American subject matter. With regard to the role of the artists within the Black Arts community, Neal advocates "the *extension* of the remembered and a *resurrection* of the *unremembered* . . . an engagement with the *selves* we know and the *selves* we have forgotten."[85] Thus Neal proposes for future generations a reinstatement of historical consciousness which derives its strength from ancestral knowledge and the wisdom it projects into the future. Remembrance involves knowledge, and knowledge emanates power.

This idea of powerfulness was one of the most significant attributes of the Black Arts movement; power needed to be generated through knowledge and pride in African American history in order to manifest resistance to oppression. Grounded in racial pride, Neal rejects derogatory terms, especially when uttered by an African American. For instance, when Don L. Lee says, "If you don't know about rats and roaches, you don't know about the black experience" in an interview in *Ebony* magazine,[86] Neal's response is:

> Why define yourself in purely negative terms, when you know that your very life, in its most profound aspects, is not merely a result of the negative? We are not simply, in *all* areas of our sensibilities, merely a set of black reactions to white oppression. And neither should our art be merely an aesthetic reaction to white art. It has finally got to exist as good art also because, in terms of the development of a national art, excellent art is, in and of itself, the best propaganda you can have. By now, we should be free enough to use any viable techniques that will allow us to shape an art that breathes and is based essentially on our own emotional and cultural imperatives.[87]

In Neal's argument there lies a deep faith in the authenticity of national art and the aesthetic value that emanates from it. Neal is partly disappointed with Ellison because of Ellison's lack of interest in the *totality* of African American sensibilities: "Ellison almost overwhelmingly locates his cultural, philosophical, and literary sensibility in the West."[88] Neal asserts that there is a range of ideas beyond those strictly of the West; neither Western nor Eastern political, philosophical, and religious attitudes can provide mankind's spiritual and psychic liberation.[89] To foster liberation, Neal asserts, what is necessary is a system of politics and art that is fluid, functional, and expansive; that derives its strength from the *whole* of African American experiences. Neal is revisiting the ideas that he first introduced in his seminal essay, "The Black Arts Movement." In that essay he emphasized the inseparable character of politics and literature. He also expounded on the role of the artist as that of a "key bearer" of culture who promotes black self-definition, as opposed to allowing definition by others. For Neal this concept of the black artist as a key bearer of culture is essential in producing a liberating national art, one in which the functionality of art and the mission of the artist are simultaneously accomplished.

Previously, in his essay titled "And Shine Swam On," Neal disagreed with Ellison's novel in terms of perspective, commenting that "the things that concerned Ellison are interesting to read, but contemporary black youth feels another force in the world today." Later he added, "We know who we are, and we are not invisible, *at least not to each other*. . . . The light is black . . . as are most of the meaningful tendencies in the world."[90]

Wright, too, had to cope with a similar problem in Neal's opinion, a problem which resulted in a contradiction between Wright's ideas and his writings. Neal explains that when Wright tried to reconcile black nationalism with revolutionary aspirations, his attempt lacked a focused approach to constructing a black ideology. Neal criticizes Baldwin on the same grounds, albeit from a different perspective. Extremely preoccupied with identity, his identity, as a black man and an American writer, Baldwin searched for a reconciliation all his life. Neal says: "He ends up begging out, or by falling back on a kind of supernormal kind of 'love.' . . . He joined the tradition of pleading with white America for the humanity of the Negro; instead of addressing himself to black people and their problems."[91]

Overall, when Neal looked at the writings of these three major authors he did not see them developing, either collectively or individually, a committed black ideology in literature. Rather they seemed to be preoccupied with the discovery and exertion of their own realms of identity and existence within an oppressive environment that did not allow them to exist freely and proudly.

THE GLORIOUS MONSTER
IN THE BELL OF THE HORN

Moving on to Neal's role as a playwright, he wrote a total of two plays: *The Glorious Monster in the Bell of the Horn* and *In an Upstate Motel: A Morality Play*, both produced while he was alive. The first is a three-scene play, or a "dirge played in three sets" as Harrison puts it, [92] about a Philadelphia musician named Herbert Robinson, Sr. and his wife Vera, a blues singer, who were killed in a traffic accident on their way to a concert in New York. [93] In the background, there is the accompaniment of continuous blues lyrics, musicians, and dances; the steady drone of fighter planes; the tenor saxophone—which ironically becomes a fatal weapon in the accident; the mention of Marian Anderson; the music of Charlie Parker and Nat King Cole; frequent references to Philadelphia's then-favorite jazz spots at Diamond and Taylor Streets; and Fairmount Park and the Schuylkill River. Through these details an authentic dramatic agency is put to work in the development of the main action. Meanwhile, in the World War II setting the audience is informed that the colored troops of the United States Army have won a major victory against the Japanese somewhere in the Pacific.

One of these soldiers, Sonny Boy Smalls, enters the stage decorated as a war-hero. It is August 6, 1945. The play opens at Cafe Blue Monster as Shammy, the lead character, introduces the main theme: "Hey y'all! This is my jitterbug song in the wind of our childhood visitations. . . . Here chants word. . . . Yes word; and the magic of the lie. . ." (P. 93). It is not coincidental that the word, that is *Nommo*, and its transformative power which inspired Neal in all of his writings, serve as a ritualistic initiation in the beginning. In addition to this motif on "word," Shammy is writing a play for Sonny Boy Smalls. He will convince Dickie, an ex-soldier, to play the part of the fugitive soldier in his play. Thus, what is striking about Neal and his play is that, unlike other playwrights who let the plot unfold independently through interaction of the characters, Neal interferes with the plot, assuming the role of the director, the actor, and the playwright behind the scenes. Moreover, the multidimensional characteristics of the play—a multiplicity of sets, time sequences, and interactive imagery—are in accord with the playwright's multi-faceted choice of material within the African American experience, from the segregation in army units to discussion of Garveyite nationalism, all merging into the stream of a North Philadelphia location. Shammy is the epitome of the *jale*, the Mandinka word for the French term *griot*: He is the archetypal spirit of artistic creativity and imagination, who is different from the rest of the people in the play. In that respect, Shammy comes closest to resembling his author, the poet-shaman-writer Neal.

Alongside the blues construct, the city of Philadelphia, particularly a North Philadelphia neighborhood where Jim Crow laws have created a deep-rooted calling, provides the essential backdrop for the interplay of love, death, war, anger, music, and chaos. As the plot(s) unfold, the characters gradually reveal their personal stories that reach out and coalesce with others', very much like the row houses of Philadelphia that extend along the city blocks, preserving in honest loyalty the history of the city and the stories of the people who inhabited them. Stories lead to other stories, both old and new; the interplay of reality and dream sequences provide a surreal atmosphere as they impart the main plot. In some senses this is a brilliant play on the nature of neighborhoods in Philadelphia where row houses are connected to each other and the intertwining of families, lives, and activities create one grand story. It is also about continuity and perseverance, because each house has its own story contributing to the story of the city just like tales of resistance, liberation, and action contribute to making a nation.

Certain segments of the play thrive on autobiographical elements which are worthy of attention because, after all, Neal spent most of his life in Philadelphia. As previously mentioned, the play may have inspired Neal's contemporaries, such as Fuller and his *A Soldier's Play*. At the same time, Neal may have been influenced by Baraka's *Great Goodness of Life* and *The Slave*. Moreover, some of his characters and their names resemble real people he had met in New York and Philadelphia during the days of the Black Arts movement. I will address these personages later in this section.

In *The Glorious Monster in the Bell of the Horn,* although the work of a first-time playwright, Neal has mastered the skill of dealing with several different settings simultaneously through adroit use of flashbacks, "flash-forwards," dance, and mime, all of which allow a transient coalescence between the scenes. The first set is titled "The

Magician's Revenge, a Colloquy on Destiny, Illusion as Method." The dialogue between Dickie and Shammy mounts to a climactic point as Dickie asks Shammy to perform at his wedding reception. Meanwhile, Shammy discloses the story of a soldier, as told by Sonny, who went crazy and started shooting people in the South and then escaped to Philadelphia. The Military Police and his own father are trying to catch him and prosecute him. Through Shammy, the audience is also informed that he and Dickie Davenport, the son of a famous physician, were childhood friends. However, it is Dickie, the neat and clean Lincoln student always favored by others, who has retained an upper hand as their lives unfolded.

Shammy's real frustration originates from his unrevealed love towards Rose, who plans to marry Dickie, but whose rape by the Brewery gang launches a bloody battle between the two gangs. The situation gets worse when the South Philly guys join in the battle against the white guys of Brewery Town. Dickie does not participate in the fights; his lack of commitment infuriates Shammy. As the poet-magician who owns mysterious powers, Shammy reveals his prophecy about the course of events that are about to begin:

DICKIE
So they catch the poor guy, eh?

SHAMMY
Not right away. . . . He must first journey through death, madness, and mirage. . . . He puts his art on the line. . . . (P. 99)

The "death-haunted" story, which Shammy calls a "pageant," somewhat disturbs Dickie because of the similarities between the protagonist and himself; his father too is a prominent physician. Meanwhile, the blaring tune of Herbie Lee's saxophone interrupts their colloquy and the audience is informed of the violent crash which killed Herbie's parents on the way to a concert in New York when he was still a baby. Their death had left the child to the care of his uncle Wally, who owns a barber shop on Ridge Avenue.

SHAMMY

... It was sudden. So sudden that Herbie's father
didn't even have time, or didn't want to take that
horn out of his mouth ... then the force of the
collision drove the horn back and down his throat,
and the steel curled up and around them, and the
horn ... pressed onto his head and his body. ...
And the state troopers came, they had to pry the horn
out of his head ... the battered instrument was
splattered with blood, and bits of Herbert's guts
clung to the keys. ... (P. 108)

Shammy the magician-dancer-poet-writer, the omniscient-shaman
figure who narrates the story, appears as a field-hand towards the end
of the first set. This time he is wearing a white beard and a straw hat,
with a corncob pipe in his mouth as he narrates another story, the story
of John and the talking bones. One day John sees a skeleton in the
forest who says, "Tongue is the cause of my being here." He runs and
informs the slavemaster about the talking skull; the slavemaster
doesn't really believe his story but still goes to the forest with his
friends. When John fails to make the skull speak they beat him to
death and leave him beside the other skeleton. The rest of the story
reads, in Neal's words, as follows:

And as the sun set redly, the buzzards was tearing
into John's liver, and as the waning sun shined
through his vacant sockets ... the bones laying
beside him commenced to shake and rattle, and then,
chillen, them bones spoke. ... They said: "Tongue,
yes tongue brought *us* here, and tongue brought *you*
here too. ... (P. 121)

As the story is known to have come from the enslavement era, its
mention in the play reinforces epic memory through tapping the
historical consciousness of the African American.
There is also the often cited story by Frederick Douglass in which
an enslaved African was walking along a path when he saw a wagon
drawing near with a white visitor. The wagon stopped and the white
visitor said to the African: "How is the owner of this plantation

treating you?" The African began to reveal all of the harm that the owner had done to the enslaved Africans, after which the white visitor continued on to the plantation. When the African arrived at the plantation after doing his chores he was rebuked by the owner, beaten, and left on the ground for dead. Douglass said: "Africans must speak with the front of their heads and never with the back of their heads if they want to live."[94]

Whereas reverence for the spoken word is highly appreciated within the cultural realm of the African people, it may not be so in a different cultural setting, as these stories imply. Neal understood all of this, as did his ancestors who knew that talking too much could be a dangerous thing. And whereas the moral lesson in this story is clear for the African American, it helps non-African Americans understand more about the underlying effects of oppression. Neal's centered vision enables the critic and the audience to reach a more inclusive vision of reality, a humanizing one, where tolerance for pluralism and a multiplicity of viewpoints is or *should be* the prerequisite for harmonious interaction between human beings.

As Asante would agree, one doesn't have an authentic story to tell without rootedness in his/her own cultural territory.[95] Given this premise, Neal's cultural location allows the audience to be informed and educated about a particular time in history from the viewpoint of the African American. Such knowledge carries healing ramifications for all parties involved, and may be liberating and humanizing too. In the last chapter of this book I provide further explanations of the inclusive nature of an Afrocentric critique; therefore, at this point I return to the discussion of the play.

As the old man leaves the stage the lights come up on Doctor Davenport's office, who is being informed by the Military Police that his son Richard B. Davenport Jr. is currently sought for several military offenses that he has committed. The doctor is puzzled; he doesn't believe the Captain:

DAVENPORT
Speak clearly, fool! What has my son done?

DABNEY
Under the aforementioned sections, and with specific reference to section seven-twelve, article one-

eighteen, chapter twenty-two, PFC Davenport is
charged with the following military crimes: Illegally
procuring weapons . . .

DAVENPORT

Oh my God!

DABNEY

. . . and the assault therewith; desertion, section six-
seventy-nine, article eighty-five; and murder . . .

DAVENPORT

Murder? Not my Richard . . . Richard Davenport?
There must be a mistake. . . .

DABNEY

It's no mistake, Doctor. (P. 124)

The second set, "Those Lyric Days, Aspects of Madness, Through
the Rivers of Fire," opens in the Gazebo at Fairmount Park, where
Herbie Lee is playing a song and Rose is watching the scull race on the
Schuylkill. The peaceful days of early youth, the innocence, subtle
friendships, and the harmony she used to know in this city are lost to
the war. Rose laments:

ROSE

I would have to make a choice . . . And it *just
couldn't be* Shammy . . . It had to be the doctor's
son . . . That's the way the Norwoods and the
Davenports had always planned things . . . That was
before the war, before we knew about chaos . . . I go
to Bryn Mawr . . . Dickie goes to Lincoln . . . And it
falls neatly into place. . . . (P. 128)

With the added impact of the assault which she suffered, Rose could
no longer be the same person. She was torn asunder, tightly gripped by
an incurable sense of loneliness and loss. It was probably this sense of
defeat and hurt that made her run away to New York.

The final scene, which Neal sub-titled "Madness and Civilization, Ideas of Harmony, Towards the Resurrection," opens at the wake of Herbie's show downtown. Simultaneously, the arsenal at Frankfort is burning. Wally, Henson, and Iverson are at the barber shop, getting ready to go downtown where Herbie plays. Dickie and Rose pass by, a married couple now. Shammy has disappeared, some say he is a preacher at Byberry, a mental asylum. President Truman's voice is heard over the radio announcing the bombing of Hiroshima:

> That bomb had more power than twenty-thousand tons of TNT. . . . It had two thousand times the blast power of the British Grand Slam: which was the largest bomb ever used in the history of warfare. . . . With the bomb, we have now added a new and revolutionary increase in destruction to supplement the growing power of our armed forces. In their present form these bombs are now in production, and even more powerful forms are in development. . . . (P. 167)

Truman's praise of the war machine, the attack on Pearl Harbor, and the following "revenge" of the atomic bomb—which corresponds with the bloody battle between the two city gangs that roamed through the streets of Philly; Shammy's ritualistic execution by Iverson's squad in the first scene, which foreshadowed his later "disappearance"; the rape incident, about which the audience is briefly informed; and the news of the explosion at the Frankfort arsenal, the symbolic self-destruction of the war machine: all contribute to the climactic resolution in the end, simultaneously inducing feelings of destruction, fear, chaos, panic, and insecurity. A few characters that are left out of this analysis are Baron Saturday, the dancer Madame Blue or Kali, and Iverson, all of whom provide the unprecedented suspense and mystery elements in the play.

The autobiographical motifs in the play are evident in numerous forms. For instance, Neal was a graduate of Lincoln University, very much like his aspiring anti-hero Dickie Davenport in the play. A less discernible element involves the character named Shammy whom Baraka mentions in his autobiography. During the early days of the Black Arts Repertory Theatre/School there was a young writer named Shammy who frequented the establishment. Resemblances between

Shammy in the play and Shammy the writer in Harlem are striking. As Baraka testifies, "Shammy was volatile and unpredictable, but he had a basic respect for me as a writer."[96]

Resemblances in names also surface when one compares *The Glorious Monster in the Bell of the Horn* with Fuller's *A Soldier's Play*. In the latter, two characters are also named Davenport and Smalls. However, in *A Soldier's Play* Captain Davenport has a law degree, is appointed investigator of the mysterious shooting at the barracks, and emerges as a hero in the final scene. The character Private Anthony Smalls takes part in the unruly killing and ends up in jail. In Neal's play Dickie Davenport, contrary to his family's expectations, proves to be an anti-hero, while Sonny Boy Smalls returns from the battlefield a war hero. Additionally, PFC Melvin Peterson in Fuller's play, who is the "model soldier," is apprehended for the murder of the Sergeant. In Neal's play, the character named Iverson—quite a resemblance name-wise—is engaged in a similar conspiracy which destroys Shammy.

Cultural and geographical locations within the play also reveal much about Neal's background and his life in the days of his Black Arts involvement. For example, as she talks to Herbie in the park, Rose mentions that she once went to a concert with a friend named Neal, the rainy night she met Richard Wright in New York.

> ROSE
>
> He's a writer, . . . a very important writer, and he's colored too. I met him in New York. . . . One night in the Village. . . . He was walking alone in the rain. . . . And, later, Neal and I went Uptown to hear the music. (P. 128)

This alludes to the real-life Neal and the places he frequented alone or with friends. Fairmount Park; the races on the Schuylkill; the arsenal at Frankfort; Diamond, Taylor, and Berks Streets; Ridge Avenue, which Neal occasionally visited to listen to old men in the barber shops; Brewery Town; South Philly; Blue Note Cafe and Cafe Blue Monster: Whether they actually existed or not, these places render the play a more specific character, a Philadelphian legacy whose imprint is charted in its playwright's own life.

Unfortunately the play never made box-office records, neither did it receive significant acclaim. *The Glorious Monster in the Bell of the Horn* was staged on May 6, 1976 in Williamstown, Massachusetts; again on July 14 in Terrace House, New York City; and finally on August 13 in Fire Island, New York. Three years later, it was staged at the New York Federal Theatre on July 6, 1979. In 1980, on July 10th it was staged again in Terrace House, probably for the last time. The play was reviewed by Stanley Crouch in *The Village Voice* in its July 23, 1979 issue, and by Richard Eder in *The New York Times* on July 11, 1979. Mae G. Henderson and Paul Carter Harrison reviewed the play in luminous essays which appeared in the special issue of *Callaloo* dedicated to Neal. Both Henderson and Harrison rightfully applauded Neal's talent and paid homage to his imprint on contemporary African American theater. Harrison in particular praised the play and charted its odyssey in the following words: "The *Monster* was Larry's great adventure, a love-child he began to nurture at his Harlem residence on Jumel Terrace in 1975; it became his constant companion during passage to Williamstown and Amherst, Massachusetts, holidays on Fire Island, and home again for the final period of incubation before turning it loose on the New York stage at the New Federal Theatre."[97]

TOWARDS AN AFROCENTRIC METHODOLOGY

As for the critical methodology whose future direction Neal had prophesied early on, it gradually metamorphosed into a new entity toward the end of the 1980s. At that time, Black Studies programs throughout the nation began to exert an unprecedented influence and gradually developed into departments within major universities at such institutions as UCLA and Temple University; similar projects followed rapidly at Harvard and Yale Universities. In Temple's case, the focus was geared towards the development of a community-based curriculum relevant to the preceding decades' activism and pan-Africanist philosophy. At the same time, emphasis was placed on the development of a critical methodology and research-oriented program. The new theory was expected to train individuals who would be capable of addressing major problems within the community. It was expected that they would bridge the gap between the community and the institutions, fostering a sense of connectedness, common heritage, historical consciousness, and locatedness.

As the study of African people from an African-centered perspective, Afrocentricity rapidly grew to become a valid response to the above-mentioned quests, and gained worldwide recognition. Temple University's Department of African American Studies has been extremely influential in its development. There the nation's first doctoral program in African American Studies was launched in 1988. The works of Molefi K. Asante, chair of the Department from 1984 to 1997, combined with those of faculty and graduates, continue to advance the theory and initiate additional discourse among the intelligentsia.

A most recent example is the debate between Asante and "classicists" such as Mary Lefkowitz, a Wellesley professor; George Will; and Roger Kimball. In the debate, Eurocentric negations once again impose themselves in the form of a purportedly universal culture that developed autonomously, without the influence of any other culture. Furthermore, Lefkowitz's book titled *Not Out of Africa* attacked African agency in Greece as well as works such as Martin Bernal's *Black Athena*, George G. M. Jones's *Stolen Legacy*, and Cheikh Anta Diop's *Civilization or Barbarism*. Apparently this is an effort to undermine not only the Afrocentric perspective, but also the global advance of multiculturalist reform movements. In return Afrocentrists, including Asante, counter-attacked Lefkowitz and others. Defending the premise of multicultural education, Afrocentrists assert that an African-centered perspective *is just one* among many viewpoints, one that rests upon a non-linear, non-hierarchical perspective. Its forward march is inevitable because it liberates the conscience and provides enlightenment even for those who are less oppressed. A powerful yet disturbing voice, it is destined to impact the past and future of human knowledge as it clarifies past philosophical inquiries into the origin of human civilizations and enhances the globalization of twenty-first-century democratic processes. The debate continues.

Neal's prophetic vision of the mission of the black writer and his indelible mark on the development of a new theory contribute to the separation of African and African American experience from that of "Negro" experience, the latter connoting a colonial superstructure laden with stereotypical allusions. His vision and distinctive mark link his work to a larger synthesis of human experiences in which the African American experience becomes one among many, without the need for hegemony. Neal explains his goal in looking at the world from an African-centered perspective in this manner:

> Finally, it should be about a synthesis of the conglomerate of world knowledge; all that is meaningful and moral and that makes one stronger and wiser, in order to live as fully as possible as a human being. What will make this knowledge ours is what we do with it, how we color it to suit our specific needs. Its value to us will depend upon what we bring to bear upon it. In our dispersal, we can "dominate" Western culture or be "dominated" by it. It all depends upon what you feel about yourself.[98]

In Asante's volume *The Afrocentric Idea*, the emphasis is also on the significance of African knowledge, but without preconceived assumptions about its superiority over other venues of knowledge. Asante contends that Afrocentricity does not claim hierarchical space; its contribution to human understanding and knowledge is neither less nor more important than that of other world views. At the same time, Asante insists on the centrality of the Afrocentric idea to African peoples all around the world. Likewise, Neal's understanding of human knowledge and the role of the African American in this realm is not only grounded in the African American perspective, but is also inclusive of other perspectives resisting the domination of a purely Eurocentric outlook.

What Baraka, Karenga, and Asante argue today on more general theoretical grounds, Neal had already articulated earlier on specific occasions, gradually laying the groundwork for the establishment of an aesthetic theory in black literature and drama. For instance, in his 1968 essay "The Social Background of the Black Arts Movement," Neal argued for the necessity of creating a separate terminology in the arts, literature, drama, and criticism. "Black people had a feeling of always being on stage for white folks. It was time, some of us thought, to be in certain contexts socially, unashamedly on our own, and to define ourselves on our own terms without someone else intervening in the definition."[99] Furthermore, on different occasions Neal would express his resentment at the lack of methodology and direction within black literary circles: "No one had developed a model form of cultural nationalism that these writers could follow"; the Harlem Renaissance failed because the writers were "caught up in the euphoria of suddenly having been discovered by the white intelligentsia."[100] He also observed that the thirties were not productive because of the overwhelming dominance of left-wing ideologies, and that "Garvey lacked a cultural philosophy."[101]

Folk culture, too, was largely left unexamined, with the exception of Zora Neale Hurston's studies. Albeit a brilliant writer, Ellison himself, in Neal's opinion, experienced an intellectual crisis because he "seemed to be awed by Western critical methodology."[102] However, unlike the state of black literature, Neal saw black music as freed from the Western critical methodology and he echoed its celebratory tone: "Bessie Smith's or James Brown's crafts are products of a non-Western sensibility . . . they carry the weight of different cosmological outlooks. . . . The music of John Coltrane, Albert Ayler, Milford Graves and Sun Ra is primarily non-matrixed. It does not conform to Western musical notation and it is not fully understandable within the context of formal European music."[103]

In his formulation of an aesthetic theory, Neal also addressed the condition of African American theater, which at the time was going through a creative and artistic drought. In his essay "Cultural Nationalism and Black Theatre," Neal asserted with disappointment: "As long as Black Theater is conceived as a means of getting to Broadway to Hollywood, we will have no theater. We will simply witness the drying up of one creative venture after another."[104] During an interview with Charles H. Rowell he said:

> . . . There was the black theatre of the 1920's, which was mostly the theatre of the musical comedy and dance type thing. There were a few other things later on in the 1930's and a few other fairly dramatic things, but mostly black theatre was the musical thing and the dancing thing. The new black theatre of the 1960's was a very engaged theatre . . . springing up in black communities, in black theatres, that was saying "We are dealing with

> black art". As LeRoi said it in that poem, "We are
> black magicians. We work something in black labs
> of the heart". There is an attempt at a kind of
> collective intimacy. It was art.[105]

As a matter of fact, Neal proposed that all of black America be perceived as one community and that cultural institutions be developed to sustain that community. He suggested: "The theater must be more than a place where we see plays. It must have an integral relationship to as many facets of the life of the community as possible."[106] In other words, in Neal's formulation theater assumed a new characteristic: Like a church or a school, it became a place for congregation. Here people could renew their self-confidence, gather spiritual nourishment, gain affirmative foresight, cherish ancestral Ma'atic wisdom, and most importantly, attain education.

Evidently there was a need to jump-start the spirit of the African American, that spirit which Neal's swift pace and *Hoodoo Hollerin' Bebop Ghosts* and *The Glorious Monster in the Bell of the Horn* could only half-awaken. It needed a louder voice, less gentle, more disgruntled; a cannon placed in the front-yard of the mainstream literary practice. If one may call Neal "the prophet of the Black Arts movement," then Baraka is well-suited to the name "arch messenger" in his development of cultural and aesthetic theory as well as his literary productivity. Neal's writings initiated a revolutionary approach to literature and the arts based upon the unity and solidarity of community, art, and politics. Baraka carried Neal's message a step further, particularly in his plays, illustrating the importance of an artistic and aesthetic sensibility fully committed to the needs of the black community. He showed that it is through the reformative, constructive, responsible attitudes of authors that the audiences/readers will experience a change of hearts and minds.

The stage was finally set for the dawning of a new era in the history of African American theater, soon to be known as the "Black Theater movement." The following chapter is therefore devoted to an analysis of Amiri Baraka's ideas and works. I examine their relationship to the advancement of the Black Arts movement, as well as acknowledge their role in the evolution of the African-centered perspective.

NOTES

[1]   Houston A. Baker Jr., "Critical Change and Blues Continuity: An Essay on the Criticism of Larry Neal," *Callaloo #23*, 8, no. 1 (1985): 70.

[2]   Larry Neal, "The Black Arts Movement," in *Visions of a Liberated Future: Black Arts Movement Writings* (New York: Thunder's Mouth Press, 1989), 62.

[3]   Ibid.

[4]   Kimberly Benston, "Introduction," *Callaloo #23*, 8, no. 1 (1985): 7.

[5]   Charles H. Rowell, "An Interview with Larry Neal," *Callaloo #23*, 8, no. 1 (1985): 13.

[6]   Ibid., 34.

[7]   Ibid., 34-35.

[8]   Ibid., 26.

[9]   Addison Gayle Jr., ed. *The Black Aesthetic* (Garden City, N.Y.: Doubleday and Company, 1971), 260.

[10]   Stokely Carmichael and Charles V. Hamilton, *Black Power: The Politics of Liberation in America* (New York: Vintage Books, 1967), 43-44.

[11]   Gayle, *Black Aesthetic*, 257.

[12]   Amiri Baraka, "The Wailer," in *Visions of a Liberated Future: Black Arts Movement Writings*, Larry Neal (New York: Thunder's Mouth Press, 1989), x.

[13]   Ibid., xi-xii.

[14]   Larry Neal, "The Black Writer's Role, II: Ellison's Zoot Suit," in *Visions of a Liberated Future: Black Arts Movement Writings* (New York: Thunder's Mouth Press, 1989), 53.

[15]   Gayle, "Introduction," in *Black Aesthetic*, xxii.

[16]   Houston A. Baker Jr., "Generational Shifts and the Recent Criticism of Afro-American Literature," *Black American Literature Forum* 15, no. 1 (1981): 8.

[17]   Larry Neal, "The Black Writer's Role: Ralph Ellison," *Liberator* 1 (January 1966): 9-11.

[18]   Larry Neal, "The Black Contribution to American Letters, Part II: The Writer as Activist (1966 and After)," in *The Black American Reference Book*, ed. Mabel M. Smythe (New Jersey: Prentice Hall, 1976), 784.

[19]   Neal, "Black Arts Movement," 259.

[20]   Gayle, *Black Aesthetic*, 12.

[21]   Neal, "Black Art and Black Liberation," *Ebony* (August 1969): 54-56.

[22]   LeRoi Jones, "The Legacy of Malcolm X," in *Home: Social Essays* (New York: William, Morrow and Company, 1966), 244.

[23]   Larry Neal, "The Social Background of the Black Arts Movement," *The Black Scholar* (January/February 1987): 14.

[24]   Ibid., 16.

[25]   Ibid.

[26]   Ibid., 17.

[27]   Ibid., 18.

[28]   Paul Carter Harrison, "Larry Neal: The Genesis of Vision," *Callaloo #23*, 8, no. 1 (1985): 193 n. 15.

[29]   Neal, "Social Background," 19.

[30]   Harrison, "Larry Neal," 177.

[31]   Neal, "Social Background," 15.

[32]   Harrison, "Larry Neal," 173.

[33]   Ibid.

[34]   Neal, "Black Arts Movement," 269.

[35]   Larry Neal, "New Space: The Growth of Black Consciousness in the Sixties," in *The Black Seventies*, ed. Floyd Barbour (Boston: Porter Sargent Press, 1970), cited in Paul Carter Harrison, "Larry Neal: The Genesis of Vision," *Callaloo #23* 8, no. 1 (1985): 173.

[36]   Larry Neal, "The Ethos of the Blues," in *Visions of a Liberated Future: Black Arts Movement Writings* (New York: Thunder's Mouth Press, 1989), 107.

[37]   Ibid., 114.

[38]   Ibid., 113-14.

[39]   Ibid., 117.

[40]   Maulana Karenga, "Black Cultural Nationalism," in *The Black Aesthetic*, ed. Addison Gayle Jr. (Garden City, N.Y.: Doubleday and Company, 1971), 36.

[41]   Ibid.

42   Neal, "Ethos of the Blues," 108.

43   Harrison, "Larry Neal," 176.

44   Ibid., 177.

45   Neal, "Black Arts Movement," 264.

46   Harrison, "Larry Neal," 178.

47   Neal, "Social Background," 22.

48   Neal, "Black Arts Movement," 264-65.

49   Neal, "Black Art and Black Liberation," 37.

50   Eleanor W. Traylor, "And the Resurrection, Let It Be Complete: The Achievement of Larry Neal (A Biobibliography of a Critical Imagination)," *Callaloo #23*, 8, no. 1 (1985): 43.

51   Larry Neal, "Some Reflections on the Black Aesthetic," in *The Black Aesthetic*, ed. Addison Gayle Jr. (Garden City, N.Y.: Doubleday and Company, 1971), 12.

52   Alice Walker, *In Search of Our Mothers' Gardens* (San Diego, Calif.: Harcourt Brace Jovanovich, 1983), 143.

53   Ibid., 145.

54   Molefi Kete Asante, "Location Theory and African Aesthetics," in *The African Aesthetic: Keeper of the Traditions*, ed. Kariamu Welsh-Asante (Westport, Conn.: Greenwood Press, 1993), 55.

55   Larry Neal, "And Shine Swam On," in *Visions of a Liberated Future: Black Arts Movement Writings* (New York: Thunder's Mouth Press, 1989), 7.

56   Molefi Kete Asante, *The Afrocentric Idea* (Philadelphia, Pa.: Temple University Press, 1987), 102.

57   Neal, "And Shine Swam On," 7.

58   Ibid., 8.

59   Ibid., 13.

60   Ibid., 14.

61   Ibid., 15.

62   Ibid., 16.

63   Ibid., 20.

64   Ibid., 21.

65   Ibid., 21.

66   Ibid., 22.

67   Ibid.

68   Ibid.

[69]   Ibid.

[70]   Ibid., 23.

[71]   Larry Neal, "Cultural Nationalism and Black Theatre / Two On Cruse: The View of the Black Intellectual,"in *Black Theatre* 1 (1968), 8.

[72]   Ibid.

[73]   Ibid., 9.

[74]   Ibid.

[75]   Larry Neal, "The Black Writer's Role, I: Richard Wright," in *Visions of a Liberated Future: Black Arts Movement Writings* (New York: Thunder's Mouth Press, 1989), 26.

[76]   Ibid., 27.

[77]   Ibid.

[78]   Ibid., 28.

[79]   Ibid., 25.

[80]   Ibid., 26.

[81]   Ibid., 24.

[82]   Ibid.

[83]   Ibid.

[84]   Larry Neal, "Black Writer's Role, II: Ellison's Zoot Suit," 51.

[85]   Ibid., 52.

[86]   Ibid.

[87]   Ibid.

[88]   Ibid., 52-53.

[89]   Ibid., 54.

[90]   Larry Neal, "And Shine Swam On," 20.

[91]   Larry Neal, "The Black Writer's Role, III: James Baldwin," in *Visions of a Liberated Future: Black Arts Movement Writings* (New York: Thunder's Mouth Press, 1989), 59.

[92]   Harrison, "Larry Neal," 181.

[93]   Larry Neal, *The Glorious Monster in the Bell of the Horn*, *Callaloo #23*, 8, no. 1 (1985): 87-170. Hereafter all references to the play are incorporated into the text.

[94]   Molefi Kete Asante, "Keynote Address," Diop Conference, October 1996, Philadelphia, Pa., Temple University.

[95]   Molefi Kete Asante, "Locating a Text: Implications of Afrocentric Theory," in *Language and Literature in the African*

American Imagination, ed. Carol Aisha Blackshire-Belay (Westport, Conn.: Greenwood Press, 1992), 19.

[96] Amiri Baraka, *The Autobiography of LeRoi Jones/Amiri Baraka* (New York: Freundlich Books, 1984), 205.

[97] Paul Carter Harrison, "Larry Neal: The Genesis of Vision," *Callalou #23*, 8 no. 1 (1985): 181.

[98] Neal, "Black Writer's Role, II, Ellison's Zoot Suit," 52.

[99] Neal, "Social Background," 22.

[100] Traylor, "And the Resurrection," 59.

[101] Ibid.

[102] Larry Neal, "Cultural Nationalism and Black Theatre," 10.

[103] Ibid.

[104] Ibid.

[105] Rowell, "An Interview," 26-27.

[106] Neal, "Cultural Nationalism and Black Theatre," 10.

III

Amiri Baraka

But my tendency, body and mind, is to make it. To get there, from anywhere, going wherever, always. By the time this book appears, I will be even blacker.

—LeRoi Jones, *Home*

Poet, dramatist, essayist, lecturer, and critic, Amiri Baraka is considered one of the most prolific authors of African American literature. He has produced a substantial body of work, particularly during the sixties and seventies, that is crucial to the analysis of the American and African American literary nexus. Despite occasional personal and professional controversy, Baraka's contribution to the Black Arts movement, both as a theorist and a practitioner, has been an extremely significant one. His influence also extends into the 1990s, as evidenced by the common themes and ideas shaping the contours of contemporary African American literature: centeredness in the African perspective, race-pride, and the promotion of African American aesthetic and cultural values at school, work, and home as prerequisites to nationhood.

Born Everett LeRoi Jones in Newark, New Jersey on October 7, 1934, he graduated from Barringer High School in Newark and attended Rutgers University on scholarship. Later he transferred to Howard University in Washington, D.C., which was a short-lived endeavor. In 1954 he joined the Air Force; there he was stationed at a strategic Air Command post in Puerto Rico most of the time, with occasional trips to American bases in Germany. He refers to his Air Force days as "the error farce"[1] because it made him understand the "white sickness," just as Howard taught him to understand the "Negro sickness." As he explains it: "When I went into the Army I saw how the oppressors suffered by virtue of their oppressions—by having to oppress, by having to make believe that the weird, hopeless fantasy that they had about the world was actually true."[2] Yet he endured and even attained the rank of sergeant, until his dishonorable discharge from the service in 1957.

Although disappointed in the politics of the Air Force, Baraka managed to collect a huge stack of papers which he believed would make a writer of him. He was right. He moved to New York's Greenwich Village and found himself among the so-called "Beat Generation" writers, painters, and poets—better known as "the post-World War II avant-garde"—such as Allen Ginsberg, Frank O'Hara, Gil Sorrentino, Joel Oppenheimer, Max Finstein, Charles Olson, and A.B. Spellman. The last figure was a poet and jazz critic who was one of Baraka's old friends from Howard University. "Poetry, literature, was our undying passion," Baraka wrote.[3] In 1958 he married Hettie Cohen with whom he ventured on several projects of publishing and editing, the first of which was *Zazen*. The couple had two daughters, Lisa and Kellie. Their first apartment on West 20th Street became the meeting ground for their circle of friends.

In July of 1960 Baraka visited Cuba. This marked a turning point in his life, as he later admitted in his autobiography. During his visit to Fidel Castro's socialist regime he was surrounded by a group of assertive Latino artists, intellectuals, and writers, including Nicolas Guillen, who questioned his apolitical stance severely. "For twelve or fourteen hours on the train I was assailed for my bourgeois individualism. And I could see, had seen, people my own age involved in actual *change,* revolution."[4] It was the beginning of a gradual but radical separation from his earlier bohemian stance and integrationist ideals as he moved towards a "blacker," separationist vision; in short, his would-be center. Following his trip to Cuba, Jones would remark: "I carried so much back with me that I was never the same again."[5] He started having intense arguments with his literary comrades. He thought: "It was not enough just to write, to feel, to think, one must act! One *could* act."[6]

Nevertheless, in 1961 he must have been still deeply embedded in his ideals of American democracy. His formation of the On Guard for Freedom Committee, an interracial group organized in Harlem, reaffirmed his faith in progress and the attainment of civil rights. That same year he established with Diane DiPrima the American Theatre for Poets, an experimental group. His first volume of poetry, *Preface to a Twenty Volume Suicide Note*, was also published in 1961.

Meanwhile, Baraka sponsored jazz concerts, featuring young musicians who were to become the elite of the "new jazz"—or as he called it, the "new Black music." Larry Neal had heard it popularized as "loft jazz." The latter name probably arose from Baraka's latest residence: 27 Cooper Square in Greenwich Village, a building that originally held several lofts and now housed the third floor apartment of his family. Archie Shepp lived in the second floor apartment; A.B. Spellman and Albert Ayler were two welcome guests. Neal said that they often had parties at 27 Cooper Square, soon making it "the place to stop when you were downtown." He continued:

> But the other thing about 27 Cooper Square was that there were concerts in one of the lofts in the building . . . we had been hearing about this music. Everyone kept saying this new thing—all the musicians kept walking around talking about the new thing. . . . I had been reading about it in *Revolution* magazine from A.B. Spellman and LeRoi. They were calling it "loft jazz" in *Downbeat* magazine. . . . You met all of the writers who were trying to get the thing together—the painters, the musicians coming in to hear this new music . . . where a lot of ideas took shape, a lot of discussion, a lot of listening, a lot of camaraderie. . . . There was something happening here. Something that was really consuming in terms of your personality.[7]

Twenty-seven Cooper Square saw the birth of the book *Blues People,* as well as those poems which would appear in a couple of years in *The Dead Lecturer*. Poetry which emerged in the early days of the Black Arts movement was a revelation, as Baraka recalls. It expressed energy, anger, rhythm, and passion for change. He admired the poems of Yusef Rahman, Neal, and Askia Toure, whom he called masters of the new black poetry and whose poetry he deemed symbolic of the movement's resilience. Baraka found these poets to be immersed in music as well:

> The fact of music was the black poet's basis for creation. And those of us in the BAM were drenched in black music and wanted our poetry *to be* black music. Not only that, we wanted that poetry to be armed with the spirit of black revolution. An art that would not commit itself to black revolution was not relevant to us. And if the poet that created such art was colored we mocked him.[8]

In 1963 he published *Blues People: The Negro Experience in White America and the Music That Developed From It*, which won him a Whitney Fellowship. The book is an analogy of "the *path* the slave took to 'citizenship' . . . through blues . . . and jazz."[9] As he writes in his autobiography, during his youth "as a set of fresh ears trailing across Belmont Avenue listening to black blues,"[10] he learned about the real language of the place. After *Blues People* was published Baraka admitted that while writing it he had to study not only the history of African American music but also the history of the people. "It was like my loose-floating feelings, the subordinated brown that was hooked to the black and the blues, were now being reconstructed in the most basic of ways."[11]

More than three decades after its publication *Blues People* is still viewed as one of the most comprehensive studies of African American cultural expression, as music constructs one of its main avenues of inquiry. However, as pointed out by critics such as Theodore R. Hudson, the author "was subject to human error and human poor judgement."[12] Hudson asserts that Baraka knows and understands the African roots and the influences on African American music, but committed errors that weakened the book. He cites Baraka's omission of early musicians, his dismissal of the close connection between religious music and jazz, and a few other historical and technical mistakes as the weak factors.[13] On a positive note, what Baraka presents in *Blues People*, besides a sociological summary of jazz, is the impeccable correlation between epic memory and the cultural/aesthetic values of the African American transferred through music.

Two forces shaped *Blues People*: Baraka's deep-rooted consciousness and nationalist perspective on his history, which required extensive research; and the unofficial black music classes he attended with his friend A.B. Spellman, held at Professor Sterling Brown's house or in the main lounge of Howard University.[14] Baraka often acknowledges the invaluable influence of these experiences on his own spiritual and aesthetic growth.

On the other hand, Baraka does not neglect to mention that Howard University also provided him with insights into what he calls "the Negro sickness." He found the institution to be mediocre, somewhat similar to his previous experience at Rutgers University (1951-52). He declared: "They teach you how to pretend to be white."[15] Yet during the time he spent at Howard University (1952-54), unlike at Rutgers, he acquired a social charisma and was encircled with friends, writers, future doctors and lawyers, parties, and other activities. At the same time, he seemed to be concerned about the avalanching socio-political developments throughout the country. The increasing volume of social unrest, persistence of racism, and intensifying anti-discrimination campaigns led by leaders such as Martin Luther King Jr., James Forman, Ralph Abernathy, Roy Wilkins, and Whitney Young, as well as the more strident voices of Malcolm X, Stokely Carmichael (later Kwame Toure), Marion Barry, and Ella Baker would soon create a personal dilemma, a self-questioning of his lifestyle and attitudes. Already buffeted and flailed by the impact of the new knowledge and awareness he was gaining through his association with the socialist front, Baraka now seemed to be open to a more nationalistic rhetoric, ready to move to a new level of spiritual growth and transformation. It is in this light that I will look at his subsequent publications.

It is often mentioned that Baraka earned a master's degree from Columbia University; however, he denies it. More accurately, he earned two fellowships: a Whitney Fellowship in 1960-61 and a Guggenheim Fellowship in 1965-66. He taught courses in American poetry between 1963 and 1965 at the New School for Social Research and at the University of Buffalo. In 1958 he had already started co-publishing with his wife Hettie the "little" literary magazine *Yugen*. This publication had a significant impact on the literature of the times.

Gregory Corso, Frank O'Hara, Charles Olson, William Burroughs,
and Edward Dorn were among the poets who contributed to *Yugen*,
which was published until 1963 and whose copies are collectors'
items. *Floating Bear* was a similar venture, which he co-edited with
Diane DiPrima. Mimeographed copies were comprised of the first
publications of some yet unknown, but promising poets. The magazine
was circulated among friends, and like *Yugen*, is cited among rare and
prized magazines by collectors.[16]

Throughout these personal accomplishments Baraka's literary
reputation was growing rapidly. Yet in the face of discrimination and
injustice, which had been left unaddressed for quite some time, he and
many of his contemporaries soon found themselves surrounded by fire,
in both the rhetorical and literal sense of the word. The escalation of
racial incidents, the assassination of John F. Kennedy and Medgar
Evers, and the explosions which murdered four little girls in a church
bombing in Birmingham, Alabama in 1963 were only the beginnings
of a tumultuous era. More agony and suffering were to follow during
the period known as the "Freedom Summer" of 1964. In the face of
these incidents Baraka was consumed, forcing his self-proclaimed
warrior spirit to announce a "blacker," more committed, more forceful
voice than he had heretofore utilized.

In March of 1964 *Dutchman*, his one act play, premiered at
Cherry Lane Theater in New York. It also received the *Village Voice*'s
Obie award, bringing further recognition to Baraka. Until then, he was
mostly known as a poet who was committed to bringing a strong voice
to the main stage of American theater. That same year he published
his second collection of poetry, *The Dead Lecturer*.

Meanwhile, numerous riots and racial confrontations broke out in
several cities and towns around the country. In the infamous summer
of 1964 the distorted bodies of three civil rights activists—James
Chaney, Andrew Goodman, and Michael Schwerner—were discovered
by FBI investigators along the muddy banks of the Mississippi. As
civil rights activities intensified Baraka became increasingly alienated
from his former allegiances. He was seeking the proper moment for
revealing his own spiritual strivings in the form of a meaningful
public cause. His desire was to see his poems, his writings, and his
thoughts act on the world. In a letter he wrote to a friend, Black
Mountain poet Edward Dorn, he expressed his inner turmoil in the
face of the happenings that surrounded him:

> 'Moral earnestness' . . . ought [to] be transformed
> into action. . . . I know we think that to write a
> poem, and be Aristotle's God is sufficient. But I
> can't sleep. . . . There is a right and a wrong. And
> it's up to me, you, all of the so called minds to find
> out. It is only knowledge of things that will bring
> this 'moral earnestness'.[17]

Probably out of his determination to act on the world, in 1964 Baraka set up a magazine called *In/formation*, which was really a handbill manifesto. Although not many copies are extant, the magazine was one of the first publications that gave agency to a new aesthetic value system in black arts and letters. It was comprised of announcements defining the role of the artist, that is, what the artist was supposed to be about. Shortly after, Baraka would announce his commitment to a new revolutionary stance that would enhance his leadership in defining the transformative role of the black artist. Unsurprisingly, *Dutchman, The Toilet,* and *The Slave,* his three most revolutionary plays, were also written in 1964.

Baraka's sudden desertion of Greenwich Village and Hettie Cohen in 1965 in the wake of the assassination of Malcolm X did not come as a surprise to those who knew him. It most likely did not surprise even Hettie, for she had been with him on several occasions when African Americans questioned him about his championing of blackness while he lived with whiteness. He could no longer contain his frustration; the pressure was too much, and Malcolm's death was the last stroke. His disappointment, anger, or sense of loss was substantial. He would later write: "Malcolm's death had thrown people up in the air like coins in a huge hairy hand."[18]

One cold morning in March 1965 he moved uptown to Harlem as a black cultural nationalist, determined to commit his energy from then on to the black community and community-related issues. The founding of the Black Arts Repertory Theatre/School (BART/S) in Harlem and later the Spirit House in Newark are two of the most important manifestations of his long term commitment to community-based programs and practices.

Towards the spring, together with Charles Patterson, William Paterson, Clarence Reed, Johnny Moore, and others, Baraka set out to

open a school in Harlem in order to "re-educate the nearly half a
million Harlem Negroes to find a new pride in their color."[19] As one of
the several antipoverty programs popularly upheld in those days,
BART/S aimed at bringing theater to the black community of New
York.[20] A government grant of $40,000 from the Office of Economic
Opportunity facilitated its establishment and allowed for the
immediate recruitment of four hundred members. In Baraka's own
words, "the school was dedicated to the education and cultural
awakening of the Black people in 'America'."[21] At its inception
BART/S staged several of Baraka's plays, such as *Experimental Death
Unit #1, A Black Mass, J E L L O,* and *Dutchman.* However, the
school was not solely devoted to dramatic performances; eighty
children ages seven through thirteen were instructed in remedial
reading, mathematics, and in Baraka's words, "hard-core
nationalism."[22] Besides poetry readings and concerts, courses in play-
writing, poetry, history, music, painting, and martial arts were some of
the activities held at BART/S. Young people in particular were
encouraged to participate so as to fulfill and popularize the educational
goals of the school.

The theater performances that they held during the summer of
1965 were carried to the streets of Harlem and down to the northern
end of Central Park. Participants used street theater techniques which
expressed a revolutionary message, calling for immediate action to end
discrimination. This theater was not confined to four walls, for a stage
and a curtain entailed too much reality—an unsettling premise for the
mainstream cultural establishment.

BART/S' funds were cut off seven months after its inception
because of a controversy. Had this not happened, conceivably it would
have achieved much more for Harlem youth and would have
accelerated the development of the Black Arts movement beyond the
boundaries of Harlem. In spite of its short duration, BART/S had an
indelible impact on the development of black drama and those
individuals involved in BART/S activities, including Larry Neal,
Yusef Iman, Jimmy Lesser, Askia Toure, Max Stanford, Sun Ra,
Albert Ayler, Jim Campbell, Milford Graves, Hugh Glover, Andrew
Hill, Barbara Ann Teer, and other young poets and actors. It also
served as "a model for the type of community theatre-workshop-school
that sprang up in black neighborhoods in other cities in the United
States."[23] Moreover, the learning experience of BART/S helped

Baraka establish the Spirit House in Newark, New Jersey, which
became his home, once again, after Harlem. Years later when he wrote
his autobiography Baraka said: "But even more than the Harlem
geography the Black Arts movement reflected that Black people
themselves had first moved to a political unity, despite their
differences, that they were questioning the US and its white racist
monopoly capitalism."[24]

In the months that followed, Baraka continued developing
community centers and groups that responded to the cultural crisis in
the inner cities. Meanwhile, in October of 1966 Huey Newton and
Bobby Seale wrote the ten-point platform and program of the Black
Panther Party for Self-Defense. The party would be launched the
following year in "the poverty center in North Oakland."[25]
Organizations such as this would have a great influence on Baraka's
next phase.

By 1967 Baraka had already become a follower of Maulana
Karenga's Kawaida philosophy, utilizing it as a cultural premise and
instrument for instruction. Kawaida literally means "that which is
customary, or traditionally adhered to, by Black people."[26] Among the
basic tenets of Kawaida are the Seven Principles of Nationhood,
known as the *"Nguzo Saba"*: *Umoja, Kujichagulia, Ujima, Ujamaa,
Nia, Kuumba,* and *Imani,* which respectively translate as Unity, Self-
Determination, Collective Work and Responsibility, Cooperative
Economics, Purpose, Creativity, and Faith. Karenga's US organization
spearheaded the Kawaida movement and popularized the seven
principles which were considered to be "the spine and total philosophy
of the US organization."[27] In Baraka's words:

> The 7 principles are 10 commandments to us—US
> because they are pre and post 10 commandments at
> the same time. If there is UMOJA, for instance thou
> cannot kill, steal, bear false witness, commit
> adultery, or any of the things the western world
> thrives on. The commandments are fulfilled by the
> initial need of blackness for unity—oneness.[28]

For Baraka, Kawaida was a new system of thought that reinforced
his reorganization efforts within the black community. In the early
seventies, through the utilization of Karenga's Kawaida theory, he was

able to establish the groundwork for his artistic, aesthetic, and literary ideas. Consequently, Baraka succeeded in reaching the audience he had already been influential in transporting to a different level of political and cultural awareness. And while it is true that since the 1970s Baraka has claimed to move away from Kawaida, it was this philosophy that gave him an initial foothold in the intellectual community of new African American scholars as he was trying to build the connection between drama and intellectual activism. Despite current distancing, he is credited with extending Karenga's ideas and ideals with the purpose of enhancing his community objectives for the Spirit House in inner city Newark.

Interestingly enough Spirit House, located on Stirling Street in Central Ward, was established in a fashion similar to BART/S in Harlem. After the remodeling and painting were finished Baraka was able to put together performances with the help of a group of amateur actors who called themselves the "Spirit House Movers." The group began staging his plays alongside those of other young playwrights. Besides dramatic productions, social, cultural, and political gatherings were also held in Spirit House.

The first activity affiliated with Spirit House was the organization of the Afro-American Festival of the Arts. This was in response to the World Festival of Negro Arts in Dakar, Senegal. Baraka had already expressed his reservations regarding the West African event: "The idea of a World Festival of *Negro* Arts was a drag. . . . But there was no mistake, Senghor *was* a prominent Negro!"[29] About the African American festival he wrote:

> The festival was my first really organized attempt to bring political ideas and revolutionary culture to the black masses of Newark. . . . The festival also connected me to many of the young people in Newark who were trying to do something in the arts and alerted some of the political types in that city that something "new" was happening.[30]

In the days following the festival they published a magazine called *Afro-American Festival of the Arts*. It had writings by Neal, Sonia Sanchez, Ed Springs, Yusef Iman, Ben Caldwell, Clarence Reed, S.E.

Anderson, and Baraka himself. Later on it was published under the title *An Anthology of Our Black Selves.*

The positive energy generated by the Spirit House activities soon led to additional influential projects. For instance, in October 1966 the *Stirling Street Newspaper* was founded by the community's youth to inform and educate the neighborhood about significant developments in the area. Baraka's main objective in this undertaking was to organize and politicize adult leadership which would take political action if necessary. The Black Community Development and Defense (BCD) which came into being in 1968 was a product of similar conviction. As explained in more detail below, Baraka's leadership role in the BCD brought him unprecedented popularity and support from the community. Moreover, alongside other community agencies, BCD played an important role in paving the way for the Black Arts movement. As Neal and Baraka repeatedly asserted, the Black Arts movement was about the people defining for themselves the nature of art, rather than allowing it to be defined by others as a remote, dysfunctional, uncommitted entity.

Meanwhile, slowly but surely the Civil Rights movement was giving way to a Black Liberation movement. The concept of Black Power reached Newark when Stokely Carmichael was arrested in Atlanta, the same year that Baraka started Jihad Publications with a slim pamphlet of poetry titled *Black Art.* Spirit House was attracting more visitors than ever before; their fifty-seat theater could hardly accommodate the throngs.

In 1966, Baraka married Sylvia Robinson, who later changed her name to Amina Baraka. That year he also published his seminal volume of essays titled *Home: Social Essays.* In 1967—some sources cite the summer of 1968—he changed his name to the Bantuized Muslim name Ameer, meaning "prince," and adopted the title "Imamu," meaning "spiritual leader." It is also reported that this title was given to him by Maulana Karenga, the political theorist whom Baraka met in 1967 while teaching at San Francisco State University. By early 1970 Baraka adopted the Swahili form "Amiri" to replace the Arabic "Ameer." Toward the end of the decade, as he gradually attained a socialistic attitude, he decided to dispense with the title "Imamu." Finally, by 1977 he preferred to be addressed as "Amiri Baraka."

Soon after his first name change, Baraka was arrested on charges of unlawfully carrying weapons and resisting arrest during the Newark riots. Initially he was convicted of a misdemeanor and sentenced to a three-year jail term. Later his conviction was reversed on appeal. After his release Baraka published *Tales,* his only collection of short stories. It was during this stage that his community-based activities gained momentum, resulting in the expansion of once moderate projects into long-lived, self-supporting commitments favored by all members of the community. The aforementioned BCD organization was one such project.

Established in January 1968, the BCD aimed to develop a new value system based upon Baraka's theory that combined ethics and aesthetics. It began with one hundred members, among whom were teachers, clerks, laborers, and housewives. Wearing traditional African dress, learning Swahili, and changing their names were popular practices among the members. They also refrained from using alcohol, tobacco, drugs, and eating pork. Baraka was not only the spiritual leader of BCD but also the master policy maker, with defense of primary importance to his organization. He said: "I am in perfect agreement with what Martin Luther King said about peace and love, but I know that what we build must be defended."[31] Baraka's solid convictions manifested themselves in his commitment and discipline, placing him alongside Neal as the most influential force in the development of the Black Arts movement. Nineteen sixty-eight was also the year in which Baraka received a Guggenheim Fellowship and published his only novel, *The System of Dante's Hell.*

In the years following his political and spiritual transition, Baraka published *Black Music* and co-edited *Black Fire* with Neal. In 1969 his first volume of black cultural poetry appeared under the title *Black Magic.* Besides these literary endeavors, in 1970 Baraka became involved in politics by assisting black candidate Kenneth Gibson during his mayoralty campaign in Newark. From 1970 through 1972 Baraka was the major organizer and participant in the Pan-African Congress of African Peoples in Atlanta and the National Black Political Convention in Gary, Indiana.

During 1974 Baraka went through another major transition which affected his political and social world view. Defying black nationalism, the author announced his conversion to international socialism. Since then, Third World Marxism with its celebration of Marxist, Leninist, and Maoist thought has become the main focus of Baraka's writing. *Hard Facts,* his collection of Marxist poetry, reflects the culmination of new trends in his artistic and intellectual pursuit in this arena. In 1979 he began teaching in the Africana Studies Department at SUNY. That same year he was arrested in Greenwich Village because of a domestic problem between him and his wife. Sentenced to spend forty-eight consecutive weekends in a Harlem halfway house, Baraka started writing his autobiography, simply titled *The Autobiography of LeRoi Jones/Amiri Baraka.* The work was not published until 1984, however.

In 1981 Baraka won a Rockefeller Foundation Fellowship and a National Endowment for the Arts Fellowship. From 1982 through 1986 he edited magazines such as *The Black Nation* and in 1987 published another book, *The Music: Reflections on Jazz and Blues.* In 1989 he won two awards: the American Book Awards' Lifetime Achievement Award and the Langston Hughes Award. Since 1990 he has been involved in promoting curricular reforms in the Newark public schools. Additionally, his first musical drama, done in collaboration with Max Roach, has been staged. Baraka continues teaching, lecturing, and occasionally reading from his works. He retains a certain amount of popularity among college students and graduates who view him as the griot of the Black Arts and Black Power movements.

TRANSFORMATION

Now that the old world has crashed around me, and it's raining in early summer. I live in Harlem with a baby shrew and suffer from my decadence which kept me away so long. When I walk in the streets, the streets don't yet claim me, and people look at me, knowing the strangeness of my manner, and the objective stance from which I attempt to "love" them.

—Baraka, "Words"

As one of the most prolific writers of the sixties and *the* most outspoken orator of the Black Arts and Black Power movements, Amiri Baraka continues to have a great impact through his work, most of which was published during the seventies and eighties. As a playwright he is known to have gradually moved from themes intended to raise social awareness to those that can be classified as radical, revolutionary, and even irritative with regard to mainstream literary norms. His poetry, however, maintained aspects of his "beat" period, although the subject matter became more and more political, touching on such issues as American politics, nuclear disarmament, and capitalism's incorrigible advance. His first book, *Preface to a Twenty Volume Suicide Note* (1961) is comprised of poems often categorized in anthologies as "beat poetry." These poems stand in sharp contrast to his later poems, both in content and style. The first poem in the collection is dedicated to his daughter Kellie, and provides the volume its title. Almost a meandering inner exploration and pessimistic in tone, the poem reflects the poet's existential quest for relevance in a chaotic world:

> Lately, I've become accustomed to the way
> The ground opens up and envelops me
> Each time I go out to walk the dog.
> Or the broad edged silly music the wind
> Makes when I run for a bus . . .
> Things have come to that.[32]

In "Notes for a Speech" his furtive longing for spiritual connections with Africa surface conspicuously:

> African blues
> does not know me. Their steps, in sands
> of their own
> land. . . . My color
> is not theirs. Lighter, white man
> talk. They shy away. My own
> dead souls, my, so called
> people. Africa
> is a foreign place. You are
> as any other sad man here
> american.[33]

His alienation from his roots, an involuntary situation, puts him at odds with the rest of the people he comes in touch with. Africa has never been so far away, he understands—perhaps for the first time.

Baraka's later poems are collected in *The Dead Lecturer* (1964). They express his growing resentment against old friends to whom he no longer feels an attachment, and against the careless bourgeoisie and irritating whites. He asks: "What had happened to me? How is it that only the one colored guy?"[34] Baraka seems to have become more aware of the growing tension in his life and his uncertainty regarding his role as a black writer. But this interpretation is itself suspect— Baraka's lines do not always render easy interpretations; they tend to be complex and obscure, addressed to an imaginary elite.

The poems in this volume are about the separation between Baraka and his old friends—his peers—and his sense of contradiction which makes him an "outsider." "An Agony. As Now" is an illustrative poem: "I am inside someone / who hates me. I look /out from his eyes. Smell / what fouled tunes come in / to his breath. Love his / wretched women." Love, even self-love, has disappeared; in his solitude, he is restless. Reconciliation—a distant idea—seems to be taken away from him forever; until the time of salvation he has to wait in purgatory. Beyond the physical pain, there exists a spiritual agony in which he can see his destiny being shaped, slowly yet strongly. It is this new awareness that breeds the anxiety in his soul; his "scream" wells up from this new realization. *The Slave*, his 1964 play, is the most illuminating example of his sense of alienation. It will be discussed later with the rest of his plays.

The poems in the *Dead Lecturer* reflect not only Baraka's personal transition but his determination to establish a *new order* for his people. In this reordering process, the poet is concerned with the moral order and its socio-economic consequences for black people. Out of these concerns Baraka repudiated the "hipsterism" with which he was identified in the early days when he associated with the beat writers of the fifties. From then on, dissent would be the trademark of his thoughts and aesthetic understanding, and would be strident, vigorous, and unapologetic. The social protest he verbalized was directed at the hearts of black people, urging them to agitate the establishment in order to spark a revolutionary change. Throughout the rest of his career Baraka's main task would be to articulate the requirements of black literature, define the Black Arts movement, and put forth numerous poems and plays in reinforcement of that ideal.

As a revolutionary writer Baraka has taken a strong interest in displaying the cosmological and etymological framework of black expression through his poetry, drama, and essays. His understanding of *Nommo's* significance for African American expression is one of the most exemplary pillars of his discourse. This has saved Baraka's work from the transience of so many other black writers who came of age during his heyday, and have already either been outdated or simply forgotten. An important reason for his continuing popularity is that Baraka has been able to come forth as a warrior: he has been straightforward, outspoken, and consistent with his premise that aesthetics and ideology are the same, and art must speak of the need for revolution and help create it. "The first thing that needs to be transformed is yourself, because either you are an example of revolution or you are an example of what the revolution needs to destroy."[35] As he later adds: "There is no middle ground. There is no neutrality. . . . We must be an example of those values ourselves because our lives are more articulate and forceful statements of our philosophy than anything we can write or create. The largest work of art is the world itself."[36] Unlike many of his contemporaries, Baraka was able to incorporate his ideology into his works; his poems, essays, and particularly his drama evidence his eventual growth towards the enhancement of a revolutionary vision. He does not write for the sake of writing; he writes to effect a change that will be to the advantage of black people. He reminds us: "What you think is good is a political good. What you think is beautiful is a political beautiful. What you think is negative is a political negativity."[37]

His revolutionary stance notwithstanding, the most frequently mentioned and sometimes the most criticized characteristic of Baraka is his transitions in terms of ideological position. These are slow, gradual changes of direction that influence his perspective and his work with regard to the black experience. For instance, his conversion from Christianity to Islam to Yoruba to Kawaida has generated new potentialities for his writings, as exemplified in his play *A Black Mass*. After his military service he had become interested in Buddhist and Zen theology, eventually concluding that Western Christianity "tends to cover truth rather than reveal it."[38] In his quest for a meaningful alternative to Christianity, Baraka was first influenced by Malcolm X who had, himself, observed a new glimpse of hope in Islam. Baraka reportedly was converted to the orthodox Muslim faith by Hesham Jaboa of the Sunni Muslims. However, his search continued through an investigation of the Yoruba religion, until in 1970 he began to advocate Kawaida ideology and the *Nguzo Saba* as the key to the new nationalism.

Following these occasional periods of transition, easily detected in his poems and essays and originally begun as the existentialist quest of a "beat poet," Baraka finally seems to have grasped wholeness with his people—the real people; that is, the average black man/woman who belongs to lower income groups, the black American who has to cope with forces of oppression on a day-to-day basis. Renewing his name, his religion, and his family, Baraka may have maintained a *new* black identity in order to *synchronize* with the life experiences of the real people. His assertion of this stance became particularly visible in his post-1965 works. His was an inner motivation, a final encounter within his own self first, which soon stamped its mark on his art and aesthetic understanding in order to cultivate the same consciousness within the African American community in Harlem and Newark.

Meanwhile, his poetry underwent significant changes, becoming increasingly militant in its tone and message, and addressed solely to the black masses. During this phase Baraka openly declared that poetry, and drama in particular, must be utilized in the struggle to defeat racial bias, oppression, and discrimination. Indeed, during this nationalist phase several of Baraka's poems reflected the crystallization of a new energy, with intense lyricism and sometimes shockingly concrete imagery.

In *Black Magic*, his volume of black cultural poetry published in 1969, poems such as "SOS," "A Poem for Black Hearts," and "Black Art" reflect his preoccupation with revolution and the anticipation of a final countdown. For instance, in "Black Art" Baraka asserts: "We want 'poems that kill.' / Assassin poems, Poems that shoot / guns. Poems that wrestle cops into alleys / and take their weapons leaving them dead / with tongues pulled out and sent to Ireland."[39] "Black People!", the last poem in the same volume, centers around an image of a riot in Newark. Taking whatever is necessary and turning everything upside down while joining hands in a ritualistic dance in the streets is the basis of the central vision which dominates the poem. More significantly, "Black People" is a call to arms:

Run up and down Broad Street niggers take the shit
you want. Take their
lives if need be, but get what you want what you
need. Dance up and down
the streets with music, beautiful radios on Market
Street, they are brought here especially for you. . . .
We must make our own World, man, our own world,
and we can not do this unless
the white man is dead
. . . let's make a world we want black children to
grow and learn in do not let your children
when they grow look in your face and curse you by
pitying your tomish ways.[40]

In the long run, as he became the public spokesman of the new
black nationalist ideology, poetry provided for Baraka the elemental
matrix which he sought to stimulate the masses. His drama, on the
other hand, was targeted to educate the masses and his people to
reclaim their historical consciousness, aesthetic and philosophical
assets that spring from the center of Africanness. Renewal of the self
and the employment of the new self to acquire a better means of
existence became Baraka's fundamental message in his plays. As a
matter of fact, at the base of his drama there lies a medium of
expression which encapsulates his idealization of the new black
identity. The following section articulates his preoccupation with
African agency, the Revolutionary Theater, and the expression of his
views on black aesthetics through the examination of a number of his
plays.

AMIRI BARAKA
AND THE AFRICAN AMERICAN THEATER

As the fifties and early sixties faded into the civil rights era, the
black revolution became a milestone in American social history
through its popularized announcement of a complete radical break
from previous decades' "nonviolent" and "pacifist" policies. Replacing

illusions of integration with strictly nationalistic policies, increasing numbers of African Americans were ready to exert power and violence using whatever means necessary as Malcolm X gained a higher status in their eyes, particularly in the aftermath of his break with the Nation of Islam and Elijah Muhammad. During the mid-sixties it became clear that the black revolution was the natural outcome of the sense of disillusionment and demoralization triggered mainly by the assimilationist policies of civil rights activists and leaders.

Disillusionment was widespread around the nation as several critical issues remained unaddressed: poor living conditions in crowded inner city neighborhoods, unemployment, police brutality, lack of funding for public school systems, injustices in court, harassment and threats during voter registration, and racial discrimination at the work place were worsening. For Baraka, these social problems provided the catalyst to shape his creative energy and formulate aesthetic principles that would be popularized with the advent of the Black Arts movement later on.

In many instances Neal called Baraka "the chief designer." Indeed, Baraka is a man of primary designs and provocative style patterns in African American literature. In *Home: Social Essays* he explicates his theories and ideas in several essays in order to illustrate the importance of a reorganization process in literature. These essays later came to provide the fundamental criteria for black literature and laid the groundwork for the general acceptance of his plays. One of the most fitting definitions that express the entirety of his work is that of uprooting and reorganizing the existing patterns. Particularly in "The Revolutionary Theatre" (1964) he proposes a theater cut off from Euro-American cultural sensibility and connected entirely to the Afro-American political and historical dynamic. He asserts that "revolutionary theater should *force* change; it should *be* change." Since change can be maintained by exposure, Baraka claims "the revolutionary theater must EXPOSE!"[41] He notes that such exposure should include the decadence of American society as observed in contemporary American theater. After all, theater is potentially the most social of all arts, as it is an integral part of one's socializing process. Moreover, it exists in direct relationship to the audience it claims to address. Since theater exists in such close proximity to society, the revolutionary theater, then, should "show up the insides of these humans, look into black skulls." Baraka further asserts: "White men will cower before this theater because it hates them."[42] However, hatred is not its sole goal; rather than merely proliferating hatred, the inherent didacticism of revolutionary theater aims at correcting the mistakes. Baraka asserts that revolutionary theater must teach people that the "holiness of life is the constant possibility of widening the consciousness. And they must be incited to strike back against *any* agency that attempts to prevent this widening."[43]

The most important role that Baraka attributes to drama, which he himself strictly adheres to in his own plays, is one of agitation and assault. "The Revolutionary Theater must Accuse and Attack anything that can be accused and attacked. It must Accuse and Attack because it is a theatre of Victims."[44] In fact, Clay in *Dutchman*, Ray in *The Toilet*, and Walker in *The Slave* are both victims and anti-heroes. Baraka states: "In the Western sense they could be called heroes. But the Revolutionary Theater, even if it is Western, must be anti-Western."[45] For example, Walker's accusations directed at his ex-wife, her husband, the middle class, the integrationists, and the oppressors all spring from the same creed, as Baraka explicates in his above-mentioned essay. Revolutionary theater has to bring change because what has been offered for centuries by the mainstream politics of America is no longer acceptable to the African American. Walker's role in the play is to exert a radical change; he claims "the point is that you had your chance, now these other folks have theirs."[46]

Throughout his writings Baraka has emphasized his break from integrationist views; his accumulated work stands as a testimony to that position. Political integration has proved to be useless in America, therefore the African American has to identify himself as separate and understand what it means to be separate. For instance, in an essay titled "What the Arts Need Now" Baraka asserts: "Show the chains. Let them see the chains as object and subject, and let them see the chains fall away."[47] Henceforth, in order to uncover the veil of deception, one needs to expose the truth. This is accomplished, as Baraka declares, by a "changing of images, of references, [which] is the Black Man's way back to the racial integrity of the captured African, which is where we must take ourselves in feeling, to be truly the warriors we propose to be."[48] For the conscious artist it means employing his art to express the feelings of his race and identifying the form which best fits into that emotional backdrop, for as Baraka remarks: "If we *feel* differently, we have different *ideas*. Race is feeling. Where the body, and the organs come in. Culture is the preservation of these feelings in superrational to rational form."[49] In fact, it was Baraka's sense of change that made him feel differently and eventually caused the radical change in his work. He stated: "My work kept changing steadily. It was based on growing, change—like everything else—until one day the whole thing just became unbearable in a physical sense and I just cut out."[50]

A robust example of Baraka's above premise—that race is feeling—is found in *Slave Ship* (1969), a psycho-drama in which the plot develops through an exploration of the subconscious and sensory media. The play is an intriguing and exhaustive appeal to the imagination; it is initiation through ritual, relying heavily on lyrical aspects of the language, expressionistic techniques, and audio-visual effects. In this play, which Baraka appropriately sub-titled *A Historical Pageant*, the impact of being kidnapped, enslaved, deprived of an identity, beaten, raped, and robbed of one's pride and culture is represented through live enactment. To reenact the horrors of enslavement, drums, rattles, tambourines, ship bells and horns, gun shots and whip cracks, the sound of the waves, the smell of the open sea, incense, urine, and excrement are utilized, adding more weight to the realistic imagery. One critic, Stefan Brecht, called it "a national epos" which has neither heroes nor individual characters.[51] It is historical in content, but it uses history metaphorically; in other words a historical dateline is used as a symbol for the present, and enslavement is a current event.

The play does not foster a negative agency for retreat or defeat; it favors survival and a determination to continue the struggle by whatever means necessary. It is made up of three scenes: the first one is boarding the slave ship, the second one is a mock marriage, the third scene is of revolt. In spite of the distressing tone of the play there is some consolation in the bonds the individuals feel towards each other: the family unit is revered; children are praised; communal solidarity is cultivated.

Slave Ship is about exposition, as Baraka claims: "I wrote it to express a certain people's feeling about what is real in the world . . . to explain exactly what the realities of the slave ship were and how they have carried over, how America . . . is a reply or continuation of that same slave ship, that it's not changed."[52] Many readers find it thought-provoking and challenging. However, it is not one of the most popularly staged Baraka plays; the reason, I believe, has much to do with the technical aspects of so complex a production.

To return to the overall impact and value of Baraka's play-writing career, it has to be stressed that his ultimate concern has always been with the political functions of drama. Drama's primary goal should be sought in its capacity to take away dreams, and replace them with a reality. Baraka's main asset since the early days of his literary career has been his ability to awaken the asleep, teach them to get rid of their fantasies, and force them to assume greater responsibility to enforce change from within. In Baraka's opinion, integration and assimilation as fantasies of annihilation not only foster unreal expectations but also initiate an eternal conflict for both parties. Those who are tempted by fantasies are victims, only to be exposed sooner or later. At this juncture, his ideas on the mission of revolutionary theater, as an integral element of the Black Arts movement, generate further insight into the meaning of art, aesthetics, and ethics in the African American experience. They are best exemplified in his essay titled "The Revolutionary Theatre":

> Our theater will show victims so that their brothers in the audience will be better able to understand that they are the brothers of victims, and that they themselves are victims if they are blood brothers. And what we show . . . will cause their deepest souls to move, and they will find themselves tensed and clenched, even ready to die, at what the soul has been taught. . . . We are preaching virtue and feeling, and a natural sense of the self in the world. All men live in the world, and the world ought to be a place for them to live.[53]

Baraka compares American theater—which he calls "escapist"—with the Revolutionary Theater, and asserts that the theater of white America refuses to confront concrete reality. He says: "There is a cultural emptiness in American society and Broadway represents its vagueness." The Revolutionary Theater, on the other hand, is more distilled and far more realistic than its contemporaries "which show tired white lives."[54] It is a radical alternative to the sterility of American theater; "anyone who wants to see real dancing and singing should go to Harlem."[55] In this essay Baraka juxtaposes reality against superficiality; action versus inaction in order to set forth a subtle alternative to mainstream American theater. In fact his loud voice, as exemplified in the following excerpt, prepares the groundwork for reorganization rather than a revolution: "We want actual explosions and actual brutality: An EPIC IS CRUMBLING! . . . We are witch doctors and assassins, but we will open a place for the true scientists to expand our consciousness. This is a theater of assault. The play that will split the heavens for us will be called THE DESTRUCTION OF AMERICA. The heroes will be . . . new men, new heroes. . . ."[56]

At the height of the Black Arts movement Baraka was considered both the theoretician and the practitioner of a new outlook in theater, with his radical propositions engendered in the Revolutionary Theater. Yet he was not alone. Ed Bullins, Ben Caldwell, Jimmie Garrett, Marvin X, Joseph White, Carol Freeman, Marvin E. Jackmon, Ronald Drayton, and Charles Patterson with their original plays, as well as Clayton Riley, Loften Mitchell, Ronald Milner, and Larry Neal with their essays on drama criticism paved the way for the development of a separate value system that sowed the seeds of contemporary African American theater. Historical consciousness; transcendence of Eurocentric negations; locatedness in subject matter, theme, and characterization; and adherence to the aesthetic values of the African American cultural experience as antecedents of the Afrocentric idea ushered in the birth of a new phase in the history of African American drama. Baraka, its chief advocate, was a man of transformative powers, anarchistic in spirit, one whose second coming was long awaited. His drama, among all his work, best portrays the *change* in his artistic and ideological aspirations along the way.

His plays titled *A Black Mass*, *Dutchman*, and *The Slave* constitute the main body of my analysis in the following section. These works best reflect Baraka's ideas on the essence of African-centeredness. Concomitantly, they collectively display the inextricable relationship between ethics and aesthetics, an imminent characteristic of his revolutionary ideology. *A Black Mass* is based on the creation myth of the Nation of Islam, in which whiteness is created in a lab by a crazy magician. In *Dutchman* Baraka exposes the story of a hero-victim whose inability to sustain a manhood grounded in a solid black identity leads to his destruction. At the other end of the spectrum, *The*

Slave is an experimental play which announces the birth of a new black leader.

A BLACK MASS

And let me once create myself.
And let you, whoever sits
now breathing on my words
create a self of your own
One
that will love me

—Baraka, "The Dance"

Completed in 1965, *A Black Mass* was first produced in May 1966 in Newark at Proctor's Theater and was directed by the playwright himself. Based upon the creation myth of the Nation of Islam as taught by Elijah Muhammad, the play attempted to evoke justification for black separatism and validate the ideals of black supremacy.

Set in a mythical framework with deliberate references to the original creation myth of the Black Muslims, the plot centers around the main character, Jacoub, who is a wicked magician of the Isle of Patmos. His heart and mind are solely fixed on "creating creatures" through his pernicious experiments on "pigmentation." His actions eventually lead to the destruction of his whole community. According to the Nation of Islam legend of creation, Yakub initiated a holocaust among the people at Patmos, unleashing a white race to conquer the world forever. Baraka's play follows a similar path with some minor twists. For instance, the white creature that Jacoub created hates black women, and whoever it touches turns into a savage beast like itself. To stop the malady from spreading at an epidemic rate, the white creature and the afflicted women are condemned to cold and desolate lands of the North.

The most striking characteristic of the play is its didactic tone through which Baraka reveals his insistence that theater be utilized as a device for edification. In Baraka's view, didacticism and the usefulness of art reinforced through myth serve to elevate one's consciousness. Concurrently these devices provide the means of inquiry into man's affiliation with his past, an important search because the past holds the secrets of the present and future.

As explained previously, myth and mythological formations played a significant role in the evolution of drama. Egyptian, Sumerian, and Greek mythologies served as essential templates, establishing human beings' relationship to the universe, as well as to the earth and deities through rites and rituals. It was from this sense of curiosity and quest that drama took its lead. Mankind has been striving to resolve the mystery of his origins since eternity, and myths provide an essential ingredient in that pursuit:

> To know how the present world order came into being, what or who caused it, and what was its meaning is of primary significance, because only a correct understanding of those long past events can enable man to take his proper place and fulfill his proper role in the circumstances brought about by those primordial events. The duties, obligations, rights and expectations of man in relation to the physical, social and spiritual realm of his existence are all anchored in that period of origins of which the myth is the authoritative account. When understood in this sense, it becomes apparent that the significance of myth is so basic, so seminal that there would be no exaggeration in saying myth makes the man.[57]

In the most general sense, then, myth provides explanations for the unexplained and fills a void in man's psyche regarding the meaning of his existence. *A Black Mass*, being a play based on a creation myth, "explains" the existence of evil in the world, and teaches black people, from a centered perspective, how to restore the order on earth. K. William Kgositsile called the drama "Jones' most accomplished play to date," whereas Hudson referred to it as "Jones' strongest dramatic statement of the original-virtue-of-black-people theme."[58]

Interestingly, *A Black Mass* opens in a chemistry lab where three black magicians are mixing solutions and preparing a potion, that is, a magic drink. The stage setting and decor evoke a mystical atmosphere with Sun Ra's music in the background and occasional glows of red, blue, and violet enveloping the stage. The drink that is being prepared is supposed to make those who drink it "dance mad rhythms of the eternal universe until time is a weak thing."[59] Among all his plays, *A Black Mass* is probably Baraka's most symbolic play with regard to the plenitude of allegorical features. Instructing the audience upon the eternal struggle between good and evil, Baraka creates three magicians, Jacoub, Tanzil, and Nasafi. The latter two represent wisdom, goodwill, and sympathy in contrast to the wicked reasoning and evil intentions of Jacoub. "Time," a hostile force which makes people "run," is shunned in the play; "the white madness" and the "animals" who bring it into the world must be destroyed.

JACOUB
It (time) is a human thing. A new quality for our minds.

NASAFI
But deadly. It turns us into running animals. Forced across the planet. With demon time in mad pursuit. What good is that?

TANZIL
We have no need for time . . . we have hatred for it. It is raw and stays raw. It drives brothers across the earth. I think it is evil. (P. 23)

Jacoub rejects Nasafi and Tanzil's plea to destroy time, asking: "Can knowledge be evil?" Jacoub is *the scientist* who strives to achieve utmost knowledge and utmost reality, not unlike Dr. Faustus, his Eurocentric counterpart. For Jacoub all creation and the act of creating for the mere pleasure of experimentation, even at the expense of human lives, is good. He is indifferent to the detrimental consequences of his creations and believes that through scientific reasoning he will be able to conquer the secrets of the universe. Nasafi and Tanzil's attempt to convince Jacoub to give up his efforts prove futile:

NASAFI

We know the myths. We know the realities. We
know what is evil and what is perfection. We know
we are black and beautiful speeding through the
universe at thousands of miles an hour. . . . We know
beyond knowing, knowing there is nothing to know.
And knowledge is repetition, and the bringing forth
again of things that were so anyway. Everything
already exists. You cannot really create. (P. 25)

Obsessed with creation and success, Jacoub is determined not to give
up his passion. For him creation has its own end; it is movement,
action, and thought combined in a dynamic thrust. The tension rises
when women start screaming, informing the audience about the bad
omens: the earth is trembling, the sea is raging, and the sky is sinking.
"There is evil riding in the air" (P. 28) they scream, and it is Jacoub's
creation that has inflicted the disaster. Explosions follow and the fear
of apocalypse suffuses the air. Nasafi shudders, calling "Deathfire,"
while Jacoub returns his call in a frenzy of joy, "Lifefire!"

Eventually, as Jacoub completes his task the creature appears on
the stage; it is a white reptile, akin to a lizard, wearing a red, lizard-
devil mask. The skinny creature jumps up and down, screams, shrieks,
vomits, chews, spits, and shouts: "White, white, white. I white" (P.
30). Soon it attacks the magicians, including Jacoub, and the women
around the stage. Tiila, grabbed by the monster, soon turns into a
similar monster. The catastrophe spreads. The evil is set loose on
earth; the creature that "comes from endless space" lacks feelings or
thought; it cannot be taught, or tamed; it is sexless yet hungry for
"female spoor and meat" (P. 31). Nasafi warns Jacoub about the
consequences of his experimentation and reminds him of his
humanness:

NASAFI

This thing is not a man. We are men, brother. And
this thing is not ourselves. But the hatred of
ourselves. Our wholeness. And this self you speak of,
and this desire, and the animals of hated time, now
these horrible beasts, all these things, Jacoub, set you
apart from your brothers. (P. 38)

The suspense reaches its height when Jacoub is convinced by his congregation to banish the disobedient and corrupt creatures to the cold caves of the North where they can continue their horrible lives without threatening the survival of humankind. They exit, howling and hopping: "White . . . white . . . me . . . me . . . White . . . !" (P. 32) After they leave, the narrator's voice is heard over the loudspeaker:

> And so Brothers and Sisters, these beasts are still loose in the world. Still they spit their hideous cries. There are beasts in our world. Let us find them and slay them. Let us lock them in their caves. Let us declare the holy War. The Jihad. Or we cannot deserve to live. Izm-el-Azam. Izm-el-Azam. (P. 39)

As the lights dim and the curtain falls, "Izm-el-Azam," meaning "God's name" in Arabic, is softly repeated over the loudspeaker.

Considered to be one of Baraka's agitprop plays, *A Black Mass* is designed to teach certain broad and communal virtues, to make the community face its essential problems, and to educate black people as to their fundamental tasks.[60] It dates from the days of Baraka's conversion to the Nation of Islam. The play continues the tradition of attacking white society, or what Baraka calls the "madness" of the West, but expressed this time in more abstract and mythic terms. Baraka's distrust and dislike of Christianity is best expressed in this play through his reinstatement of several Nation of Islam concepts and the teachings of Elijah Muhammad. Most importantly, the play serves to elucidate Baraka's didactic lessons promulgated in his earlier essays, that is, black nationalism and consciousness can be raised through symbolic expositions. For instance, in the play Baraka expounds on the difference between good and evil, but with the added complication that the Blatant Beast still exists even though physically banished from the earth. Through a symbolic addition to the original myth, Baraka achieves his ultimate goal by warning his audience that the "ultimate evil is assimilation of the beast within the black self."[61] Only if black people recognize the "evil" both within and outside their realms, will the true renewal begin. Baraka implies that the real black mass will take place when old myths that are relevant to the black man's socio-historical consciousness, with their generative power for the good and the beautiful, are reinstated.

A Black Mass chronologically fits in with the rest of Baraka's works written during his Black Nationalist phase. Naturally the essays, poems, and plays he wrote from 1965 through 1974 clearly reflect his most revolutionary ideas and theories, promoting black nationalism and its invigorating influence on culture, aesthetic values, and ethics. "Black Art" is one of those essays in which Baraka speaks of "cultural aggression," a concept that coincides with the moral taught in the play. "Cultural aggression," as Baraka defines it, is the cause of the "bad institutions, bad ideas and negative values" that have been implemented in the black community by the colonizer.[62] While it is true that oppression often causes miseducation, sometimes oppression also results in the dislocation of internal values; ultimately those ethics will need to be reoriented through a revolution. *A Black Mass,* in essence, is about self-purification, the cleansing within. As Baraka explains:

> Cultural aggression could also be listening 24 hours a day, on a soul station, to some marionette spin records for us that would tell us to kill ourselves, to put on our wigs, drink our wine, snort our dope, to ride around with the Cisco Kid, to pervert our lives as an exact brown replica of American degeneracy.[63]

In Baraka's view the "bad" and the "evil" which teach wrong values are the same as the forces which symbolically create the evil in a chemistry lab: they are the atomic bomb mushrooming over Hiroshima, the nuclear tests in the deserts and oceans of our earth, the crack cocaine on the street blocks, and all that is hostile to one's own self-image. Baraka understands the correlation between ethics and aesthetics; the connection between positive ideology and positive politics is an important one.

The title of the play also generates a symbolic reference. It deliberately plays on the double-meaning of "mass," one being that of the Christian church service,[64] and the other referring to the Black Mass, including its connotations of witchcraft. Assumedly Baraka is comparing the sterile atmosphere of the Christian church to that of a black church, and is suggesting an alternative to his audience—that is, a return to black holiness and power.

A Black Mass, in its final analysis, reconstructs the basis of the theoretical grounds on which the Revolutionary Theater, as one of the pillars of the Black Arts movement, rested. As a propaganda play which attempts to explain the source of evil in the world, it warns black people to pursue the positive wisdom of African agency and beware of the dangers of betrayal and seduction in a general sense. After almost three decades, the play remains one of Baraka's most interesting and original creations.

DUTCHMAN

The recipient of the ninth annual Obie Award for the Best American Play produced off-Broadway in the 1963-64 season, *Dutchman* first opened at the Cherry Lane Theatre in New York City on March 24, 1964 and was staged there until February 1965. The movie version, directed by Anthony Harvey, appeared in 1967.

Highly symbolic in its theme, plot, and characterization, both scenes of the play take place in a moving subway car. The tension that typifies any urban landscape is accelerated with Baraka's introduction of his characters, Lula and Clay. In *Home: Social Essays* Baraka argued against the critics' interpretation and stated that the white girl and the black man are not symbols. "She is not meant to be a symbol—nor is Clay—but a real person, a real thing, in a real world. She does not represent any thing—she is one. And perhaps that thing is America, or at least its spirit."[65] In reality, America has been the land of "homelessness" for African Americans, a place where they have been usurped of their birth rights and made into spiritual exiles. Baraka claims: "America [is a place of] unsolved murders happening before one's eyes on television; it is a land of victims."[66] He continues: ". . . ALL KINDS OF VICTIMS. People being burned. . . . These pictures should make anybody think. This is what America looks like now. Where is the hope? Why does this terrible place not fall? Who can *dare* defend it?"[67] Baraka further compares America to an "insane asylum" in which blacks are held captive by "mad white keepers," the "Hollow Men, Paper Tigers, Closet Queens of the Universe."[68]

Dutchman, in Baraka's own words, is a play about black manhood; "it is about the difficulty of becoming a man in America."[69] On the surface, the play can be considered a retreat within Baraka's theoretical frame of reference, a framework that usually carries a victorious tone. The surprise ending does not contribute much towards the resolution of the eternal conflict between the good and the bad. However, it does fulfill an important task by implying the arrival of a new black man in a distant future, despite the protagonist's useless death. The young black man whose life is prematurely cut short at the hands of a white woman in *Dutchman* pursues his reincarnation in a different play as Walker, the leader of the revolutionary forces in *The Slave*. The black man is determined to strike back and get even. Henceforth, *Dutchman* and *The Slave* can be looked at as parts of the same play whose plot centers around becoming a man, specifically a black man. Furthermore, whereas *Dutchman* is about the difficulty of becoming a black man, *The Slave* is the watershed between the death of an assimilationist and the birth of a black nationalist.

There has been much discussion surrounding the origins of the title "Dutchman." One of the most popular interpretations refers to a half-legendary flagship of a Dutch East India Company, called "Flying Dutchman," which is known to have transported enslaved Africans from West Africa in the seventeenth century. Another popular interpretation relies on the legend of the Flying Dutchman which has inspired many authors, poets, and composers. According to this legend, a Dutch captain blasphemously declared during a raging storm at sea that he would sail round the Cape even if it took him until Judgment Day. He is taken at his word and an evil curse is laid upon him, dooming him to continue sailing forever with a crew of living-dead who obey his orders without resistance. Another version of the myth relates that the central character is ever in pursuit of a prey that can never be caught.[70]

In the context of the myth, the subway train in which the whole event takes place in *Dutchman* resembles the slave ship in the legend; its voyage defines a ritualistic cycle destined to proceed unceasingly, even after the protagonist is murdered. Lula represents Clay's inescapable destiny, because she is both the cruel temptress and the cold-blooded murderer. Clay and his young replacement who boards the train right after the murder scene essentially represent victims of assimilationist fantasies, of which Baraka is strongly critical.

The names of the characters are highly symbolic, explaining Baraka's long-lasting preoccupation with poetry and his long years of experimentation with association through language, symbol, and imagery. Lula, also known as "Lamia" or "Lilith" in Euro-American literature, is generally believed to be "*la belle dame sans merci*"—the merciless woman. According to a legend, she was once a beautiful queen turned into a wild beast who devours children, or entices young men into her arms to destroy them. Both as "terrible mother" and "female vampire," it is believed that she often "rides" her victims to destruction.[71] Lula is also related, in a symbolic manner, to Adam's first wife, Lilith, who later haunted pregnant women and kidnapped children.

It is possible to look at Clay as the natural man[72] whose innocence is corrupted and whose destiny is forged in the hands of Lula-Lilith-Lamia. He is a man whose fate resembles or is symbolic of the new Adam, that is, Jesus Christ.[73] Along these lines, according to some critics the play is a modern version of the Adam and Eve story whereby Lula is identified with Satan, and whose path to Clay's seduction again ironically resides in an apple. Needless to say, *Dutchman* is rich with symbolism and allegory, yet its characterization and dialogue also contribute to its wide acclaim. The whole play should be read or observed as a ritual unfolding the secrets of the hidden truth. Once the shroud is lifted, a fatal image forged in the irony of the promise of love reveals itself. Clay is willing to receive this gift and therein resides Baraka's deepest resentment.

As the play opens, Lula—age thirty-two, blond, vivacious, tall and flirty—gets on the subway train and sits next to Clay, who is twenty, middle class, young, and eager. Such an introduction could very well be an overture for a modern Romeo and Juliet scenario if they were different people. However, Lula's whiteness and Clay's blackness do not mix in the dramatic setting prepared by this particular playwright. When Clay accepts the apple offered by Lula, his inevitable descent begins. His assimilationist fantasies and willingness to join Lula foreshadow his terrible end.

Clay can be categorized as a victim because he has adopted typical middle-class values. He lives in New Jersey with his parents. He has been educated in a colored college where he thought "he was Baudelaire." His three-button suit, his tie and white shirt, mirror his determination to "make it" in corporate America. Lula, not the least impressed, makes fun of him:

> LULA
> What've you got that jacket and tie on in all this heat for? And why're you wearing a jacket and tie like that? Did your people ever burn witches or start revolutions over the price of tea? . . . What right do you have to be wearing a three-button suit and striped tie? Your grandfather was a slave, he didn't go to Harvard. I bet you never once thought you were a black nigger. . . . A black Baudelaire.[74]

Still engaged in flirtatious talk, seemingly unoffended by Lula's remarks, Clay invites her to come along with him to a party. Afterwards, as Lula suggests, they may even go to her apartment. The fantasy she creates persists throughout the first scene and lasts into the second. Lula sketches the picture of a wild night, a pretense that they both enjoy sharing, a promise that revolves around Clay's "manhood." However, what is inimical is that Clay does not know her nature yet; he not only does not know that she will soon display uncontrollable schizophrenic behavior, but is unaware that she will also force him to attack her. "Clay, you got to break out. Don't sit there dying the way they want you to die. Get up" (P. 31). When Lula wants to "dance," Clay refuses; therefore she calls him "dirty white man." As Clay tries to calm her down Lula increases her belligerence and this time calls him "Uncle Thomas Woolly-Head."

> LULA
> There is Uncle Tom . . . I mean, Uncle Thomas Woolly-Head. With old white matted mane. He hobbles on his wooden cane. Old Tom. Old Tom. Let the white man hump his ol'mama, and he jes' shuffle off in the woods and hide his gentle gray head. Ol' Thomas Woolly-Head. (P. 32)
> . . . .
> You're afraid of white people. And your father was. Uncle Tom Big Lip! (P. 33)

The passengers' laughter provokes Clay to slap Lula and drag her to her seat. Thus he starts on a long soliloquy in which he discloses his long-delayed anguish against white society's oppression, humiliation, and stereotypical allusions.

In the final scene Clay challenges Lula and all she represents: the white world; those who preach integration and yet do not know what they are integrating with. The souls of the black folks and their aspirations constitute an entity which has been overlooked by the dominating culture. Clay's address is a historical one, portraying him fully centered in epic memory and in the socio-political consciousness. His transcendence of Eurocentric negations is manifest in his speech which attacks whites as well as middle-class blacks. He is aware of his cultural heroes, heroines, and his music. He is also aware that while the aesthetic taste of whites has brought fame and recognition to black artists, it has indignantly refused to accord them respect.

Clay's point is clear; he may be a little romantic and somewhat innocent but he is not a fool. The problem is one of respect and understanding which will never take place. This soliloquy almost renders him a hero, if only he would hesitate less, and act instead.

CLAY

. . . You don't know anything except what's there for you to see. An act. Lies. Device. Not the pure heart, the pumping black heart. You don't ever know that. . . . They say, "I love Bessie Smith." And don't ever understand that Bessie Smith is saying, "Kiss my ass, kiss my black unruly ass. (P. 34)

Clay also mentions Charlie Parker, who had captured white audiences with his music, but in reality played to audiences who did not understand what he was saying.

CLAY

And they sit there talking about the tortured genius of Charlie Parker. Bird would've played not a note of music if he just walked up to East Sixty-seventh Street and killed the first ten white people he saw. Not a note! (P. 35).

Metaphors would be unnecessary if Bird and Bessie Smith could only tell those people what they really think of them! But they could not and therefore they said it with their music, through the notes of blues and lyrics of jazz. For Lula and the majority of whites, Clay is a "type"; he is not truly a person, just a type. His anonymity does not even prompt Lula's curiosity; she says: "I know you like the palm of my hand" (P. 17). Indeed Lula knows Clay very well; she has been pursuing him since his arrival on the ship. She is the haunting spirit, the deadly virus, messenger of death. Remember her hand which is "dry as ashes" and "cold" like death? On ship or train, Clay is her destined prey; it has been like that since the beginning of time. A moment of weariness and all his bravura disappears. He is no more the man whom he would like to be; he gives up. Battles are not his realm, for he is the "great would-be poet."

CLAY

When all it needs is that simple act. Murder. Just
murder! Would make us all sane. Ahhh. Shit. But
who needs it? I'd rather be a fool. Insane. Safe with
my words, and no deaths, and clean, hard thoughts,
urging me to new conquests. My people's madness.
Hah! That's a laugh. My people. They don't need me
to claim them. They got legs and arms of their
own. . . . They don't need any defense. (P. 35-36)

Clay is right in the sense that his people do not need him; they can defend themselves and they do. Many of them would have avoided the trap Clay is caught in. Before he can get off the train and disappear into his own middle-class values, Lula stabs him. While he bleeds to death Lula orders the passengers to throw him out. As Clay's cold body lands on the rails the train disappears into the night with a new passenger on board. On a symbolic level Clay's death ends the ritual. It is a drama of sacrilege reinstated by the playwright to illustrate the inevitable consequences of assimilationist fantasies.

Besides themes of assimilation and integration another issue that needs to be examined in *Dutchman* is Baraka's effort—a deliberate one, I believe—to evidence the dangers of interracial liaisons. This is a direct reflection of the spirit of the early sixties, a period when he himself had been transitioning towards his Black Nationalistic phase. His artistic and intellectual growth exposed an inner urge to change which was confirmed by exterior circumstances. First produced in 1964, *Dutchman* debuted in the infamous year of the murder of three civil rights activists. The following year, in February 1965, Malcolm X was killed. In March Baraka left Greenwich Village and his family for Harlem. Thus *Dutchman* needs to be analyzed, at least in part, as the culmination of his growing awareness of America on a personal level.

A piece that succinctly illustrates this personal awareness is an essay titled "American Sexual Reference: Black Male," published in *Home*. In that essay Baraka explains why some black men are attracted to white women, stating that "the wildly 'protective' attitude white society has for the White Woman" initiates the cycle for a certain kind of black man to be drawn to the white women. "Because of this protective (defensive) odor the white man spread around the white woman, she became in a sense, one of the most significant acquisitions of white society for a certain kind of black man."[75] Further on Baraka explains that in order to attain power in America, some black men prefer to establish a connection with the white female: "For the black man acquisition of a white woman always signified some special power the black man had managed to obtain (illicitly, therefore with a sweeter satisfaction) within white society. It was also a way of participating more directly in white society. One very heavy entrance into White America. (No matter if any of these directions said "Love.")[76]

Apparently Baraka went through a similar routine, and it was the residue of his accumulated guilt—or to put it in a different context, his "earned wisdom"—that prompted his creation of Lula and Clay. Indeed, Lula knows all the initiation rites; she knows that she has to define in order to be in control. As Baraka had said, "the ability to define, of course, is the ability to control. Who defines, controls."[77] However, her definitions of blackness are misconstrued; she knows only what she has been taught—lies. Consequently she is blind to Clay's "pumping black heart," as she is blind to Bessie Smith who died on the way to a colored hospital, and to Charlie Parker and his melody, as well as to the rest of the world. Her ignorance, however, is a shield behind which she hides her real intentions of destruction. Clay, on the other hand, starts his journey in renouncement of his black identity, a stance that carries him into the delusion of the white mainstream. The revelation comes when Lula starts insulting him; it deepens suddenly with his recovery, that is, with the attainment of reality. Yet his recovery is short-lived. Clay restrains his feelings and contains his rage; his retribution is his death at Lula's cruel hands.

In 1965 Baraka wrote: "The black man is weakened by any friend-contact with whites simply because his concerns will shift (if he is 'influenced') and the raw problems of survival—mindsoulbody—will be obfuscated, and replaced by unwhite hallucinations."[78] Therefore, integration becomes nothing more than the "beatified decadence."[79] In keeping with this realization, Baraka foregoes forever the possibility of integration when he starts writing *The Slave*, the last play to be discussed in this section.

A play can be interpreted in various ways, one of which is an Afrocentric analysis, the overarching theme in this book. The Afrocentric analysis involves certain assumptions which are at the foundation of the Afrocentric critical method; they involve generative possibilities for other ways of looking at drama as well. The assumptions are: 1) centering discourse in the historical literatures/oratures of the particular people; 2) transcending Eurocentric negations of the people's culture, which involves counterargument, transcending Eurocentric preoccupation, and embracing more inclusive visions of reality; 3) using the three fundamental themes of transcendent discourse, which are human relations, human and supernatural relations, and the human relationship to self; 4) presenting the principal contexts of resistance, liberation, and action; 5) addressing the work to a particular audience; 6) employing the cultural mythoforms that inform the creative expression; 7) the social/political context which shapes the work; 8) lyrical qualities in the work; and 9) the ideas of unity and harmony. A more detailed explanation of the assumptions is provided in chapter four. In the meantime, these assumptions provide a means for looking into the ways a playwright or a writer produces his work, his center of operation, and the constituent elements of the work, all of which make it a production of a particular cultural entity. In Afrocentric analysis it is important to examine the author and the work from an African-centered base because the evaluative standards that have been applied to drama, fiction, film, and art heretofore were established far outside the culture.

An Afrocentric analysis of the *Dutchman* reveals that Baraka is historically located in African American history through the orature he embeds in his characters. Clay's entrapment in Lula's well-organized scheme is not a surprise to anyone but Clay; integration, after all, is not a new dream. Baraka presents the counterargument in Clay's dramatic soliloquy, but Clay still fails because of his hesitation to embrace more inclusive visions of reality. Clay displays resistance, yet liberation is never realized because he is too weary.

Baraka addresses his work to both black and white audiences, warning them about delusions of assimilationist fantasies. In keeping with the Afrocentric paradigm, lyrical elements are prevalent in Clay's references to jazz and blues figures such as Bessie Smith and Charlie Parker. Lastly, a non-Afrocentric aspect of the play is its failure to invite ideas of unity and harmony in the end because of Clay's brutal murder by Lula, the merciless woman.

THE SLAVE

First presented at St. Marks Playhouse, New York City, in December 1964, *The Slave* is the projection of the conflict in *Dutchman* from an integrationist perspective to what Baraka perceives as its resolution. It opens with a Prologue which serves as a commentary on the play as a whole. The protagonist, dressed as an old field hand, enters the stage, weary and drooping. His speech is inarticulate, his thoughts are unclear. He might be speaking for both sides, the white liberal and the black protagonist.

The plot centers around the conflict between Walker Vessels, the leader of a black revolutionary army, and Bradford Easley, a university professor married to Walker's ex-wife, Grace. Easley and Grace, both white liberals, are upset about Walker's unexpected visit. They fear for the children sleeping upstairs, for his visit during the height of the uprising signals that he has come to see his daughters. The Easleys do not want to believe that he has become a bandit just like "those" outside because they remember him as an intellectual, a poet, and even a friend. However, things have changed: Walker is no longer polite; he plans to take over.

Once upon a time, before Grace left Walker, they must have had good times, and even love. As Walker began to adopt a political stance that leaned increasingly towards black nationalism, his friendships and ideology disturbed Grace. In *The Slave* Grace accusingly explains: "You began to align yourself with the worst kind of racist and second-rate hack political thinkers."[80] Her point makes sense from her perspective as she continues: "Walker you were preaching the murder of all white people. Walker, I was, am, white. What do you think was going through my mind every time you were at some rally or meeting whose sole purpose was to bring about the destruction of white people? (P. 72). Walker's response, contradicting both his behavior and his words, catches Grace by surprise too: "Oh, goddamn it, Grace, are you so stupid? You were my wife. . . . I loved you. You mean because I loved you and was married to you . . . had had children by you, I wasn't supposed to say the things I felt. I was crying out over three hundred years of oppression; not against individuals" (P. 72). However, a previous exchange between the two reveals a different impression of their relationship.

GRACE

You're not going to take the children, are you? You wouldn't just take them, would you? You wouldn't do that. You can't hate me so much that you'd do that.

WALKER

I don't hate you at all, Grace. I hated you when I wanted you. I haven't wanted you for a long time. But I do want those children. (P. 65)

In reality, this couple is engaged in a typical love-hate cycle. Yet, at the same time, the above statements by Walker can be interpreted within the realm of power politics between the two races. As we observed in *Dutchman*, the protagonist seems to be chasing the power ideal in the white woman's persona. If this is true, then Walker's initial attachment to Grace was initiated to attain power. When he married her he didn't necessarily love her; he "loved" what he hoped she could bring to him—a sense of power, acceptability within the mainstream, and upward mobility. It was only after their marriage ended that Walker could realize she represented a false sense of achievement for him because he saw that he could attain power without her. Throughout the scene, Walker has been drinking heavily. When intoxicated, he reminiscences about the past: the years at the college where he apparently met Grace, and the season they both acted in a play in which he was Othello, Grace played Desdemona, and Easley was ironically Iago. Ultimately, in Walker's eyes Easley becomes Iago, not only because he married his ex-wife but because he is the symbol of white supremacy whose dynamics will be demolished by Walker's revolutionary army. Walker attacks Easley because he finds him to be a passive man, unable to perform what he preaches. Easley is the epitome of all the obstacles Walker has ever encountered; Walker is overly familiar with Easley's type, for these are the people who have prevented him from coming into his own since the beginning of his life. His people's freedom has been delayed by these people and now is the time for him to get even. The "great white fog" has to disappear and it will, at least in Baraka's revolutionary context for theater.

Walker is an angry young man, apparently dissatisfied and confused about his own life. Yet he still has compassion for his family, particularly for his daughters whom he admits loving deeply. On the other hand, he has murdered Easley, his ex-wife's husband, the motive being either jealousy or his lack of tolerance for white liberals. Moreover, he has denied Easley the opportunity to "go out [die] with any kind of dignity" (P. 82). He implies that he might even kill Grace because "the cause demands it" (P. 83).

With regard to the symbolic texture of the play, the protagonist's name is, according to one critic, "fraught with symbolic implication."[81] Walker's last name connotes a container that is either full or empty. Walker is filled with hatred as well as love and a strong desire to bring about social change; there is a reason for him to be the way he is. But the words he uses are not his own words; he admits that he has learned them: "I swear to you, Grace, I did come into the world pointed in the right direction. . . . I learned so many words for what I've wanted to say. They all come down on me at once. But almost none of them are mine" (P. 53).

Out of this exchange I conclude that Baraka is informing the audience that some black men do not have the opportunity to be whoever they want to be because both black and white society dictate their character long before they can decide who they are. The old man who appears at the beginning and at the end of the play may well stand as the symbolic spokesman, the "age-less" representative of all black men, for his age is unknown. He delivers the Prologue, a speech which sets the tone for the psychological and ideological paradigm in which Baraka places his protagonist. Ideas and concepts which are not Walker's own will send him on an imaginary quest whose possibilities are already limited. Walker is a finished product, a forlorn "vessel" on the high tide of revolution. As the title of the play suggests, he is "the slave" who cannot change the destiny of his people. The revolution needs better heroes.

References to Richard Wright's *Native Son*, whose protagonist Bigger Thomas reminds Grace of Walker, is another symbolic twist in the play. In that context Easley can be called Mr. Dalton, and his death justified in Walker's eyes. In the novel, Bigger Thomas' greatest hindrance is his fear of the white man. When Grace calls Walker "a second rate Bigger Thomas" (P. 57) it is understood that Walker cannot escape from the reality of facing Bigger Thomas. Although his drinking is not the most characteristic feature of Walker, it seems to provide a commentary on some people's habits of drinking and the explanations they offer as an excuse. Whereas a quick conclusion such as "he drinks because the society is oppressive" can serve many ends, Walker's motives may be more varied than that. Looking at the human aspect alongside the premise of racial discrimination and oppression, Walker has been alone so long, without his daughters and his wife, that drinking probably became his sole consolation. Furthermore, he harbors the personal fear that the revolution may fail, and he may not be able to take his daughters with him. All or some of these factors may provide valid explanations for Walker's heavy drinking. What is indisputable, however, is that his drinking is one of the factors which brings disharmony to the general atmosphere of the discourse he engages in throughout the play.

There is a deep sense of distrust between Grace and Walker which provides a commentary on human relations, and thus brings in the Afrocentric idea. In an Afrocentric analysis of any play the critic is asked to look into human relationships to assess the playwright's location. References that provide insight into the socio-historical background of this playwright frequently reveal a denial of the African world view operating in the communication among the characters. For example, Grace often calls Walker "liar!", or shouts at him "You're lying!" and "You're out of your mind." A cosmological analysis of the dialogue between the two reveals a lack of African cultural referents on Walker's part; he simply does not respond the way he is supposed to. First of all, there is no hint of the power of the word in his speech. As the rhetor in the play he is expected to use African cultural referents and evidence psychological connectedness in his creation of messages, yet none of his responses are aligned with an African cultural base. When Grace tells him that he has killed too many people, even his own people, Walker's response falls far short of an African perspective.

> . . . in spite of the fact that I, Walker Vessels, single-handedly, and with no other adviser except my own ego, promoted a bloody situation where white and black people are killing each other; despite the fact that I know that this is at best a war that will only change, ha, the complexion of tyranny . . . (*laughs sullenly*) . . . despite the fact that I am being killed in my head each day and by now have no soul or heart or warmth, even in my long killer fingers, despite the fact that I have no other thing in the universe that I love or trust, but myself . . . despite, the resistance in the large cities and the small towns, where we have taken, yes, dragged piles of darkies out of their beds and shot them for being in Rheingold ads, despite the fact that all of my officers are ignorant motherfuckers who have never read any book in their lives, . . . in spite of all the drunken noises I'm making, despite . . . in spite of . . . I want those girls, very, very much. And I will take them out of here with me. (P. 66-67)

Later, when Grace tells him he is out of his mind, Walker answers in weariness: "Turn to another station." He continues: "Out of my mind is not the point. . . . The way things are, being out of your mind is the only thing that qualifies you to stay alive. The only thing" (P. 83). At one point Grace calls Walker "the nigger murderer," to which Walker mockingly responds: "When you taught the little girls to pray . . . you'd have to whisper, 'And God Bless Mommy, and God bless Daddy, the nigger murderer'" (P. 54). He laughs hysterically, amused at what he heard and what he said.

Throughout the play Walker sounds confused and dislocated, belonging neither to his own base nor to any other base. His fury seems to be the driving force for his frenzy of killing, which is plausible even if he genuinely cares for his daughters. But these are not the ways of a revolutionary leader, and in that sense Walker fails.

The physical confrontation between Walker and Easley which was mounting to an inevitable climax finally leaves Easley dead. Meanwhile, Grace is left under the debris and beams which fall as a result of the explosions outside. As she dies she asks Walker to save the girls but Walker replies that they are already dead. However, just as he is leaving a child's crying is heard between the explosions which continue sporadically, implying that there is still some hope for reconciliation.

In applying an Afrocentric analysis to *The Slave*, one sees that throughout the play Walker attempts to explain the counterargument in his paradoxical rhetoric. He may even have transcended Eurocentric negations in his own mind, but can he manage to establish an inclusive vision of reality after so much killing and bloodshed? Moreover, he claims that he is "dead," has neither soul nor heart, and does not trust anyone but himself. Such individualistic bravura has no place in African cosmological and etymological discourse wherein the goal is to attain the best for the community.

Walker exhibits resistance to oppression but his own liberation is the result of wanton violence. Of course, the social political context that shapes the play is definitely connected to the memories of social unrest during the sixties in locales such as Watts, Detroit, and Kent State. And admittedly, during any time of upheaval, confusion and chaos are inevitable side effects. What is problematic from an Afrocentric perspective is that Walker does not provide any solutions for the aftermath of the uprising; he leaves the stage stumbling as unsteadily as the old man at the beginning of the play. Nor are there any lyrical qualities in the work, cultural mythoforms, or ideas of unity and harmony.

Apparently, in *The Slave* Baraka continues the stream of thought he started with his previous plays. He denounces Eurocentric negations, meaning stereotypical allusions bred by racial hatred and discrimination—a task he had started with *Dutchman*. Walker's entire act is a testimony to the destruction of the domination of Eurocentric beliefs and value systems. However, the protagonist fails to place the Eurocentric world view in a perspective which would lend itself to building an Afrocentric perspective. Instead, he is caught in the denial of the Eurocentric negation, neglecting to move on to a different level of preoccupation for the African American. Thus, throughout the play Walker's discourse is full of contradictions, driven by feelings of hatred and revenge, nullifying any hope for the delivery of unity, harmony, a new order, and reconstruction. In the midst of this, Baraka is not only the playwright but the instructor as well, with an obvious didacticism at the forefront of all his arguments. However, he fails to provide any explanations as to why *The Slave* ends on a blurred note. It is clear, through the subtitle of the play—*A Fable*—that he intended it for moral instruction, yet the play falls short of its implied aim.

Then what is the message of *The Slave*? Is it the ultimate triumph of anger that Baraka wants to communicate to his audience? Is the play about the sanctification of the new black man whose growing process Baraka sees as complete? Or does he want his reader to believe in the image of Walker Vessels, a confused lonely man, who will achieve what Clay in *Dutchman* failed to do? These questions do not allow for quick answers, yet they all contribute to our general understanding of Baraka's ethical, political concerns combined with his dramatic imagination at that specific time in his life.

Before I conclude this section it is possible to look into Baraka's methodology for a social, political theater and draw additional critical insights. For instance, in his essay "The Revolutionary Theatre" Baraka said: "What is called the imagination (from image, magi, magic, magician, etc.) is a practical vector from the soul. It stores all data and can be called on to solve all our 'problems' . . . Imagination (image) is all possibility . . . possibility is what moves us."[82] In this context, *The Slave* can be looked at as simply the culmination of a dramatic series of possibilities enacted within the soul of the playwright.

An image worth pursuing further is that of Walker Vessels, the commander of the revolutionary army, wearing an armband that is the insignia of the attacking army. As Baraka explains: "It is a big red-lipped minstrel, grinning like crazy."[83] Moreover, the protagonist is clad as an old field-slave at the beginning and at the end of the play, walking as if he is in a daze. Through the interaction of these elements Baraka might have planned to elucidate his utmost conviction that a mock-hero cannot save the African American people from the domination of Eurocentric values. A mock-hero cannot help even himself; it is futile to expect relief for others. Furthermore, a lack of socio-historical consciousness causes confusion and mental instability.

A last point that Baraka is making is that assimilationist ideas are outdated and of no use to African Americans. Members of the African American community must get to know themselves and then decide on a method to carry out a full-fledged cultural revolution. Moreover, they must be willing to suffer some loss for the advancement of their people and society as a whole.

NOTES

[1]   Theodore R. Hudson, *From LeRoi Jones to Amiri Baraka* (Durham, N.C.: Duke University Press, 1973), 11.

[2]   Ibid.

[3]   Amiri Baraka, *The Autobiography of LeRoi Jones/Amiri Baraka* (New York: Freundlich Books, 1984), 155.

[4]   Ibid., 164.

[5]   Ibid., 165.

[6]   Ibid., 166.

[7]   Larry Neal, "The Social Background of the Black Arts Movement," *Black Scholar* (January/February 1987): 15.

[8]   Baraka, *Autobiography*, 237.

[9]   LeRoi Jones, *Blues People: The Negro Experience in White America and the Music That Developed From It* (New York: William Morrow and Company, 1963), ix.

[10]   Baraka, *Autobiography*, 173.

[11]   Ibid.

[12]   Hudson, *From LeRoi*, 96.

[13]   Ibid., 96-97.

[14]   Baraka, *Autobiography*, 173.

[15]   Hudson, *From LeRoi*, 9.

[16]   Ibid., 15.

[17]   William J. Harris, ed., *The LeRoi Jones/Amiri Baraka Reader* (New York: Thunder's Mouth Press, 1991), xxi-xxii.

[18]   Baraka, *Autobiography*, 202.

[19]   Hudson, *From LeRoi*, 21.

[20]   Genevieve Fabre, *Drumbeats, Masks and Metaphor: Contemporary African American Theater* (Cambridge, Mass.: Harvard University Press, 1983), 16.

[21]   Hudson, *From LeRoi*, 21.

[22]   Ibid.

[23]   Ibid., 24.

[24]   Baraka, *Autobiography*, 204.

[25] Bobby Seale, *Seize the Time: The Story of the Black Panther Party and Huey P. Newton* (Baltimore, Md.: Black Classic Press, 1991), 59.

[26] Amiri Baraka, "'7 Principles of US and Maulana Karenga and the Need for a Black Value System," in *Kawaida Studies: The New Nationalism* (Chicago: Third World Press, 1972), 12.

[27] Ibid., 11.

[28] Ibid.

[29] Baraka, *Autobiography*, 235.

[30] Ibid., 236.

[31] David Llorens, "Ameer Baraka," *Black Revolution: An Ebony Special Issue* (Chicago: Johnson Publishing Company, 1970), 78.

[32] Harris, *LeRoi Jones Reader*, 3.

[33] Ibid., 14-15.

[34] Baraka, *Autobiography*, 157.

[35] Amiri Baraka, "Black Art," *Black Scholar* (January/February 1987): 29.

[36] Ibid.

[37] Ibid.

[38] Hudson, *From LeRoi*, 34.

[39] Harris, *LeRoi Jones*, 219.

[40] Ibid., 224.

[41] LeRoi Jones, "The Revolutionary Theatre," *Home: Social Essays* (New York: William Morrow and Company, 1966), 210.

[42] Ibid.

[43] Ibid., 211.

[44] Ibid.

[45] Ibid.

[46] LeRoi Jones, *Dutchman and The Slave* (New York: William Morrow and Company, 1964), 73.

[47] Hudson, *From LeRoi*, 170.

[48] Jones, "The Legacy of Malcolm X and the Coming of the Black Nation," in *Home*, 247.

[49] Ibid., 246.

[50] Hudson, *From LeRoi*, 20.

[51] Stefan Brecht, "LeRoi Jones' *Slave Ship*," *The Drama Review* 14, no. 2 (1970): 212-19, cited in Kimberly W. Benston, *Baraka: The*

Renegade and the Mask (New Haven: Yale University Press, 1976), 248.

⁵² Hudson, *From LeRoi*, 172.

⁵³ Jones, "The Revolutionary Theatre," in *Home*, 213.

⁵⁴ Ibid.

⁵⁵ Ibid., 212.

⁵⁶ Ibid., 214.

⁵⁷ Raphael Patai, *Myth and Modern Man* (Englewood Cliffs, N.J.: Prentice Hall, 1972), 71.

⁵⁸ Hudson, *From LeRoi*, 166-67.

⁵⁹ Amiri Baraka, *A Black Mass*, in *Four Black Revolutionary Plays* (Indianapolis, Ind.: Bobbs-Merrill, 1969), 17-39. Henceforth all references to the play will be incorporated into the text.

⁶⁰ Kimberly W. Benston, *Baraka: The Renegade and the Mask* (New Haven: Yale University Press, 1976), 217.

⁶¹ Ibid., 240.

⁶² Baraka, "Black Art," 24.

⁶³ Ibid.

⁶⁴ For further information on the mass see *An Encyclopedia of Religions*, 1970. The word "mass" is derived from a Latin word *missa* which is another form of *missio*, meaning "dismissal." To obtain grace from God, or getting rid of evil might have been an extended meaning.

⁶⁵ Jones, *Home*, 187.

⁶⁶ Ibid., 188.

⁶⁷ Ibid., 189-90.

⁶⁸ Ibid., 199.

⁶⁹ Ibid., 188.

⁷⁰ Hudson, *From LeRoi*, 152.

⁷¹ See "Lamia" in *Dictionary of Symbol and Imagery*, 1974.

⁷² See Tom S. Reck, "Archetypes in LeRoi Jones' *Dutchman*," *Studies in Black Literature* 1, no. 1 (Spring, 1970): 66-68.

⁷³ See George R. Adams, "'My Christ' in *Dutchman*," *College Language Association Journal* (Spring, 1970), n.p.n.

⁷⁴ Jones, *Dutchman and The Slave*, 18-19. Hereafter all quotations will be incorporated into the text.

⁷⁵ Jones, "American Sexual Reference: Black Male," in *Home*, 222.

⁷⁶ Ibid., 223.

77 Baraka, "Black Art," 23.
78 Jones, "American Sexual Reference: Black Male," in *Home*, 225.
79 Ibid., 226.
80 Jones, *Dutchman and The Slave*, 72. Hereafter all quotations will be incorporated into the text.
81 Henry C. Lacey, *To Raise, Destroy and Create: The Poetry, Drama and Fiction of Imamu Amiri Baraka* (Troy, N.Y.: Whitson Publishing Company, 1981), 83.
82 Jones, "The Revolutionary Theatre," in *Home*, 213.
83 Ibid., 214.

IV

Charles Fuller

Perhaps Charles Fuller is the best example in African American drama of the playwright who spans the evolution from the Black Arts movement to the Afrocentric movement. In his own way, Fuller is the bridge between the incipient move toward agency and the fulfillment of that agency in the dramatics of possibilities and the theater of the real. He knows that African Americans, in order to be considered significant and powerful as human beings, must be taken seriously—a goal that can be attained only if they are seen as agents, subjects, and centered human beings. This translates into the need for characters that exhibit accountability and responsibility, and that are open to all of the dangers and evils as well as good and comforts of any other human group. In this respect, Fuller is the preeminent sign of the times of Afrocentricity in drama. Furthermore, his friendship with Larry Neal (whom Molefi K. Asante considers to be the "precursor of the Afrocentric movement"); their long conversations and stipulations about the future of the Black Arts movement; and the discourse they created among young, committed, pumping black hearts contributed immensely to the development of the Afrocentric school of thought.

Born in 1939 in Philadelphia, Pennsylvania, Charles Fuller attended Roman Catholic High School and graduated in 1956. His early years were greatly influenced by the coming of World War II. This war made Philadelphia one of the chief hubs of the Northern migration of African Americans from the South, an influx which impressed him with the diversity of roles played by African Americans in real life. Fuller was shaped by the churches, the social climate, and the economic prospects that engaged the minds of the newly arrived

African Americans. Added to these focal points were the guitars, wailing horns, and rhythm and blues matrix of the groups of men gathered at every street corner or in every other hallway. The Philadelphia of that time had a tempting mobility and anonymity to offer a young man like Fuller, but he was able to escape most of the dangers that accompanied the intense gang activities occurring with increased frequency as more people moved closer and closer to each other. All of this was dramatic material for the keen historical observer.

The first seventeen years of Fuller's life were full of the dynamism that attended a bustling Philadelphia created by the many new immigrants arriving to work on the waterfront at the large naval yard. In subsequent years he would attend Catholic colleges in and around Philadelphia such as Villanova (1956-58) and LaSalle (1963-68). He received two honorary doctoral degrees from these institutions in 1982. Combined with his idealism and a strong sense of discipline, commitment, and obligation, in Fuller one could observe—particularly during his early years—the development of a moral perspective which would color his dramatic works and suggest that he believed in the possibility of each human being taking responsibility for him/herself. With what might be called a missionary zeal, Fuller used his earlier education and training to infuse his works with the idea of noble humanity where one's character, not race, plays a great role in his/her interaction with others.

Theater had been Fuller's favorite hobby since his early youth. During his high school days he frequently visited the old Walnut Street Theater in Philadelphia to watch plays, observing how playwrights used the stage for the presentation of dramatic ideas and ethical values. Although he was deeply influenced by the Catholic religion, it was a Yiddish play which most impressed him and made him decide that he wanted to be a playwright. In an interview he told Jean Ross that "it was fascinating!"[1] True, he did not understand a single word of it, but he liked what he saw. He said: "It was live theater, and I felt myself responding to it." Fuller understood for the first time that the theater could become the vehicle for his own social consciousness—a consciousness that was growing rapidly because of the Civil Rights movement led by Dr. Martin Luther King Jr. The playwright's response would turn into a lifelong commitment, a reality that would guide the rest of his creative ventures. Alongside his commitment would be his love for history and historical materials, which would become particularly evident in his works of the 1970s and 1980s. In Fuller's mind the basic ingredients of drama would be the events and personalities of the ordinary people who operated as agents in a world of great diversity and experience. After attending Villanova University for two years, Fuller left the United States in 1958 to work as an Army petroleum laboratory technician in Japan and South Korea; this took him on a four-year-journey. Fuller doesn't reveal much about his overseas experience, yet its impact surfaces in some of his best-known plays about Army life. On his return from Asia he worked as a housing inspector in Philadelphia's Ludlow section. There he discovered the depth of poverty, social disintegration, and moral desperation which surrounds so many people living without a substantial income. He also found homes where the poor people of North Philadelphia exhibited unusual courage, determination, and spiritual fortitude in the face of their desperate economic situations. Working as a housing inspector would enrich his dramatic characterizations on the basis of what he saw and heard, and eventually provide a rich depository of material to be occasionally utilized in his future dramatic career. Meanwhile, from 1965 to 1968 he attended LaSalle College and continued writing.

Subsequently, Fuller became involved in the artistic scene in Philadelphia which consequently led to his affiliation with local playwrights, civil rights leaders, and political activists. The mid-sixties were productive years for Fuller, a time in which he wrote increasingly popular plays. Several plays from that era did not bring Fuller immediate recognition. There was *Love Song for Robert Lee* in 1968, followed in 1969 by *Ain't Nobody, Sarah, But Me*; *Cabin*; *Indian Givers*; and *J.J.'s Game*. Meanwhile, the season was ripe for what would come to be known as the Black Arts movement, and in the midst of this Fuller felt involuntarily drawn into an expanding vortex where art was to be employed for the sake of human transformation. Reflecting upon those early days Fuller says: "We needed a place out of which to operate, to be a part of building the community. . . . At that time I wasn't really writing plays, but skits connected to community issues. I was interested in how you save your community."[2] Fuller was at once in the middle and on the fringes of the movement; that is, he demonstrated a philosophical allegiance to the role drama could play in defining the nature of society and in making the life of

African Americans better. During this period the young Fuller was reading continuously and concluded that there must be a different quest for the intellectual than for the strict activist. He was a committed political person who viewed his intellectual and dramatic work as a form of activism, wherein action took place on the stage rather than in the streets. He took on the role of spokesperson for the enlightened participants in the drama arena.

By 1972, Henry Street Settlement's New Federal Theater staged Fuller's play, *In Many Names and Days*. This was followed in March 1974 by the play titled *The Candidate*. Meanwhile another play, *First Love*, opened in the Billie Holiday Theater in Brooklyn the same year. While his plays were gaining wide acclaim, Fuller himself was working as the co-founder and co-director of Afro-American Arts Theater in Philadelphia. In October of 1968 McCarter Theater in Princeton, New Jersey produced his first play, *The Village: A Party*. The production, which was later called *The Perfect Party*, centered around interracial marriages and racial intolerance. Since 1970 he has periodically taught at educational institutions such as Yale University, Hunter College, and Temple University and has lectured widely in America, Canada, and Europe on various aspects of African American culture.

Fuller is a person with enormous interest in various forms of art presentation. His interest in television scripts and radio programs began in the early seventies. He created "Roots, Resistance and Renaissance," a twelve-week television series, in 1968 for WHYY-Channel 12. It was followed by "Mitchell," a teleplay for WCAU-Channel 10 the same year. During 1970-71 Fuller directed a one-half hour show for WKYW-Channel 3, called "Black America." In fall 1978 he created an American Short Story Series titled *Sky is Gray: Learning in Focus* for PBS. In September 1984 Columbia Pictures released his screenplay for his Pulitzer-winning-drama, *A Soldier's Story*. And lastly, he made a television drama out of *Ceremonies in Dark Old Men* in 1987.

Fuller's native town, Philadelphia, became the center for most of his television-related interests until the 1980s. The focal point changed when his fame as the Pulitzer Prize Winner for Drama in 1982 brought him a much wider national audience and he began writing for national television programs. For instance, prior to his Pulitzer he wrote and directed a radio show, "Black Experience," for WIP radio station, and worked as a consultant and format-designer for a ninety-minute talk show titled "Speak Out" for a local television station. After his prize he won contracts and commissions for television drama from NBC and ABC. He also received, between 1974 and 1978, fellowships and grants such as Creative Artists in Public Service, N.Y. (1974); National Endowment for the Arts (1976); Rockefeller Foundation Grant in Playwriting (1977); and a Guggenheim Foundation Fellowship (1978).

Although his early years were important in establishing his recognition, Fuller's play-writing career was particularly successful in the wake of his cooperation with the Negro Ensemble Company (NEC). Started in 1967 by Douglas Turner Ward—himself an accomplished actor and playwright (*Day of Absence* and *Happy Ending*)—the Negro Ensemble Company became the most significant contributor to off-Broadway as the premier source of production and publicity for African American theater. Ward is also known as an actor's director because he has directed and in some cases introduced to the public some of theater's most talented actors, including Adolph Caeser, Denzel Washington, Phylicia Rashad, Roscoe Lee Brown, and Billy Dee Williams. As director of the NEC Ward created a place where authors, actors, dancers, musicians, set designers, costume and lighting designers, stage managers, production managers, technical directors, and theater administrators would have a permanent place to learn and sustain their craft. Since their inception the group staged numerous plays, such as *The Sty of the Blind Pig* and *The Great MacDaddy* by Paul Carter Harrison; *The River Niger* by Joseph Walker; *Ceremonies in Dark Old Men* by Lonne Elder; *Home* by Samm Art Williams; *Eden* by Steve Carter; and *A Soldier's Play* and *We* by Fuller himself.

In later years the NEC would receive many praises for not surrendering to "propaganda" or "agitprop." However, it would also be severely criticized, alongside Ward and Fuller. Amiri Baraka levied harsh criticism in an essay titled "The Descent of Charlie Fuller into Pulitzerland and the Need for African American Institutions." Baraka argued that the NEC "became a real force in the black community by means of the bourgeoisie's money," and added: "When Negro artists say, as did Ward and Fuller recently, that they wanted 'a theatrical rather than a polemical event,' they lie. They have created as political a theater as any in the Black Arts movement, only it is the politics of our enemies!"[3] But Baraka's objection had a lot to do with Ward's search for plays with multidimensionality. Furthermore, throughout its history the NEC has been viewed by the general public as the rival organization of the Black Theater movement.

On the other hand, it can also be asserted that the NEC has been supportive of both the Black Theater and the Black Arts movements simply because the NEC has managed to keep its doors open for black plays for nearly two decades, despite numerous setbacks originating from various sources. In order to prove this point, Ward is known to have adopted a non-conformist policy and to have said that until the ghettoes are rebuilt, their theaters would be islands.[4] Richard Gilman in a 1982 review of *The Soldier's Play*—the opening production of the NEC's fifteenth season—asserted that "the Negro Ensemble Company can no longer be regarded as an exotic enterprise on the fringe."[5] Moreover, contrary to what Baraka said in his 1983 essay regarding the NEC's role within the black community, Gilman argued that the NEC was born out of the void within established American theater which seemed to have no place for the black experience. Gilman, who mentioned that in the beginning the company encountered some difficulty creating an identifiable style of its own, stressed that *A Soldier's Play* was instrumental in helping the NEC to change: to overcome most of its parochial quality and maintain a more flexible repertory reflecting its socially oriented realism.

The NEC may not have been as politically active as Baraka would have demanded but it was certainly a player in the raising of consciousness of the public regarding the creative spirit of African people. Fuller's support of NEC was given mainly because Ward provided a place for the African American artist when other companies kept him/her out of the Broadway theaters. Hence, to criticize Ward and the NEC remains a short-sighted argument when done without an understanding of the NEC's instrumental role in the struggle. This is despite the fact that the NEC was supported, as is most theater, largely by those who had money to spend on entertainment. Indeed, Fuller's *A Soldier's Play* brought a diverse crowd to the small theater and helped give other African American playwrights an opportunity to showcase their works.

Fuller wrote his first play for the NEC, *In the Deepest Part of the Sleep*, in 1974. By the end of the seventies the NEC had staged three additional plays by Fuller, all of which received popular acclaim throughout the nation. In succeeding years the NEC became a sort of alma mater for Fuller, and he insisted that his plays would continue to have their stage debuts at the NEC In choosing the NEC as the first repertory company for his productions, Fuller was making a political statement about the need to support African American theater companies. This was in response to the limited number of professional theatrical outlets available to African American dramatists. However, even Fuller would find this arrangement impossible to maintain as the demand grew for his works. Reflecting on these early years Fuller says: "I decided then that I wanted to do something bigger and beyond myself, something historical, that would stand *outside* normal black theater. I wanted to open up black theater so that it couldn't be labeled that easily."[6] He was searching for the ultimate dramatic instrument to stage elements of African American life.

For the NEC's tenth anniversary Fuller wrote *The Brownsville Raid*. The play became a hit on off-Broadway soon after it opened on December 5, 1976; it had a long run of 112 performances. *The Brownsville Raid* is based on a mysterious 1906 shootout in the town of Brownsville, Texas, which resulted in the dishonorable discharge of 167 soldiers from the all-Black 25th Infantry stationed in the town. The incident left a Mexican and a white man dead, and the townsfolk suspected that a black soldier, perhaps more than one, was the assailant. However, without any concrete evidence the Army, with President Roosevelt's indignant concurrence, ordered the whole company to be dismissed without an honorable discharge. The ranking member of the company was Sergeant Major Mingo Saunders, successfully played by Ward. Saunders had been in the service for more than twenty years, with prior assignments in Cuba and the Philippines. After the shootout he was ordered to solve the mystery. He insisted that his men were innocent, but his request for an open trial was categorically denied and he was also dismissed with his men.

Harold Clurman in his review of *The Brownsville Raid* praised Fuller's writing, as well as the cast and the director, Israel Hicks. "What makes the play stirring is that all its characters—the white officers as well as each of the blacks—are honestly, incisively and often humorously drawn. . . . The writing is apt: there are no routine or wasted words." Clurman added: "We are confronted with facts which are not merely faithful to the record but fleshed in the living matter of authentic individuality."[7] Most critics praised the play for its authenticity and particularly for the conclusion, in which the names of the discharged soldiers and their fates were read in roll-call fashion.[8]

In 1980 Fuller's second outstanding play opened in Theater Four. Directed by Ward, the NEC's production of *Zooman and the Sign* brought Fuller an Obie Award. Centering around an important dilemma of urban life, the plot revolves around the violence and terror that haunt the streets of urban America. What makes *Zooman and the Sign* different from the rest of Fuller's plays is its thematic examination of one of the paradoxes of modern life, that is, the breakdown of the social fabric in urban areas and the triumph of fear, indifference, and callousness in its aftermath. In the play, silence and a noncommittal attitude in the face of human suffering among people who live in the same neighborhood easily give way to truncated relationships. Fuller's goal is to improve the climate of sharing and cooperation; therefore his plays strike at intolerance and bigotry in order to foster healing within communities. The process of examination, reexamination, and redescription is a continuing quest, a noble act in the making. It is with such vigor and enthusiasm for renewal that Fuller seeks to engage his audience.

Fuller received greater acclaim and was finally recognized as a major playwright after *A Soldier's Play* (1981) brought him a Pulitzer Prize for Drama in 1982. First staged at the NEC's Theater Four, it opened on November 28, 1981 and ran for 481 performances. It continued to be staged for thirteen consecutive months until early 1983. Later it was presented at the Mark Taper Forum in Los Angeles for a long run, until it went on a successful thirteen-city tour. The tour began at the Goodman Theatre in Chicago in June 1983, and ended at the Coconut Grove Playhouse in Miami in May 1984. *A Soldier's Play* won several awards, including the New York Drama Critics' Circle Award as the Best American Play; the Outer Critics' Circle Award; the Best Off-Broadway Play; and the Theatre Club Award as the Best Play of the Year. It was also selected by the Burns Mantle Theatre Yearbook *Best Plays* series as a "Best Play" of 1981-82. In 1984 the screenplay appeared under the title *A Soldier's Story.*

A Soldier's Play is based on a mysterious shooting of a black sergeant just outside a segregated army camp in New Orleans in 1944. The suspects are numerous, embodying the Ku Klux Klan, the white army officers, and a black soldier from the same company. Captain Davenport, who is also an attorney, is sent to investigate the murder.

Despite a racially hostile climate of mistrust between the two groups, he conducts a thorough inquiry that eventually leads to the discovery of the murderer and the motives for the crime.

Throughout his career as a playwright Fuller has always sought to magnify his characters so that they achieve universal recognition. Davenport and C.J. Memphis in *A Soldier's Play*, and Rachel in *Zooman and the Sign* are characters in this tradition. Nevertheless, his quest to achieve the "universal" is based upon his belief in the perfectibility of man. Fuller was not influenced by any particular author or playwright, although he admired "Joyce, Stendhal, Hermann Hesse . . . wanted to duplicate something like Franz Kafka's *Metamorphosis* . . . imitate *Ulysses*, writing stream-of-conscious [*sic*] thought."[9] However, he read anything that he could get his hands on in order to expand his vision beyond the boundaries of the American Northeast and its urban paradoxes. Upon these self-developing strategies Fuller reflects as follows: "I made it a point to try and read everything. So plays were part of that process. After a while, it wasn't any individual's influence, it began to be the influence of literature in the world, and wanting to be a part of this great body of work that survived everything. I read to learn about history, about what people were doing."[10]

Fuller's goal, particularly in *A Soldier's Play*, was to display the timeless nature of human relations which cannot be assessed with preconceived ideas and judgments. Furthermore, he sought to explore the puzzling impact of environment upon behavioral patterns and the urge in the human heart to discover the truth, no matter how costly it may be. Howard Kissel of the *Daily News*, in praise of Fuller, said: "Charles Fuller's strength is his ability to dramatize the moral dilemmas of a black man caught between a rock and a hard place."[11]

Fuller proceeded to pursue the same line of thought and dramatic effect in his later plays, namely *Sally, Jonquil*, and *Prince*. These constitute three of the five works that make up a cohesive series produced under the title *We*. This series reflects Fuller's desire to trace a portion of African American history from the Civil War until the turn of the century.

His Catholic upbringing and lifelong concern for providing solutions to problems that *ordinary* people encounter in their daily lives has steered Fuller towards certain professional affiliations. For instance, he has worked as a housing inspector in Ludlow, and as a student consultant at Temple University. Theoretical remedies rarely nourish practical solutions, and it is Fuller's work experience that has provided him with the material he was seeking—that is, a reexamination of the roles played by African Americans at certain crossroads in American history. He believes that reexamination needs to be reinforced with redefinition, because a rethinking of the past may change how black and white people perceive each other in the future.[12] In an effort to improve the racial climate within the United States, Fuller acts on his belief that he can at least overturn stereotypes through his writing. "All the stereotypical things white people used to believe about black people just can't be true in the light of reason. . . . In examining the world, you find that stereotypes of white people don't exist either."[13] Certainly, *We* demonstrates in dramatic grandeur Fuller's discontent with "everything that was written about those recently freed slaves" which reflected merely the biased opinions that white people held concerning black people.

Fuller confers the largest responsibility for the creation of stereotypes on historians and social scientists. However, in Fuller's judgment some African Americans have also been guilty of accommodating stereotypical images of blacks by producing plays with one-dimensional characters. Similarly, he points out that the history of the African American in general mainstream theater has been one of presenting either clichéd or stereotypical images of the black character, even when that image has been one of blacks as perfect beings.

By trying to demonstrate the humanity of the African person, that is, a person capable of the range of human emotions and behaviors, Fuller has created controversy and caused even some African American writers to criticize him. His goal, consistently, is to uncover the pretensions and dispel myths. Of the time period that inspired his creation of *We*, the playwright asserts: "The social sciences at the time, describing the truth of the negro, have to be understood in terms of who was telling it, the advantage to him or her in the telling."[14]

Fuller's devotion to presenting facts from the perspective of African Americans rather than from that of Eurocentric scholars and writers constitutes the gist of his Afrocentric quest. It is particularly in his convictions and dramatic style that Fuller best represents the culmination of the Afrocentric idea in African American theater. He has developed a pattern that was initiated by the Black Arts movement, a movement wherein Neal and Baraka were not only the prophets but practitioners as well. Fuller's significance within the development of the Afrocentric paradigm lies in the fact that by underscoring in his art the conviction that history has a role to play in dramatic interpretations of human experiences, Fuller reaches new heights in Afrocentric creative production. In addition, Fuller's unique contribution to African American drama has been his insistence on the accountability and responsibility of his characters. His characters are not simply protesters, but activists in a moral and ethical tradition; they are people with families, private and public concerns, and a sense of wholeness, even if that wholeness is sometimes disrupted by personal flaws. There are no paragons of virtue in Fuller's human characterization; there are evils, bitterness, complaints, misdeeds, and racism. On the other hand, Fuller's intention is not to eliminate the audience's sense of hope; rather, as he explains, "it is about putting what you believe to be the truth, no matter how wild and fantastic it is." He asserts, "people are benefited by the truth, no matter how ugly it is. Anything that we are misled by or misinformed about or afraid to confront limits us."[15] And in all of these situations Fuller is able to find the quintessential human quality. We see in his works the true New African American, rounded as a full human, with the agency that is predicted in Afrocentricity.

I am claiming Fuller as a modern Afrocentric playwright because he combines historical context with self-critical analysis. In a pre-Afrocentric phase of African American drama one might see plays with a historical context, but without an attendant self-critical analysis; or conversely, one might find plays, particularly during the Black Arts movement, that contained self-critical analysis but lacked a deep historical context other than an examination of racism in American society. The majority of plays written during the Black Arts movement—for instance Baraka's *Experimental Death Unit #1, Great Goodness of Life,* and even *A Black Mass*—convey a certain message to the audience which idealizes the African American experience to the extent that other perspectives, particularly the white experience, do not exist at all. Whereas there is nothing surprising in Baraka's dramatic idealization of the African American perspective at the expense of other probable perspectives, his critique of Fuller in the essay titled "The Descent of Charlie Fuller into Pulitzerland" illuminates their differences in theory and practice. In his essay

Baraka attacks *A Soldier's Play* as having a limited vision, and also blames the NEC as being "a house slave's theater, eschewing struggle for the same reason that the house niggers did—because they didn't have it so bad."[16] In Baraka's definition of revolution and struggle, fierceness, violence, and didactic dogmatism are fundamental tactics. This has led one faction of the black community to reject a more humanizing effort within the liberation movement, like that of the NEC and Fuller. On the other hand, Baraka's art has also suffered from the above-mentioned traits. It has been labeled by some critics as "agitprop," "sloganeering," and even "racist" or "sexist."

At first glance Fuller may not seem to be adequately revolutionary or confrontational. However, his strength lies in his refusal to let his own experience as an African American man interfere with his understanding of human phenomena in general; at the same time, he does not alienate himself from the historical African American experience. Fuller says: "I write about dramatic situations involving black people in the creation of American history. I do that because black American history so often is depicted as an isolated phenomenon."[17] In other words, Fuller believes that the African American experience exists as just *one* among other experiences of other peoples. It is not less important, but it is necessary to reach a concession with regard to the multi-cultural experiential range. Fuller seems to be willing to uphold this stance through his plays in order to suggest the possibility of a new type of revolution; Baraka seems to be unwilling to acknowledge such possibility. These differing outlooks constitute a major divide between the two playwrights.

Fuller is today recognized, by a heterogeneous group of audiences, as a successful playwright whose contribution to American drama lies in his ability to convey a realistic picture of the black experience in its multiplicity. His portrayal is often from the standpoint of analytical historicism, avoiding both racially biased and Eurocentric preoccupations. Additional elements of his Afrocentric paradigm are further analyzed later in this chapter. Suffice it to say at this point that Afrocentric theory is a multi-dimensional approach to collective human experience, and as Asante asserts, its power lies in its unerring emphasis on pluralism without hierarchy. Furthermore, Asante contends that "ascertaining the view of the other is important in understanding human phenomena."[18]

Whereas Fuller is not much different from Baraka in his emphasis on the centrality of the African American experience, his characters are not always ideal human beings. Some of them have flaws, misjudgments, temperaments, and weaknesses which often put them in adverse relations with the rest of humanity. Lester in *Zooman and the Sign* is a typical example; Fuller generates first disapproval, resentment, compassion, and finally even pity in the last scene. Likewise, a whole street block who chooses to remain silent at the expense of an innocent child's murder—because, Fuller implies, they are either scared, or selfish, or indifferent—manifests a human situation, incredibly sad yet within the possibility of human nature. In *A Soldier's Play* it is possible to observe Fuller's preoccupation with the idea of creating not flat types but fully rounded, multi-dimensional characters. This is evident in his characterization of the black sergeant who vainly attempts to "purify" his race, and even more distinctly in Captain Davenport's unrelenting pursuit of the truth and justice. Both of these characters fit what has become a trademark in Fuller's drama: realistically drawn, truthful characterizations which exemplify a variety of human situations in different environments, ungoverned by primeval concerns such as loyalty to the race or kinship relations.

In this respect Fuller's works differ from some of his contemporaries, particularly those of Baraka whose characters generally appear to have a one-dimensional quality which inhibits their adaptability and accountability. Baraka's Court Royal in *Great Goodness of Life*, Lula in *Dutchman*, and Walker in *The Slave* are examples of this premise. Their common trait is an inhibition in their actions, a lack of resourcefulness and flexibility which reflects not only upon these characters' accountability but upon the playwright's vision of the human situation. In contrast, Fuller's preoccupation with realistic characterizations has won his writing recognition as possessing a "universal" quality in drama circles. In Afrocentric terms, such a focus reveals not only Fuller's centeredness but also his rare ability to embrace more informed visions of reality that transcend Eurocentric negations. It should be noted that transcendence, in Afrocentric ideology, is one of the essential steps in bringing about solutions to human crises.[19] Charles Fuller's plays represent, as do those of August Wilson, an ardent advocacy of historical realism. Both playwrights have written cycles of history plays, which render them a distinguished place within contemporary African American theater. In particular, Fuller's *We* displays the playwright's vision in this realm. Thus, a brief analysis of the plays which comprise the *We* cycle is necessary at this point.

We: A History in Five Plays spans African American history from the Civil War through the turn of the century. It holistically reflects Fuller's basic concern with revealing the truth and demolishing all stereotypes, with the aim of acting as a catalyst for change in the audience. It is through his vision and ability to deal with this vision on stage that Fuller transcends Eurocentric negations. The epitome of his Afrocentric quest is his embracing of more inclusive visions of reality that allow for the identification of solutions for varied human crises. Through the agency of this Afrocentric perspective, which rests upon the conception that the African American mission is one of humanizing the world,[20] Fuller sets out to transform "reality" into a better informed, more humanizing one: "How people see black people must change. That we are two-dimensional, length-and-width type people that have no depth is simply not true. And I think it's important to display that sense of having more to us than simply the stuff of protest or of being victimized. There's much more to us than that. I'm simply expressing what is real, not what people like to think we are. So far we've been the victims of a compendium of stereotypes about ourselves. The very idea that black people are complex psychological beings is simply not dealt with."[21]

Sally, the first play in the cycle, started the series on November 9, 1988 at the NEC's Theater Four in New York City under the direction of Douglas Turner Ward. It was soon followed by the second and third plays in the series, namely *Prince* and *Jonquil*, which validated Fuller's recognition as an emerging force in African American theater. *Sally*, as the opening piece which sets the stage for the rest of the cycle, takes place in 1862 around Beaufort, South Carolina. It involves black soldiers who are objecting to the hypocritical Union Army which has reneged on promises of equal payment. The two-act play consists of twenty-one short scenes that shift from the battlefields to the Union General's office and then to Sally's quarters. Sally is the leading female character in the play. Based on a revenge plot, the drama at the same time explores the possibilities of love and compassion in times of crisis, as symbolized in Sally's relationship with Sergeant Prince Logan.

The second play in the cycle is named *Prince* after the leading male character. It centers around his flight from the Ashford Plantation in South Carolina where he was the landowner's driver. In addition to numerous negative forces which surround Prince and his relationship with Sally in a hostile environment, Fuller brilliantly depicts the psychological shock and the sense of loss that newly emancipated people suffered in the aftermath of the Emancipation Proclamation in early 1863. In the play, after being told that they are "free" and can go wherever they want, African American men, women, and children find themselves in the midst of total chaos—unprepared, perplexed, yet exuberant. They are anxious to enjoy their long-delayed freedom, but without money or identification cards freedom seems a vague promise to these people. Fuller's characters display courage, energy, and perseverance in overcoming great odds, yet as a playwright he does not allow his characterizations to gloss over the discrepancies in the historical record.

Fuller's third play in the cycle, *Jonquil,* was staged in the fall of 1989. Receiving mixed reviews as "a sometimes awkward, sometimes murky play,"[22] *Jonquil* did not generate as much publicity as the previous plays in the cycle. Yet *Burner's Frolic,* the fourth play in the series, was scheduled to open in New York the next season when Fuller started working on a screenplay about Malcolm X.

Although the plays in *We* did not attain record box-office yields, they single-handedly managed to bring to life a less known era in African American history—that is, the Civil War and its aftermath—from the perspective of African American people. In a mysterious way these plays force the audience to look closely and more understandingly at a nation of people who went through various life experiences in a conglomeration of ways typical of human beings: sometimes exhibiting an unyielding Herculean determination to persevere and survive; sometimes displaying a cunning, selfish, or arrogant attitude; and at other times showing a humble, passive, or even cowardly surrender to the forces surrounding them. These myriad snapshots make Fuller's characters all the more plausible and realistic.

Fuller's other plays are also indicative of his commitment to historical realism in drama, with certain variations in style and subject matter. Likewise, August Wilson—another African American Pulitzer Prize winner—as mentioned earlier, is renowned for his mastery of historical realism. This is evident in his "decade plays" which capture certain eras in African American history, such as *Jitney, Ma Rainey's Black Bottom, Fences, Joe Turner's Come and Gone, The Piano Lesson,* and *Two Trains Coming.*

In the following section I will mainly focus on two additional Fuller plays: *Zooman and the Sign* and *A Soldier's Play.* Since I believe Fuller's works to be the best example of the Afrocentric idea as delineated by Asante, I will approach the analysis from an African-centered perspective, highlighting the value of an Afrocentric critique for African American drama in general.

ZOOMAN AND THE SIGN

When will Black men learn that
fist & feet against the teeth
is like removing the heart of a people.
who will teach us that slaps & kicks & verbal lashings
detour sharing, stops bonding
destroy unifiers, retard respect & eliminate
connecting vision.

—Haki Madhubuti

When the curtain rises Zooman appears on the stage wearing a mesh and plastic green and white baseball cap tilted to the side. He is wearing a red T-shirt with the inscription "Me" on it. His carefree attitude and the disco sound in the background inform the audience that he belongs to that group of "thugs" who value their own selves above anything and anybody else. He carries a knife with which he confesses to having wounded a West Indian man on the subway the other day. Moreover, he also mentions that he has just killed a little girl who was sitting on her front porch while he was after Gustav.

ZOOMAN

But I had told Gustav if I eva' saw his ass around the
"Avenue" I'd blow him away. So I started shootin'
and she jes' got hit by one of the strays, that's all.
She ain't had no business bein' out there. That street
is a war zone—ain' nobody see her. . . She was in

the wrong place at the wrong time—how am I
supposed to feel guilty over somethin' like that?
Shiiit, I don't know the little bitch anyway. And in
that neighborhood you supposed to stay indoors,
anyway.[23]

Proud and arrogant, he boasts: "They call me Zoo-man! From the
Bottom! I'm the runner down thea'. I fight like a panther, strike like a
cobra! Stomp on. . . like a whole herd of Bison! Zooman!" (P. 7-8).

Zooman's appearance, attitude, and words blasphemously
symbolize the malady of terror and cruelty that has struck many
American neighborhoods within the last three decades of the twentieth
century. Due to drug and crime wars, these neighborhoods have been
afflicted with vicious atrocities ranging from death to burglaries. As a
result of such occurrences some neighborhoods have been totally
abandoned, leading to an increased festering of crime in those areas.
Thus, block by block many urban areas are involuntarily declared "war
zones" where, because of criminal activities, "stay-indoors" has
become a genuine lifestyle. Fuller illustrates the fear and anxiety that
follow a shooting through his characterization of the Tate family and
their neighbors. The emotions and concerns portrayed reflect the real
life experience of too many American people in various urban areas.

Rachel, who has just lost a daughter to the crime war on her
street, naturally does not want her son Victor to go out—not even to
the front steps.

RACHEL
Where's he gonna go? Out on the same street so they
can kill him too? (To Victor) No! You stay in here—
we just got back into the house. You just stay in. (P.
11)

Rachel is hurting; she feels guilty—she had an argument with Jinny
just before the child went out. Her husband tries to console her,
assuring her that the death was not her fault. On the other hand, their
marriage is not working well, and Rachel blames her husband for not
being home when disaster hit. Apparently, he prefers being out to
being home. She asks her spouse: "Are you going to stay this time—or
leave—or what? . . . because I really can't take it, Reuben! It's too

much to ask me to do by myself right now." Then she adds: "I can't deal with this and not know what's on your mind!" (P. 12).

Meanwhile, Victor tries to gather information about the murderer of his sister and finds out that Zooman is a cruel young man who even beats up his own mother. This gives us some insight into Zooman and his kind. They prey on the weakest—his mother, the West Indian, Jinny—and could not exert an influence if their victims were not as fragile as they are. In other words, what allows a vicious murderer to roam freely is the unwillingness of his family members, neighbors, and citizens to have him arrested. Indifference, fear, and lack of sensitivity to human suffering let Zooman grow bigger than life itself and surround himself with a superficial veil of protection. Yet, liberty and the pursuit of happiness are inalienable rights of every human being, and should not be curtailed by terrorists or anyone else. The role of the police also comes into play, a subject I will pursue later.

As Fuller introduces the major conflict in the play—that is, the harshness of the urban landscape and mass disorientation—he also presents a variety of other issues, including alienation, negligence, and lack of respect and caring among members of the same community. Reckless behavior and incongruences within the system cause Emmett and Reuben to feel dislocated. For instance, Reuben is a bus driver and he dislikes the way the doors operate on the new buses. The new technology not only has failed to bring much of an innovation, it has unnecessarily complicated the way his business is conducted. Emmett, on the other hand, works at Bellevue Hospital where he observes how ignorance and illiteracy endanger the lives of the patients and the staff.

EMMETT
Ain't no different at Bellevue—they hire all these no-readin' niggahs, instead of teachin' 'em somethin' . . . and the other day, this kid been in my section 'bout four-five weeks, takes a bottle of acid off the shelf—how it get there I'll never know—pours it into a bucket and damn if he don't start moppin' the floor with it! The tiles started turnin' brown—couple nurses shoes start burnin'. I caught it . . . he told me he couldn't read—imagine that? (P. 16)

Indifference and carelessness seem to have paralyzed the system from the top to the bottom, with social deterioration more clearly evident among the lower social strata. In actuality, Reuben's complaint about the doors that do not open with the push of a button is a reference to his own sluggishness. Meanwhile, the unions protect all without discriminating between the hard-worker and the slacker.

Another social problem that Fuller sees as a threat to community ethics is the indifference of people to crime. They prefer to remain deaf, mute, and blind to a senseless murder in the midst of their community. The loss of a sense of sharing and togetherness, and the consequential alienation among members of that particular community, is probably the most important social message Fuller imparts in *Zooman and the Sign*. Broken family bonds appear to be at the core of social disintegration in the play. This is evident in that not only is Zooman a loner, but the panic-stricken Tate family is left helpless and forlorn in an ocean of pain and grief.

In a feeble attempt to rationalize his loneliness, Zooman claims he has friends and relatives available to him all over the United States, including two "half-sistas" whose parents are also separated.

ZOOMAN
I got picked up 21 times last year! Everytime somebody black did somethin' and the cops didn't have a name? They busted me!. . . . Tomorrow's my little sista's birthday! Not my sista' here . . . a half sista in Birmingham. . . . I gotta' notha' half-sista' who's married. I got people everywhere. Detroit. California. I got an Uncle in Buffalo. . . . Plus I got friends in town! PJ, Mooky, Christine—so I got plenty of places to go if I want to! Plenty. I just don't want to. (P. 22)

In reality Zooman doesn't have anywhere to go; he has been disowned, spiritually and probably physically too. Since he has not received guidance, warmth, and affection, he is incapable of nourishing anyone else. Added to this is the common stereotype applied to all African American men, that is, the allegations they must face whenever something goes wrong with the law enforcement system.

Ironically Zooman—whose real name is Lester Young—is the epitome of a social disease for which he is not solely responsible. A naturalistic interpretation of the play provides a better understanding of Zooman's dilemma and breeds sympathy for him. However, any chance of reconciliation is nullified by the final heinous crime he has committed. At the same time, the Tate family is also victimized by the circumstances which bred Zooman and his type. This is unsurprising given that the majority is afflicted with the same malady, leaving the people surrounded by a spiritual wilderness.

Ash, who represents common sense in the play, verbalizes her criticism of the neighborhood as follows: "It's a shame how we Negroes have changed through the years . . . from one extreme to the next, like Jekyll and Hyde!" (P. 23). Ash blames the food stamps, and is nostalgic about the old times when things were different.

ASH
When the "Negro" was hungrier, we treated each
other better. Nowadays everybody's got their bellies
full and we sit up belchin', watching those damn
Soap Operas and Game Shows all day—hot dog in
one hand, the phone in the other, a beer—or a Pepsi
on the floor beside us—the baby crawlin' around
dirty, the whole house filthy, and honey don't give a
damn about nobody! . . . Those food stamps got all
these children eatin' cookies, candy and potato
chips! (P. 25)

Later on Ash adds that if people don't care about themselves, their own health, and their bodies, it is unlikely that they will care about Jinny or anyone else. Reuben disagrees with her and asserts: "It's not food stamps, all right? Not one food stamp answered anybody's door on this block, Ash!" (P. 25). He believes food stamps never solved any problems or met the people's needs. Moreover, he is somewhat offended that Ash perceives the problem with a limited vision. By the end of the first act he has hung a sign on his front porch which reads: "The killers of our daughter Jinny are free on the streets because our neighbors will not identify them" (P. 32).

Grace, a neighbor who came to express her sympathy, sheds more light on the stigma which plagues the neighborhood. According to her,

it is the result of a mutual and ongoing process whereby people have
long forgotten the tradition of giving and sharing. She recalls that in
the past there have been many instances where neighbors were
indifferent to rising problems and turned their backs on each other,
refusing to alleviate the suffering by sharing.

> GRACE
> The Tates ain't no better than nobody else! Rachel
> and Reuben didn't come to Myrtle Coleman's
> layout—or to Mr. Stewart's funeral either! I didn't
> see the Tates get excited when those hoodlums raped
> Lou Jefferson's little girl—or robbed my place! Why
> should anybody go out of their way for them? I
> didn't hang up no sign! (P. 40)

Meanwhile, Rachel is already upset about the sign. Suddenly two
bricks and a bottle break through the front door screen and crash on
the living room floor. Victor pulls his gun but Rachel snatches it out of
fear of losing her second child. In the midst of the crisis situation
Grace reminds them all that no one wants to be wrongly accused and
it's better if the sign is taken down. Meanwhile, Rachel feels angry,
lonely, and completely engulfed by the real drama in her life.
However, she manages to hold back her emotions until Reuben
receives a phone call inviting him to a local TV channel for an
interview about the sign.

> RACHEL
> Guns, fights, signs on telephone poles—TV
> interviews and all in the name of Jinny? Hallelujah!
> Well Jinny was gentle, Reuben—did you forget that!
> A shy child—and this is her time! The last little bit
> of her time we have left, and someone in this family
> better pay her some attention, you know that?
> Somebody better pay some attention to her! (P. 46)

Besides Rachel and Grace, the entire neighborhood is upset about the
sign and wants it removed. Rachel is concerned about her family;
specifically, she is afraid that Reuben will be killed because of the
sign. She says: "We just got through sitting in front of Jinny—and

Reuben I don't want to wind up sitting in front of you. If you don't
take it down—I want you to leave!" (P. 57). Yet she loves her
husband; her fear is that she might lose Reuben or Victor to another
stray bullet.

Meanwhile, police arrest a fifteen-year-old boy named Stockholm
who told on Zooman. This adds fuel to the fire in terms of Zooman:
now he is upset not only about the sign, but about the arrest of his
friend as well. Zooman fully intends to tear down the sign and take
revenge upon the Tates. When he reaches the Tate house he starts
yelling as he rips and tears at the sign. Emmett hears the sound and
fires his gun through the living room window; the bullet immediately
hits Zooman and knocks him down on the sidewalk with the sign in
his hands. Rachel moves forward to see her daughter's killer.

RACHEL

Who is it, Reuben?

REUBEN

Zooman—I heard him yell it.

RACHEL

Zooman? This is the one who killed my baby? Get
up! I'ma kill him! Get up goddamnit!

REUBEN

He's dead, Rachel!

RACHEL

Oh, Reuben—oh my God, Reuben—

REUBEN

I know, baby. I know. (P. 61-62)

As the lights fade out slowly, another sign is projected which reads as
follows: "Here, Lester Johnson was killed. He will be missed by family
and friends. He was known as Zooman" (P. 62).

The symbolism in the play ranges from characters' names to
names of streets. "Zooman" spreads fear and anxiety like a wild beast
loosed on urban civilization. He wreaks his havoc on *Titan* Street, a

reference to the Titans of Greek mythology, primeval deities who are gigantic creatures linked with immense, extraordinary, evil acts. Fuller cleverly juxtaposes Titan Street, Lester's superficial kingdom, with Jinny's innocence and fragility. Due to the fear he instigates Zooman is symbolically identical to a Titan. He has neither friends nor relatives with whom he can communicate; all he has is a radio. He is always accompanied by the disco sound on stage, an ironic twist that accentuates his loneliness. On the other hand, Victor, as his name suggests, is the embodiment of the positive values Fuller wants the audience to see in black youth.

Zooman and the Sign is a family drama which might have taken place not far from the Freedom Theatre in North Philadelphia where the play opened in early 1982. As a social drama the play suggests that the black community is suffering from a breakdown of shared pride and identity. Still, the play is not a criticism of African American society. Rather, it is a therapeutic exposition on the ailing part meant to induce healing. Fuller's Catholic upbringing is also at play in *Zooman and the Sign*. The Bible teaches that "you must purge the evil from among you" (Deuteronomy. 24:8), a purging the audience witnesses in the removal of Zooman from Titan Street.

In the play numerous concepts are questioned and emphasized, such as family unity, love and respect, black youth and its values, sharing and caring for others. An Afrocentric critique of the play provides further insight into Fuller's depiction of a modern-day dilemma. The next section is devoted to a focused analysis of the play according to the nine assumptions of the Afrocentric critical framework.[24]

The first critical insight in the Afrocentric framework is that of "centering discourse in the historical literatures/oratures of the particular people." The principal aim is to determine whether or not the author/playwright possesses a historical consciousness. During an interview Fuller said: "History has become for me a way of reexamining black people in the long journey of the United States."[25] Thus, for Fuller history acts as a conduit for expressions arising from the African American point of view. For example, *Zooman and the Sign* reexamines a segment of the African American people in an urban area, highlighting the scope of their plight through a merciless killing in their neighborhood.

The second assumption, "transcending Eurocentric negations of the people's culture," is also directed towards the author/playwright. It is important to note whether he/she transcends the common positions taken by Eurocentric analysts in such areas as ethics, values, morality, equality, history, and justice. Fuller juxtaposes several issues in the play which are somehow interrelated with each other as well as with the question of moral values. For instance, in the play Zooman mentions that he was arrested twenty-one times in one year as an automatic suspect each time a black man committed a crime for which there were no other suspects. The most important task Fuller undertakes in the play is that of demolishing stereotypical allusions and drawing a more realistic picture of African American society. While carelessness and indifference towards the Tates' suffering is observed with a critical eye by the playwright, Zooman's frequent arrests by the police for crimes he did not commit provide critical insight into the ways stereotypes persist within society.

However, the playwright presents a complicated message, one in which Zooman is not to be viewed as a scapegoat within society, despite rampant racism. Fuller uses counter-argument and the transcendence of Eurocentric preoccupations as tools for determining how the text relates to the particular context it represents. Concomitantly, he embraces more inclusive visions of reality. In this way Fuller provides, at least in the very end, a humanizing insight. By the close of the play Rachel and Reuben have found quiet consolation in each other's company, and Zooman has been terminated by Emmett. Victor has been warned about the dangers of owning guns and the neighborhood seems to be a safer place after the halt of drug trafficking.

Through Fuller's characterizations the play draws heavily upon the significance of human relations and human relations to the self. He employs the principal contexts of *resistance, liberation,* and *action* in order to establish alternative images to society's stereotypes. For example, Zooman's monologues reveal that he has a guilty conscience, and that his friends and relatives do not care where he is or what he is doing. He is a loner throughout the play, with his conversations carried on with himself only. The Tates, with the help of their relatives, form an alliance to resist their neighbors' lack of caring. Reuben puts up a sign to prompt the neighbors to come forward with information about the murder of Jinny, and following the killing of

Zooman the fear which haunted Titan Street disappears. However, the vital question still lingers in everybody's mind: Is there true relief from random violence? How can the chain of violence be stopped?

Fuller also illustrates the significance of responsible acts as guiding principles that sustain social harmony in a community. In *Zooman and the Sign* he addresses a general audience for whom violence is part of modern urban living. Simultaneously, by dealing with a complex situation for which there are no ready-made, clear-cut resolutions, Fuller achieves a universal quality. Indeed, this feature commonly inspires most of his dramas because disintegration of the social fabric is neither characteristically African American nor American. Rather, the disintegration is a social phenomenon that plagues modern societies in general.

Nevertheless, Fuller focuses on and succeeds primarily in explaining the motives and impact of violence within African American society. His preoccupation has always been with "describing black people in a new way," his goal being "to destroy all the stereotypical ideas about black people." Fuller continues: "It's very important for me as a black writer to change how Western civilization—which includes black people—perceives black people."[26] It is obvious that Fuller is fully cognizant of the socio/political context and the prevailing issues that shape his work. For instance, the drug war that entraps Zooman and Stockholm contributes negatively to the disintegration and erosion of moral values within the community, a dilemma that neither the police nor the political power system is capable of resolving. Moreover, the social network—the neighborhood—seems to have been "dead" for so long that moral inertia and social callousness have become ordinary life experiences.

Despite the moral inertia, resistance against oppression is evident in *Zooman* in the form of a central mythoform. Although major cultural myths of the African American community revolve around defending the people against various types of oppression, whether they be physical, political, psychological, or cultural, a secondary mythoform deals with the subduing of the "bully" who engages in terror. The bully appears in many forms and is always defeated by the collective will of the people, resulting in a heroic act. This mythoform shares some key elements with the legend of the "signifying monkey." The monkey which succeeds in getting the lion embroiled in a dirty fight with the elephant represents, in a symbolic manner, the triumphant spirit of the oppressed, whose resistance is one supreme negation of the imposition of a racist and oppressive discourse.[27] Emmett becomes the signifier, as the community is cleansed of the oppressive discourse of Zooman. Still, when the play ends everyone has lost something of value.

Lyrical qualities are also present in the dramatic work. In *The Afrocentric Idea* Asante states that the African American's approach to language is principally lyrical, and this is the basic poetic and narrative response to reality.[28] Fuller is living proof of this; growing up in Philadelphia with its jazz, rhythm and blues matrix in the background shaped his creative skills. The Black Arts movement and his friendship with Larry Neal, whose poetry and poetic ideas constituted one of their favorite topics of conversation, further molded Fuller's creative output. Added to this was his Catholic upbringing in the heart of North Philadelphia during the turbulent sixties and seventies, all of which empowered Fuller to capture with great success the musical speech of the African American. Lyrical qualities may be as obvious as the disco sound which accompanies Zooman's monologues whenever he appears on the stage, or as subtle as Rachel's style of expression even in her grief.

RACHEL

Glass all over the porch! Did you hear him—the Tates! Will somebody please tell me what good that sign is accomplishing? Are we supposed to take turns sitting guard on the front steps? We're supposed to be in mourning for our daughter— there's a wreath on the door, and where the hell is he? Comes back three days, disrupts everything— turns things inside out. Putting up signs, it's—it's disrespectful! I almost wish I had let him beat up a few of them. (P. 41)

Naturally Rachel's speech does not retain the same effect in print as it has when presented orally. Nevertheless, Fuller takes full advantage of the pauses, cadences, and rhythms of African American speech. Zooman in particular exhibits lyricism more than any other character in the play. His speech is spiced with expressions from the popular culture, the musical context, and the drug industry.

ZOOMAN

Once upon a time, while the goose was drinkin'
wine? Ole' monkey robbed the people on the trolley
car line. I carry a gun and a knife. A gun in this
pocket—and ole' 'Magic' in this one! Now you see
it—(Makes a stabbing gesture.) Now you don't! (P.
6)

Moving on to the issue of harmony, according to Afrocentric
theory the writer must seek to advance the ideas of unity and harmony
within the African American community as well as the outside world.
The author achieves this quality by expressing the fundamental values
of the people in such a way that the resolution of conflict and the
creation of ideas for community reconstruction are clearly observed.
This concept relies on the element of participation which takes into
consideration that each member of the community is responsible for
maintaining harmony. Since disharmony is seen as destructive, the
main objective is the maintenance and restoration of harmony within
the society. In the final scene Fuller brings forth the kind of harmony
that derives from the catharsis of a family still feeling the tragedy of
their loss, but at last relieved and united because the terrorizer has
been silenced.

Fuller's play received favorable reviews as well as a few
unfavorable ones, such as the aforementioned 1983 essay by Baraka,
"The Descent of Charlie Fuller into Pulitzerland." Baraka criticized
Fuller not only for creating a monstrous character, a black teenage
"animal," but also for misrepresenting the consciousness of black
people. He says: "Because that is what Charlie Fuller seems to want to
represent in *Zooman: the Negro Consciousness,* the consciousness of
the black people who have been so washed out mentally by white
supremacy that they think other blacks are the problem!"[29]

Whether Baraka is justified in thinking Fuller is misrepresenting
the African American consciousness, Fuller, I submit, makes a
genuine attempt to explain the reasons for the disintegration of the
social fabric within some black communities, and to provide a picture
of conflict resolution that will lead to a peaceful environment for its
residents. During an interview on July 21, 1989 Fuller stated that "for
uncleanliness, violence, separation, and misunderstanding, we blame

white people. In order to be close to understanding what we want to do we have to understand and be aware of who we are."[30] On the other hand, Fuller has always expressed his faith in self-determination and race-pride. He believes that there is nothing wrong with raising consciousness for the sake of education, improvement, and reformation. What is more problematic, however, is not knowing where to start or postponing the effort forever out of fear of retaliation. In fact, his sympathy is not limited to the heroic Reuben Tate or Emmett, but is also extended to Lester who is driven into crime because of the cycle of poverty and loneliness around him.

Contrary to what Baraka claims, I believe that Fuller's goals as a dramatist lie far beyond the creation of damaging criticism. He has a genuine interest in seeing the world become a better and safer place for African Americans as well as for other human beings. This mission is central to his work and clearly in accord with the social function of drama as it should be.

A SOLDIER'S PLAY

It was the play which brought Charles Fuller national recognition in 1982 when it was awarded the Pulitzer Prize. *A Soldier's Play* had a lengthy run at the NEC and was also cited as the "Best New American Play" by the New York Drama Critics Circle.

The central fictional incident takes place in April of 1944 at Fort Neal, Louisiana in a segregated army camp where the soldiers are stationed waiting to be transferred to Europe. The play opens as Tech/Sergeant Vernon C. Waters is suddenly shot to death in a wooded area not far from the camp. The rest of the play tracks the investigation of the murder through flashbacks and reveals staggering facts about the cause of the murder. Contrary to stereotypical assumptions, the play portrays the interactions of African American soldiers within the circle of social prejudice and color barriers established by white army officers and soldiers. *A Soldier's Play* establishes a balance in terms of including both blacks and whites, a quality lacking in *Zooman and the Sign*.

A month after the shooting Captain Richard Davenport, a lawyer from the 343rd Military Police Corps Unit, is appointed to investigate the incident at Fort Neal. The unofficial consensus is that Sergeant Waters has been killed by the local Ku Klux Klan. In order to prevent any retaliations against the townspeople, all military personnel are forbidden from entering the town, Tynin, and the Friday night dance is canceled.

The arrival of Captain Davenport at Fort Neal causes some displeasure among white officers because he is the "first colored officer they have ever met," and has a law degree from Howard University. Captain Taylor does not hesitate to express his resentment.

> TAYLOR
> Your daddy a rich minister or something?
> (Davenport shakes his head no) I graduated the
> Point—We didn't have any Negroes at the Point. I
> never saw a Negro until I was twelve or thirteen.
> (Pause) You like the army, I suppose, huh?[31]

Taylor cannot liberate his mind; he is overcome with prejudice and confusion. Firstly, he is shocked to see an African American officer. Secondly, he is surprised at Davenport's determination to investigate the murder and discover the identity of the murderer, as he listens to Davenport clearly state: "Captain, like it or not, I'm all you've got. I've been ordered to look into Sergeant Waters' death, and I intend to do exactly that" (P. 19). Apparently Davenport's arrival poses a serious problem for the camp because Taylor warns him: "You go near that sheriff's office in Tynin in your uniform—carrying a briefcase, looking and sounding white, and charging local people—and you'll be found just as dead as Sergeant Waters! People around here don't respect the colored!" (P. 19).

Despite serious resentment against his presence at the camp Davenport conducts his investigation by questioning the soldiers in the unit. The incidents which took place prior to the murder are revealed in a series of flashbacks, the first of which is the dispute between Waters and his confidante Sergeant Wilkie. It is important in the sense that it reflects Waters's latent feelings toward his own self, his men, and his race. Moreover, the incident foreshadows other developments which shed light on the main plot of the play. Waters sends Wilkie to jail for ten days and takes his stripes away because Wilkie got drunk while he was on duty.

WATERS

You wind up drunk on guard duty—I don't blame
the white man—why the hell should he put colored
and white together in this war? You can't even be
trusted to guard your own quarters—no wonder they
treat us like dogs—Get outta' my sight, *Private!* (P.
25)

Needless to say Waters is a strict disciplinarian, with no tolerance
for disorderliness. On the other hand he is a family man too; Wilkie
states that he often writes letters to his wife and carries pictures of her
with him. His greatest ambition is to send his children to one of those
"big white colleges and let'em rub elbows with the whites, learn the
white man's language—how he does things" (P. 28). Otherwise,
Waters believes, "we'll be left behind—you can see it in the army.
White man runnin' rings around us" (P. 29). Waters also asserts that
the only way to challenge the white man is to use "his weapons,"
which means gaining an education, and having lawyers, doctors, and
generals to fight him "in his arena" (P. 29).

In the following days C.J. Memphis, the best ball player in the
group and a singer and guitar player, commits suicide in his jail cell.
He was sent there by Sergeant Waters on charges of a shooting, after
which the gun was discovered under C.J.'s bed. His self-inflicted death
comes as a surprise because in the past C.J. was a soldier favored by
Sergeant Waters who loved the way he played the guitar. Whether it
was his blues or his baseball skills, Sergeant Waters seemed to care a
great deal for C.J. However, the audience learns through another
flashback that a previous incident sparked these infamous
developments in the play.

During the first year of the war hundreds of African American
soldiers enlisted hoping that they would be given the chance to take
part in their country's war. However, segregation crippled their spirits
as well as their desire to combat. Nausea and inertia replaced their
patience and hope. During this tense period Private Melvin Peterson
dares to challenge Waters because of his arrogant attitude, pejorative
language, and continuing intolerance toward his own race. It is C.J.'s
intervention which unleashes Waters' rage.

PETERSON
You ain't got to come in here and call us names!

WATERS
The Nazis call you schvatza! You gonna tell them
they hurt your little feelings?

C.J.
Don't look like to me we could do too much to them
Nazis wit' paint brushes, Sarge. (P. 39)

Men laugh; Waters is badly humiliated. The next day he beats
Peterson in a public fight. Peterson never reports the incident because
Waters leaves him alone after that day. Interestingly, it would be C.J.
who would encounter Waters's spite and accordingly be sacrificed to
satisfy his ego and heal his injured pride.

Meanwhile, Davenport questions two white officers, Lieutenant
Byrd and Captain Wilcox, who had a brief encounter with Waters the
night he was killed. At first Davenport believes that he has arrested
the murderers but dismisses the possibility quickly. The murderer(s)
must have had a different motive than just racial animosity because,
after all, Sergeant Waters was a disciplined soldier who always obeyed
orders and supported the status quo in his effort to be white. The men
whom he mocked and belittled were probably more inclined to kill him
than whites because they hated him, particularly after what he did to
C.J. This realization marks a turning point in Davenport's
investigation.

Eventually the news of deportation arrives at the same time as
Davenport's decision to arrest Private James Wilkie for assisting
Sergeant Waters in planting the incriminating gun under C.J.'s bed;
and Private Tony Smalls and Pfc. Melvin Peterson for murdering
Sergeant Waters. It is Smalls who discloses that Peterson shot Waters
on the way to the camp and dragged his body to the woods thinking
that everyone would believe he was killed by white people. Peterson
flees the camp in panic only to be arrested one week later in Alabama.
Davenport completes his task and returns to his post. Sergeant
Waters's family is informed that he died in action. C.J. leaves an
unimportant legacy behind: during 1945 a style of guitar-picking and a
dance called "C.J." catch on in Tynin saloons. As to the men in the

221st Chemical Smoke Generating Company, they are all wiped out in combat in Germany.

"They still hate you!," shouted Waters before he was shot twice. His "split-personality" made him both a cold and a warm person. While his African self admired C.J.'s guitar-strumming, his American self longed to merge with the mainstream culture in denial of the other half. Although his inner dynamics bid him to return to his roots, the forces beyond his control gripped him at the core of his being, pulling him to the other side. Power and its acquisition by whatever means necessary was the quintessential motive of his existence within a society which does not even let him fight in a major war. As a child he was abused, probably neglected too. As an adult he grew to be spiteful, a man burdened with an inferiority complex who sees the whole world as an arena where his right to compete on fair grounds was taken away at birth. He felt he was in a losing game from the beginning; his disorientation was a natural outcome of his psychological impotence.

Conversely, C.J. was gentlemanly, romantic, and sentimental; a musician, a baseball player, and a soldier. He was so grounded in his cultural heritage that it would not be an exaggeration to call him "the blues character." Unlike Waters, C.J. was serene, down-to-earth, natural, uncomplicated, and close to his Africanness. The blues matrix constructed an important venue for C.J. that went beyond a mere affinity with its lyrical aspects. As Baraka stated: "Blues could not exist if the African captives had not become American captives."[32] This musical form was a reactionary mode of expression; it was an aesthetic response to oppression and strengthened the spirits of the oppressed.

Along these lines, C.J. believed his "Farmers Dust" amulet would protect him from evil and that he had "Bird" in his blood. These were the epistemological variables of his existence as much as they stood for the forces which attached him to the cosmological powers above and the roots below. In short, C.J. was a Southerner, a complete rural man comfortable with the powers he possesses. He did not feel dispossessed among his people, nor was he "a singin', clownin'—yas-sah bossin'— homey kinda' niggah," as Sergeant Waters labeled him (P. 72). C.J. was grounded in his roots, and expressed himself in sports and music. Centered in his own culture, he was almost the opposite of Waters.

Having examined the plot, characters, and themes, it is appropriate to now examine broader dimensions of the play within the

Afrocentric framework. To begin with, Fuller's *A Soldier's Play* is located in the historical activities of the African American people; he has chosen to focus on the plight of African American soldiers in the U.S. Army. The setting is essentially historic and raises the audience's consciousness, whether black or white, regarding the nature of African American involvement in the United States military in the mid-1900s. However, it must be remembered that African American participation in this country's war efforts is as old as the nation itself. For instance, the first American to die in the American Revolution against the British was an African, Crispus Attucks. Yet the African American military person was discriminated against in every American war until the Korean War. Fuller is keenly aware of this history as he situates the play in the military context, utilizing a major historical motif to heighten audience appeal and creative power.

The segregated army which kept black and white soldiers apart even when on military campaigns was a source of anger for many of America's citizens. Beyond the play's actual reference to a problematic time period in American history, it also gains power in that all of the characters have a relationship to the military setting. Fuller's brilliance is demonstrated by his ability to center the play in the lives of African Americans, the group from whom he derives his cultural power, while simultaneously showing us the possibilities within all peoples and cultures.

Although Fuller uses a full range of characterizations from African American culture, he is never pedestrian or trite in his employment of characters. In the Afrocentric context his characterizations can best be described as noble, for Afrocentric theory seeks to uncover the noble even in the common.[33] When Fuller depicts the rural C.J. Memphis, he infuses the character with grace, honor, intelligence, tradition, music, passion, beauty, and determination—all elements that raise the character to a noble level.

A Soldier's Play transcends the negations which are often created by white authors whose visions of Africans are too frequently obstructed by racial and cultural prejudice. Fuller gives the audience the character types in their most natural form rather than as they might be perceived or conceived by authors who are unfamiliar with the culture. What is evident in *A Soldier's Play* is the well-rounded and complete quality of his African American characters. This is true of C.J. and other characters as well. The maintenance of such characterization reflects Fuller's intention to provide a foundation for a more diversified interpretation of African American life. He demonstrates in his transcending discourse, that is, discourse which raises the level of our expectations, that African Americans are fully capable of any behavior, even the murder of Vernon C. Waters. More than any other contemporary playwright Fuller seems to make the most effective case for racial and cultural equality. While his dramatic ethos is not self-serving and does not necessarily engage in wishful thinking, it is grounded in the most profound reality—that Africans are, as is the rest of all humanity, capable of the most honorable and dishonorable human acts. In creating *A Soldier's Play* in this fashion Fuller authenticates the African American's humanity without resorting to rhetoric and bombast. Thus, he transcends naive racial theories that would make the African American a superhuman incapable of evil and merely the victim of white racism. Indeed, as an American playwright engaged in the quest for an honest dramatic portrayal of African American culture, Fuller, by virtue of his work in the historical genre, virtually stands alone.

In African-centered critical methodology it is the writer's duty to explore human relationships, human relations to the supernatural, and intrapersonal relationships. The only unusual or less familiar component as compared to Western drama—with the exception of tragedy—is probably human relations to the supernatural, a category that encompasses spiritual and supra-rational activities and interests. While all cultures have some response to the supernatural, the African culture, even as it is seen in America, relies on various amulets, potions, and spiritual powers for effective discourse. Fuller displays that he is aware of all of these aspects of the culture as the play unfolds.

Human relations constitute the principal grounds for the dramatic energy of the play. Fuller employs relationships in such a complex manner that the entire focus of the play is initially on the chief drama in American social relations: the historical suspicions between blacks and whites. The Ku Klux Klan, a white supremacist group founded in the South in 1866, initially becomes the main target for the anger surrounding the death of Sergeant Waters. The history of white opposition to African American equality and human rights is such that the implication of the Ku Klux Klan in the murder seems reasonable to whites as well as blacks, particularly in the context of the 1940s.

A more revealing aspect of the play is the relationship of Sergeant Waters to his men. Waters, as the audience discovers through flashbacks, is deeply troubled by his own inability to make his soldiers like himself. He attacks whatever he considers to be the most fundamental elements of genuine African American culture. In the end he has little credibility with his soldiers because he becomes a racist against his own kind.

Through Davenport's relationships with the white officers and black soldiers Fuller shows the audience clear-cut evidence of white dislike of black authority, particularly when it is assertive, no-nonsense, and competent. Meanwhile, Fuller does not miss the opportunity to demonstrate the surprise and pride of black soldiers when they meet Captain Davenport. Here is a black man whose handling of the investigation as well as his relationships with others prove to be superb.

The intrapersonal relationship refers to whatever psychological transformations the dramatist shows us in the characters. *A Soldier's Play* becomes, in the final analysis, what the title implies. This is Waters's play, or Peterson's or Davenport's or C.J. Memphis's—it is clearly a soldier's play in terms of the intellectual ideas that are engraved within the dialogue.

The supra-rational or supernatural aspect of the play can best be seen in the characterization of C.J. who loses his Dust after he enters the jail cell and consequently fears for his life. He believes that the Farmer's Dust he wears around his neck has supernatural powers which can make a person "strong as a bull." He loses his strength when he is arrested and condemned to a cell where he cannot "breathe." His jail cell becomes his tomb; he ironically replaces the amulet with his belt and hangs himself.

Fuller juxtaposes Peterson's groundedness in reality with C.J.'s passive resistance, particularly when Peterson scolds C.J. for not speaking out against Waters. For Peterson, what is essential is the courage to stand up against any kind of oppression, no matter which direction it comes from. In his forthright attack against any "backwater crap" Peterson reminds the audience of a Malcolm X type.

Maulana Karenga said that unless African Americans win the war for the minds of the people they cannot hope to win any other.[34] The play presents the most dynamic form of resistance to racism in its conceptualization of liberation and action. Liberation does not develop as a reaction to white oppression; on the contrary, it may necessitate, as in the case of Sergeant Waters, a cleansing from within. It is only through the transformation of minds that African Americans can be freed from all kinds of oppression, whether imposed by whites or blacks. In the play, Private Peterson obviously felt that the only way to eliminate white racism as it infects black minds such as Sergeant Waters's was through the destruction of the receptacle. Fuller achieves victory over oppression and stereotypical depictions by attacking the source of that oppression closest to the African American at that moment in time.

In determining the audience to whom the work is addressed, it is critical to acknowledge that *A Soldier's Play* is located in the cultural milieu of black America. Fuller explores the ways African Americans have articulated all of the contradictions of living in a nation that has refused them citizenship rights routinely granted whites. Fuller's intent in *A Soldier's Play* seems to be the demonstration of the heroic quality in the African American people by suggesting that internal problems must be dealt with internally, and that whenever they fail to do so they limit possibilities within the African American community. Therefore, the play both draws from and gives to the African American community, not only because its intellectual and cultural materials are derived from that community, but because its primary audience becomes that community. It is the African American community which understands the symbols and motifs without intermediaries. Thus the text gains an organic relation with the writer and the audience. As Larry Neal would agree, the artist whose work demonstrates alienation from his or her community is not a *committed* artist, nor is his or her art collective or functional. He said: "National and international affairs demand that we appraise the world in terms of our own interests."[35]

Part of the success of *A Soldier's Play* was due to the way in which it employs the cultural mythoforms pertinent to the African American experience. Fuller engages a variety of cultural elements, such as the legendary hero myth, as in Stagolee; exaggeration; and signifying. For instance, Peterson is the defiant, rebellious, militant man who is brave, outspoken, and has an orientation towards direct action. Peterson represents the radical impulse to challenge an authority that seeks to repress freedom, improvisation, and harmony.[36] Through his direct-action orientation, toughness, and a strong sentiment for justice and emancipation, and subsequently his dynamic verbal alertness that restores human dignity, Peterson resembles Malcolm X, a figure who embodies in many instances the Stagolee myth. Peterson loses the one-to-one combat with Waters but eventually rallies against him and regains his dignity.

Waters, on the other hand, is a confused, troubled, self-hating African whose actions and words prompt Peterson to ask: "What kind of colored man are you?" (P. 39). This becomes one of the most revealing questions in the play. In this respect Fuller exposes the overriding issue of identity and adds a universal quality to his drama. In fact, Waters is the kind of black man C.J. does not know or understand; Waters may not have been an Uncle Tom but he is certainly a Cousin Tom. In contrast, Peterson represents a Malcolm X figure who is capable of heroic and brave acts. C.J. is the young man from the deep South who represents the oldest, blackest folk ties of the African American. He is a "blues character," enacting the lyrical qualities and centeredness of Southern culture. Waters hates this Southern quality that connects, through enslavement, directly to Africa. Waters believes that the real problem is the obstruction built not only by white supremacy, but by the black middle class and the black bourgeoisie. In his eyes, the latter group keeps qualified blacks from advancing or receiving recognition. He feels that such obstructions are more disdainful when erected by other black people, especially Southern black ones who sing the blues. Waters has taken upon himself, albeit pathologically, the duty of refashioning the black image with a missionary zeal in order to bring about change. Waters recounts an event which occurred during the First World War in Europe:

WATERS

Do you know the damage one ignorant *Negro* can do? (Remembering) We were in France during the First war . . . We had won decorations, but the white boys had told all the French gals we had tails. And they found this ignorant colored soldier. Paid him to tie a tail to his ass and parade around naked making monkey sounds. . . . And when we slit his throat, you know that fool asked us what he had done wrong? (P. 90)

Waters's obsession is to "purify" the race, get rid of the "ignorant colored soldier" image. The irony is that his focus on purification corresponds with the Nazi Germany in the background waiting to consume additional lives once the soldiers reach Europe. As a matter of fact, as Davenport reports at the end of the play, the entire team is wiped out during a German attack in the Ruhr Valley of Germany. It is interesting to observe Fuller's clever deployment of the Waters character as the messenger of doom. A collective "We Shall Overcome" feeling abounds in the hearts of the men who challenge Waters. When he is killed by Peterson, who represents resistance and liberation, there is a sigh of relief in spite of the widespread suspicion that he might have been killed by white people.

Regarding the political context that informs the play: It is set during World War II, a time when the United States Army was still segregated. It was not until President Harry Truman desegregated the U.S. Army in 1948, after the war, that blacks and whites were integrated. The date of the action in the play is 1944, during President Franklin D. Roosevelt's administration. In *A Soldier's Play* we see that there is also a war going on at Fort Neal itself. Larry Neal would have appreciated Fuller's choice of names, because the agency he gives to "Neal," as a symbol of struggle wherein African Americans succeed in establishing their identity as resilient and capable human beings, is a victorious action. Furthermore, *A Soldier's Play* acquires additional significance within the African American drama tradition as a contemporary play that deals with two aspects of the social and political context: the external and internal.

In terms of the external forces, the playwright introduces the race question with all its implications at the onset of the play. Even though the entire action takes place on a segregated army base the characters recognize that the larger entity of America impacts their isolated lives at Fort Neal. They also know that World War II is really a big European war and not at all a world war. They are fully aware of the paternalistic maneuvers in which their realities are overridden by a political context dominated by Europe. They know, as does Waters, that the black man's role in the army is conceived by whites as supportive and not substantive. Yet these black soldiers realize that their people fought in every American war with distinction and valor despite the frequent lack of recognition and appreciation. As the war rages in the Pacific and the Atlantic regions, these soldiers are still in Louisiana, almost midway between the Atlantic and Pacific Oceans, an ironic twist that credits Fuller's understanding of the social and political context shaping a particular crisis.

Fuller also excels in establishing the internal politics, with Captain Davenport as the lone voice of logic and reason. As soon as he arrives at Fort Neal he is confronted with the racial prejudices of the white officers, yet succeeds in establishing his authority unequivocally. As a graduate of Howard University Law School, the only black college in the 1940s, Davenport draws unfavorable attention from white soldiers. They assume that he is the son of a Christian preacher since it is common knowledge that they usually sent their children to college. Captain Taylor verbalizes the outrage of whites at seeing blacks in positions of influence and power. Fuller tactfully places the problem in a Southern white rural background by having Taylor state that people in Tynin would not charge a white officer with a crime if it was investigated by a black officer. What Fuller seeks to do through this dramatic episode is to highlight the political and social context in which the wrenching black-on-black infighting takes place. Thus, the smaller context of Fort Neal is situated within the larger context of the American society at war with itself.

As mentioned previously, the blues as a motif is present throughout the play and the use of its lyrical qualities to provide space and artistic relief from the tension in the play is an effective strategy. According to literary and dramatic canons of expression represented in the works of Neal and Asante, Fuller's use of blues represents an appeal to the fundamental structure of the culture in America. No matter how debilitating conditions may become, blues as a musical form still offers a glimpse of resolution, victory, and hope in the end. For instance, C.J. strums his guitar and sings: "I got me a bright red zoot suit / And a pair a' patent-leatha' shoes / And my woman she sittin' waitin' / Fo' the day we hea' the news! Lawd, lawd, lawd, lawd!" (P. 37). In fact, Houston A. Baker asserts that the blues theme emerges as a major motif in African American life: "The blues seemed to me the prod and spur that compelled us to 'get away' from any position—literary critical or culturally political—that failed to raise oppressive heels from our collective neck."[37] Baraka in *Blues People* refers to blues as the "parent of all legitimate jazz."[38] Baraka adds it is impossible to say exactly how old the blues is, although it is "certainly no older than the presence of Negroes in the United States. It is a native American music, the product of the black man in this country." Later he remarks: "Blues could not exist if the African captives had not become American captives."[39] Thus it is clear that the blues is and has become, for the African American, a platform providing an "eternal return to the source."[40]

Blues as a matrix that emerges from African American culture reveals its presence in Fuller's drama mainly through two characters: C.J. Memphis and Zooman. C.J. the guitar player and the natural athlete, appears as the symbolic victim or scapegoat in a society which does not tolerate his individuality. Lester, the Zooman, is the "anti-blues" character, obviously implying lyricism with the dissonant disco music that accompanies him in the form of a radio. However, apart from that Lester is the embodiment of violence, terror, lack of centeredness, and value disintegration.

A Soldier's Play opens, according to Fuller's stage directions, with the Andrews Sisters singing "Don't Sit Under the Apple Tree." The play excels in its use of lyricism when one would not normally consider a poetic and lyrical tone to be consistent with military settings. Fuller rises to a new challenge to invest his work with the purest form of African American lyricism in his characterization of C.J. Memphis. But after his death, lyricism surrenders to the directness of Captain Davenport.

As the play closes Fuller does not attempt to bring all the characters into agreement and unity. He does, however, manage to achieve resolution with the dramatic possibilities of the play itself. If one takes Afrocentric theory as an explanation of what is most acceptable in African American culture for the dramatist, writer, or orator, then eliminating disharmony emerges as a cardinal principle. Fuller achieves this end by the elimination of Waters and the discovery of the killer. The suspense which was built throughout the play around who killed Waters turns into relief when it is discovered that Waters was killed by a black man. It provides relief in the sense that African Americans are capable of cleaning-up their own problems, without the intervention of whites. Propitiation comes as a result of death; irresponsible attitudes need not be tolerated. Waters shares the same destiny as Zooman, and in both cases some loss is inevitable.

Walter Kerr, the critic, argued that *A Soldier's Play*'s "particular excitement . . . doesn't really stem from the traditional business of

tracking down the identity of the criminal. It comes instead from
tracking down the identity of the victim."[41] Indeed, despite his sinister
attack on C.J., Waters realizes in the end that he has been "dislocated"
all along. He feels sorry for what he has done, and his drinking is
evidence of such repentance. In a drunken stupor he challenges the
white establishment.

> WATERS
> Followin' behind y'all? Look what it's done to
> me!—I hate myself! . . .My daddy said, "Don't talk
> like dis'—talk like that!" "Don't live hea'—live
> there!" I've killed for you! And nothin'
> changed! . . . And I've tried everything!
> Everything!" (P. 52-53)

Waters knows that he is guilty and that he cannot live with this shame.
Therefore, he almost begs for justice. His murder/execution does not
come as a surprise; it is a retribution for all his past crimes which he
himself practically instigates.

As the epitome of internal fighting within a segregated army unit,
A Soldier's Play reflects Fuller's concern with exposing the myths in
order to redefine what people hastily accept as truths. As an African
American playwright who is aware of his society's aspirations, Fuller
challenges his audience to engage in a rational reevaluation and
possibly a reconciliation of the differences between the two races. As
Fuller would agree, violence is generated at all levels in all societies
and it has yet to disappear from the face of the earth. What is
remarkable about Fuller is his directness in verbalizing human
conditions and drawing the line between what he sees as just and
unjust. However, while he is doing that he is also aware of the
historical, social, and political circumstances that shaped the African
American experience in the United States. "I don't spend a lot of time
trying to make Black people unreal. . . . Violence in the Black
community is a fact of life. Not that I think it ought to be glorified, but
I think we need to be responsible for what goes on in our
community. . . I can not see how any growing people would want to be
continually portrayed as sweet and innocent."[42] Fuller as a playwright
has always been involved in a historical project. His aim is to explore
the African American experience in its *fullness*, that is, with all the

humanity it embodies. He is consistently more Afrocentric than someone who portrays African Americans as only good or bad; Fuller is aware that the human predicament does not yield to such rigid classifications.

Fuller's drama achieves a further realistic outlook through his portrayal of the arrogance of white officers in *A Soldier's Play*. In this drama he explores the depth of contempt directed at those who worship the white power system and yearn to be included in the establishment. Fuller juxtaposes Sergeant Waters's character with C.J. Memphis, the blues character, who is as vulnerable to destruction as Jinny is to Zooman.

Needless to say, as his plots, themes, and characterization demonstrate, Fuller is located clearly in the center of African American culture and history. His symbols, motifs, language, and style are truly reflective of his groundedness in his cultural heritage. His audience is primarily the African American community. On a larger scale his audience is all humanity, with a particular emphasis on the renewability of human dignity, justice, and harmony. Few playwrights achieve what he has in terms of rendering a slice of reality with honest concern. Whatever the viewer's reaction, Fuller does not deliberately aim to alienate audience members. Nevertheless, some will shrink from his message, others will be irritated by it, but all will learn from its exposition. Ultimately, this learning is the goal of Charles Fuller.

NOTES

[1]   James P. Draper, ed. "Charles Fuller," in *Black Literature Criticism*, Vol. 2 (Detroit: Gale Research Inc., 1992), 824.

[2]   David Savran, "Charles Fuller," in *In Their Own Words: Contemporary American Playwrights* (New York: Theatre Communications Group, 1988), 72.

[3]   Amiri Baraka, "The Descent of Charlie Fuller into Pulitzerland and the Need for African American Institutions," in *Black Literature Criticism*, Vol. 2, ed. James P. Draper (Detroit: Gale Research Inc., 1992), 825.

[4]   Ibid.

[5]   Richard Gilman, "A Soldier's Play," *The Nation*, 234, no.3 (January 23, 1982): 90-91.

[6]   Fuller, interview by the author, July 21, 1989.

[7]   Harold Clurman, "Theatre," *The Nation*, 223, no. 22 (December 25, 1976): 701-02.

[8]   Draper, *Black Literature Criticism*, 824.

[9]   Savran, "Charles Fuller," 73.

[10]   Ibid.

[11]   Howard Kissel, "Negro Ensemble: Fuller's Plays Need Filling Out," *Daily News* (December 20, 1988): 41.

[12]   Savran, "Charles Fuller," 79.

[13]   Ibid.

[14]   Ibid.

[15]   Ibid., 81.

[16]   William W. Demastes, "Charles Fuller and 'A Soldier's Play': Attacking Prejudice, Challenging Form," cited in *Black Literature Criticism*, Vol. 2, ed. James P. Draper (Detroit: Gale Research, 1992), 832.

[17]   Charles Fuller, Negro Ensemble Company 22nd Annual Season subscription brochure. New York, November 30, 1988.

[18]   Molefi Kete Asante, *The Afrocentric Idea* (Philadelphia, Pa.: Temple University Press, 1987), 11.

[19]   For an explanation of the Afrocentric themes of transcendent discourse as pertains to rhetoric, see Asante, *The Afrocentric Idea*,

164-67. For instance, Asante asserts: "Rhetoric must transcend ideologies, whether political or racial, in order to perform the task of continuous reconciliation" (P. 167).

[20]   Asante, *The Afrocentric Idea*, 170.

[21]   Charles Fuller, interview by Esther Harriott, in *American Voices: Five Contemporary Playwrights in Essays and Interviews*, cited in *Black Literature Criticism*, ed. James P. Draper (Detroit: Gale Research, 1992), 827.

[22]   Edith Oliver, "Post-Bellum," *New Yorker* LXV, no. 50 (January 29, 1990): 83.

[23]   Charles Fuller, *Zooman and the Sign* (New York: Samuel French, n.d.), 7. Henceforth all references to the play will be incorporated into the text.

[24]   For further information on Afrocentric critical methodology see Nilgun Anadolu-Okur, "Ma'at, Afrocentricity and the Critique of African American Drama," in *Molefi Kete Asante and Afrocentricity: In Praise and in Criticism*," ed. Dhyana Ziegler (Nashville, Tenn.: James C. Winston Publishing Company, 1995), 137-51. In this essay, a radical attempt is made to evaluate the inherent qualities of African American drama within its own sphere of axiological, epistemological, and cosmological referents, rather than through a set of culturally unfamiliar value systems and standards. The result is a framework of analysis dependent on nine assumptions: 1) centering discourse in the historical literatures/oratures of the particular people; 2) transcending Eurocentric negations of the people's culture; 3) using the three fundamental themes of transcendent discourse; 4) presenting the principal contexts of resistance, liberation, and action; 5) addressing the work to a particular audience; 6) employing the cultural mythoforms that inform the creative expression; 7) the social/political context which shapes the work; 8) lyrical qualities in the work; and 9) the ideas of unity and harmony.

[25]   Savran, *In Their Own Words*, 79

[26]   Ibid., 75.

[27]   Asante, *Afrocentric Idea*, 27

[28]   Ibid., 43.

[29]   Baraka, "Descent of Charlie Fuller," 830.

[30]   Fuller, interview by the author, July 21, 1989.

³¹   Charles Fuller, *A Soldier's Play*, (New York: Hill and Wang, 1981), 17. Henceforth all references to the play will be incorporated into the text.

³²   LeRoi Jones, *Blues People: The Negro Experience in White America and the Music That Developed From It* (New York: William Morrow and Company, 1963), 17.

³³   Molefi Kete Asante, "Using Afrocentric Creative Motifs," lecture, University of Maryland, February 9, 1994.

³⁴   Maulana Karenga, *Kawaida* (Los Angeles: US Organization, 1971).

³⁵   Larry Neal, "The Black Arts Movement," in *The Black Aesthetic*, ed. by Addison Gayle Jr. (Garden City, N.Y.: Doubleday and Company, 1971), 259.

³⁶   Asante, *Afrocentric Idea*, 106.

³⁷   Houston A. Baker Jr., *Afro-American Poetics: Revisions of Harlem and the Black Aesthetic* (Madison: The University of Wisconsin Press, 1988), 143.

³⁸   Jones, *Blues People*, 17.

³⁹   Ibid.

⁴⁰   Baker, *Afro-American Poetics*, 143.

⁴¹   Demastes, "Charles Fuller and 'A Soldier's Play'," 835.

⁴²   Charles Fuller, "Zooman and the Sign," Interview, *New York Times* (September 1980): n.p.n.

Conclusion

The drama of the African American experience in a collective sense, as opposed to the more personal examinations of individual reactions to the reality as found in the works of Adrienne Kennedy and Ntozake Shange, has thrust Larry Neal, Amiri Baraka, and Charles Fuller into the forefront of a social theater. It can be said that through their works the African-centered perspective and critique is illuminated, as a theoretical framework that corresponds to the collective, functional, and committed art styles of the Black Arts movement during the sixties.

The generative spirit that gave birth to this work springs from a literary and cultural inquiry into the roots of contemporary African American theater through an Afrocentric methodology. The principal metaphor in the critique of African American drama involves the determination of the *location* of not only the playwright, but the critic(s) as well. This determination reveals whether the playwright operates within the historical experiences of African people within the larger world arena. Whereas Afrocentricity does not dismiss other methodologies as valid approaches to literary criticism, when it comes to issues of African cosmology, epistemology, axiology, and aesthetics, an Africa-centered perspective is required.

African Americans have consistently maintained spiritual connections with Africa. Thus, the sensibilities that are common to African/African American art forms—whether speaking of music, dance, drama, or literature—reflect this African connection. The central pillars of Afrocentric methodology include Maulana Karenga's Kawaida and its seven principles of *Nguzo Saba*; along with Kariamu Welsh-Asante's seven aesthetic senses, that is, polyrhythm, polycentrism, curvilinearity, dimensionality, epic memory, repetition, and holism. Implicit in this methodology is a recognition of the oral principle which constitutes the essence of the African American aesthetic realm. It also confirms the legitimacy of African American language, that is, Ebonics.

Historical consciousness mandates one's groundedness in his/her own culture. It shuns escape from one's own center while at the same time opposing attacks on other forms of consciousness. Thus with its emphasis on historical continuity and cultural/aesthetic groundedness, Afrocentricity is a methodology which provides agency in the evaluation and interpretation of African American drama. The Black Arts movement has played an active role in the development of Afrocentric theory, particularly in its emphasis on the collective, committed, and functional nature of art. As a theory of social change, Afrocentricity professes that art can be employed to change human conditions for the better through meaningful interaction between the artist and the community. In this manner, art can fulfill its primary goal to inform, educate, transform, and establish political and cultural dialogue. Drama, as the most social of all arts, holds infinite potential for change. Moreover as one critic indicated, "any drama is the servant of two masters—the playwright whose vision it makes public and the public whose way of seeing the world must be met and moved."[1]

Neal, Baraka, and Fuller, each in his own way, has demonstrated African agency in an effort to make art respond to human conditions. They are located in the historical, political, social, and artistic center of African American culture and their art expresses what they see as the collective will of the African American people. Theirs is a liberating art, but more importantly, it is theater taken from the leading edge of the culture itself, lifted to the stage for all to see and learn. It is theater that deals with social issues and is generally historically oriented, as in the majority of Fuller's works. Baraka demonstrated his transformation from an avant-garde artist to one who exhibited spiritual commitment and heightened empowerment. Accordingly, he forcefully expressed concrete ideas revolving around change, transition, and a reconnection to Africa. For Neal, reaffirmation meant immersion in the process of redefining the Black Aesthetic. For him, the role of the black artist should be one of implementing the changes necessary for improving society. All three authors believed in art's transformative power to replenish and affect change; its ability to transcend Eurocentric negations. They persistently highlighted its socio-political connotations, its revolutionary, functional and liberating characteristics. While they

observed the way(s) black art and aesthetics were influenced by the
Civil Rights and Black Power movements, they did not neglect to look
into the works of scholars, authors, and activists who paved the way
for the sixties' engaged theatrical forms. Moreover, as Neal and Fuller
occasionally expressed, in their analysis they were also aware of the
forces that were distinctly American, which rendered contemporary
African American theater different from typically African or European
theatrical forms. As jazz took shape on the American landscape and
came to be recognized as a distinctly African American musical form,
so did African American theater. A unique amalgamation of African
American art and aesthetic sensibilities, African American theater was
free of Euro-American theatrical parentage, expressing its distinction
through the works of the Black Arts movement authors, artists, and
poets. What they have achieved, that is giving credence to the
importance of cultural and historical consciousness in artistic
creations, has not been attempted by previous African American
artists.

The future of theater in the African American community will be
governed in part by the school of art and aesthetic sensibility
epitomized by Neal, Baraka, and Fuller. While their subject matters
and styles may be different, they collectively pose a challenge for the
future. This challenge combined with the critics' questioning of their
works and philosophies has the potential to generate a functional art
that addresses society's needs.

Within this realm the Afrocentric idea as a methodology provides
an expressive and interpretive medium for contemporary African
American drama. The nine assumptions presented in this book provide
a springboard for critical assessments with regard to the playwright,
the audience, and the work itself. As the theory indicates, these
assumptions are not meant to be rigid categories; there is room for
revision, extrapolation, and augmentation.

Larry Neal's prophetic emphasis on the generative power of
African American folklore, poetics, blues, and lyricism; Amiri
Baraka's centered concentration on the need of theater to engage the
social consciousness of the audience; Charles Fuller's characterization
of African Americans as fully developed participants in society, foster
a new insight into African American theater. With its articulation of
the American experience through the lives of Africans in America,
and varied themes, plots, and styles, the contemporary African

American theater remains one of the best cultural assets of the American nation.

NOTES

[1]   Helene Keyssar, *The Curtain and the Veil: Strategies in Black Drama* (New York: Burt Franklin and Company, 1981), 207.

Selected Bibliography

Adams, George R. "'My Christ' in *Dutchman*." *College Language Association Journal* (Spring, 1970), N.p.n.

Aksit, Ilhan. *Ancient Treasures of Turkey*. Istanbul, Turkey: Haset, 1985.

Anadolu-Okur, Nilgun. "The Beginning Before the Beginning." *International Journal of Black Drama* 2, no. 1 (1996): 1-6.

——. "Ma'at, Afrocentricity and the Critique of African American Drama." In *Molefi Kete Asante and Afrocentricity: In Praise and Criticism*, edited by Dhyana Ziegler. Nashville, Tenn.: Winston Publishing Company, 1995.

Asante, Molefi Kete. *The Afrocentric Idea*. Philadelphia, Pa.: Temple University Press, 1987.

——. *Afrocentricity*. Trenton, N.J.: Africa World Press, 1988.

——. *Kemet, Afrocentricity and Knowledge*. Trenton, N.J.: Africa World Press, 1990.

——. "Keynote Address." Diop Conference. Temple University. Philadelphia, Pa. October 1996.

——. "Locating a Text: Implications of Afrocentric Theory." In *Language and Literature in the African American Imagination*, edited by Carol Aisha Blackshire-Belay. Westport, Conn.: Greenwood Press, 1992.

——. "Location Theory and African Aesthetics." In *The African Aesthetic: Keeper of the Traditions*, edited by Kariamu Welsh-Asante. Westport, Conn.: Greenwood Press, 1993.

——. "Using Afrocentric Creative Motifs." Lecture. University of Maryland, February 9, 1994.

Baker, Houston A., Jr. *Afro-American Poetics: Revisions of Harlem and the Black Aesthetic*. Madison: The University of Wisconsin Press, 1988.

——, ed. *Black Literature and Literary Theory*. New York: Methuen, 1984.

—. *Blues, Ideology and Afro-American Literature: A Vernacular Theory.* Chicago: University of Chicago Press, 1984.

—. "Critical Change and Blues Continuity: An Essay on the Criticism of Larry Neal." *Callaloo #23*, 8, no. 1 (1985): 70-87.

—. "Generational Shifts and the Recent Criticism of Afro-American Literature." *Black American Literature Forum* 15, no. 1 (1981): 3-21.

Baraka, Amiri. *The Autobiography of LeRoi Jones/Amiri Baraka.* New York: Freundlich Books, 1984.

—. "Black Art." *Black Scholar* (January/February 1987): 23-30.

—. *A Black Mass.* In *Four Black Revolutionary Plays.* Indianapolis, Ind.: Bobbs-Merrill, 1969.

—. "The Descent of Charlie Fuller into Pulitzerland and the Need for African American Institutions." In *Black Literature Criticism*, Vol. 2, edited by James P. Draper. Detroit: Gale Research, 1992.

—. "7 Principles of US and Maulana Karenga and the Need for a Black Value System." In *Kawaida Studies: The New Nationalism.* Chicago: Third World Press, 1972.

—. "The Wailer." In *Visions of a Liberated Future: Black Arts Movement Writings*, Larry Neal. New York: Thunder's Mouth Press, 1989.

Benston, Kimberly W. *Baraka: The Renegade and the Mask.* New Haven: Yale University Press, 1976.

—. "Introduction." *Callaloo #23*, 8, no. 1 (1985): 5-7.

Bernal, Martin. *Black Athena: The Afroasiatic Roots of Classical Civilization.* New Brunswick, N.J.: Rutgers University Press, 1987.

Bierbrier, Morris. *The Tomb-Builders of the Pharaohs.* Cairo, Egypt: American University in Cairo Press, 1989.

Branch, William, ed. *Crosswinds: An Anthology of Black Dramatists in the Diaspora.* Bloomington: Indiana University Press, 1993.

Brecht, Stefan. "LeRoi Jones' *Slave Ship.*" *The Drama Review* 14, no. 2 (1970): 212-19. Cited in Kimberly W. Benston. *Baraka: The Renegade and the Mask.* New Haven: Yale University Press, 1976).

Brockett, Oscar G. *The Essential Theatre.* New York: Holt, Rinehart and Winston, 1984.

—. *History of the Theatre.* Boston: Allyn and Bacon, 1991.

Budge, E.A. Wallis. *Egyptian Ideas of the Future Life: Egyptian Religion.* New York: University Books, 1959.

—. *From Fetish to God in Ancient Egypt.* New York: Dover, 1988.

Carmichael, Stokely and Charles V. Hamilton. *Black Power: The Politics of Liberation in America.* New York: Vintage Books, 1967.

Chandler, Wayne. "Of Gods and Men: Egypt's Old Kingdom." In *Egypt Revisited,* edited by Ivan Van Sertima. New Brunswick, N.J.: Transaction Publishers, 1989.

Clurman, Harold. "Theatre." *The Nation,* 223, no. 22 (December 25, 1976): 701-02.

Demastes, William W. "Charles Fuller and 'A Soldier's Play': Attacking Prejudice, Challenging Form." Cited in *Black Literature Criticism,* Vol. 2, ed. James P. Draper. Detroit: Gale Research, 1992.

Diop, Cheikh Anta. *Civilization or Barbarism: An Authentic Anthropology.* Translated by Yaa-Lengi Meema Ngemi. Edited by Harold J. Salemson and Marjolijn de Jager. Brooklyn: Lawrence Hill Books, 1991.

Draper, James P., ed. "Charles Fuller." In *Black Literature Criticism,* Vol. 2. Detroit: Gale Research Inc., 1992.

Ethnic Notions. Produced by Marlon Riggs. 56 min. San Francisco: California Newsreel, 1987. Videocassette.

Fabre, Genevieve. *Drumbeats, Masks and Metaphor: Contemporary African American Theater.* Cambridge, Mass.: Harvard University Press, 1983.

Fletcher, Banister. *A History of Architecture on the Comparative Method.* New York: Charles Scribner's Sons, 1963. Cited in Carlton Molette and Barbara Molette, *Black Theater: Premise and Presentation* (Bristol, Ind., 1986).

Fuller, Charles. Interview by the author. July 21, 1989.

—. Interview by Esther Harriott. In *American Voices: Five Contemporary Playwrights in Essays and Interviews.* Cited in *Black Literature Criticism,* ed. James P. Draper. Detroit: Gale Research, 1992.

—. Negro Ensemble Company 22nd Annual Season subscription brochure. New York, November 30, 1988.

—. *A Soldier's Play.* New York: Hill and Wang, 1981.

—. "Zooman and the Sign." Interview, *New York Times* (September 1980): n.p.n.

—. *Zooman and the Sign.* New York: Samuel French, n.d.

Gates, Henry Louis, Jr. "Criticism in the Jungle." In *Black Literature and Literary Theory*, edited by Gates. New York: Methuen, 1984.

Gayle, Addison, Jr., ed. *The Black Aesthetic.* New York: Doubleday and Company, 1971.

Gilman, Richard. "A Soldier's Play." *The Nation*, 234, no.3 (January 23, 1982): 90-91.

Griffiths, J. Gwyn. *The Origin of Osiris and His Cult.* Leiden, Netherlands: E.J. Brill, 1980.

Haigh, Arthur Elam. *The Attic Theatre: A Description of the Stage and Theatre of the Athenians and of the Dramatic Performances at Athens.* 3rd ed., in part re-written by A.W. Pickard-Cambridge. Oxford: Clarendon Press, 1907.

Harris, William J., ed. *The LeRoi Jones/Amiri Baraka Reader.* New York: Thunder's Mouth Press, 1991.

Harrison, Paul Carter, ed. *Kuntu Drama: Plays of the African Continuum.* New York: Grove Press, 1974.

—. "Larry Neal: The Genesis of Vision." *Callaloo #23*, 8, no. 1 (1985): 170-95.

Herodotus. *Histories.* Translated by David Green. Chicago: University of Chicago Press, 1987.

Hudson, Theodore R. *From LeRoi Jones to Amiri Baraka.* Durham, N.C.: Duke University Press, 1973.

Ignatieff, Michael. "Fault Lines." Review of *The Clash of Civilizations and the Remaking of World Order*, by Samuel P. Huntington. *New York Times Book Review* (December 1, 1996): 13.

Jacobus, Lee A. "Imamu Amiri Baraka: The Quest for Moral Order." In *Modern Black Poets*, edited by Donald B. Gibson. Englewood Cliffs, N.J.: Prentice Hall, 1973.

Jahn, Janheinz. *Muntu: African Culture and the Western World.* New York: Grove Weidenfeld, 1961.

Jones, LeRoi. "American Sexual Reference: Black Male." In *Home: Social Essays.* New York: William Morrow and Company, 1966.

—. *Blues People: The Negro Experience in White America and the Music That Developed From It.* New York: William Morrow and Company, 1963.

—. *Dutchman and The Slave: Two Plays.* New York: William Morrow and Company, 1964.

—. *Home: Social Essays.* New York: William Morrow and Company, 1966.

—. "The Legacy of Malcolm X and the Coming of the Black Nation." In *Home: Social Essays.* New York: William Morrow and Company, 1966.

—. "LeRoi Jones Talking." In *Home: Social Essays.* New York: William Morrow and Company, 1966.

—. "The Revolutionary Theatre." In *Home: Social Essays.* New York: William Morrow and Company, 1966.

Karenga, Maulana. "Black Cultural Nationalism." In *The Black Aesthetic,* edited by Addison Gayle Jr. Garden City, N.Y.: Doubleday and Company, 1971.

—. *Kawaida.* Los Angeles: US Organization, 1971.

Keyssar, Helene. *The Curtain and the Veil: Strategies in Black Drama.* New York: Burt Franklin and Company, 1981.

Kissel, Howard. "Negro Ensemble: Fuller's Plays Need Filling Out." *Daily News* (December 20, 1988): 41.

Lacey, Henry C. *To Raise, Destroy and Create: The Poetry, Drama and Fiction of Imamu Amiri Baraka.* Troy, N.Y.: Whitson Publishing Company, 1981.

Llorens, David. "Ameer Baraka." *Black Revolution: An Ebony Special Issue.* Chicago: Johnson Publishing Company, 1970.

Meyerowitz, Eva L.R. *The Divine Kingship in Ghana and Ancient Egypt.* London: Faber and Faber, 1960.

Molette, Carlton and Barbara Molette. *Black Theater: Premise and Presentation.* Bristol, Ind.: Wyndham Hall Press, 1986.

Morrison, Toni. *Playing in the Dark: Whiteness and the Literary Imagination.* Boston: Harvard University Press, 1992.

Neal, Larry. "And Shine Swam On." In *Visions of a Liberated Future: Black Arts Movement Writings.* New York: Thunder's Mouth Press, 1989.

—. "Black Art and Black Liberation." *Ebony* (August 1969): 54-56.

—. "The Black Arts Movement." In *The Black Aesthetic,* edited by Addison Gayle Jr. Garden City, N.Y.: Doubleday and Company, 1971.

—. "The Black Arts Movement." In *Visions of a Liberated Future: Black Arts Movement Writings*. New York: Thunder's Mouth Press, 1989.

—. "The Black Contribution to American Letters, Part II: The Writer as Activist (1966 and After)." In *The Black American Reference Book*, edited by Mabel M. Smythe. Englewood Cliffs, New Jersey: Prentice Hall, 1976.

—. "The Black Writer's Role, I: Richard Wright." In *Visions of a Liberated Future: Black Arts Movement Writings*. New York: Thunder's Mouth Press, 1989.

—. "The Black Writer's Role, II: Ellison's Zoot Suit." In *Visions of a Liberated Future: Black Arts Movement Writings*. New York: Thunder's Mouth Press, 1989.

—. "The Black Writer's Role, III: James Baldwin." In *Visions of a Liberated Future: Black Arts Movement Writings*. New York: Thunder's Mouth Press, 1989.

—. "The Black Writer's Role: Ralph Ellison." *Liberator* VI.I (January 1966): 9-11.

—. "Cultural Nationalism and Black Theatre/Two On Cruse: The View of the Black Intellectual." *Black Theatre* I (1968): 8-10.

—. "The Ethos of the Blues." In *Visions of a Liberated Future: Black Arts Movement Writings*. New York: Thunder's Mouth Press, 1989.

—. *The Glorious Monster in the Bell of the Horn*. *Callaloo #23*, 8, no. 1 (1985): 87-170.

—. "New Space: The Growth of Black Consciousness in the Sixties." In *The Black Seventies*, edited by Floyd Barbour. Boston: Porter Sargent Press, 1970. Cited in Paul Carter Harrison "Larry Neal: The Genesis of Vision". *Callaloo #23* 8, no. 1 (1985): 170-94.

—. *Hoodoo Hollerin' Bebop Ghosts*. Washington D.C.: Howard University Press, 1974.

—. "Kuntu." In *Visions of a Liberated Future: Black Arts Movement Writings*. New York: Thunder's Mouth Press, 1989.

—. "Rhythm is a Groove, #2." In *Hoodoo Hollerin' Bebop Ghosts*. Washington, D.C.: Howard University Press, 1974.

—. "The Social Background of the Black Arts Movement." *Black Scholar* (January/February 1987): 11-22.

—. "Some Reflections on the Black Aesthetic." In *The Black Aesthetic*, edited by Addison Gayle Jr.. Garden City, N.Y.: Doubleday and Company, 1971.

—. *Visions of a Liberated Future: Black Arts Movement Writings.* New York: Thunder's Mouth Press, 1989.

Oliver, Edith. "Post-Bellum." *New Yorker* LXV, no. 50 (January 29, 1990): 83.

Patai, Raphael. *Myth and Modern Man.* Englewood Cliffs, N.J.: Prentice Hall, 1972.

Pickard-Cambridge, Arthur Wallace. *Dramatic Festivals of Athens.* London: Oxford University Press, 1968.

Reck, Tom S. "Archetypes in LeRoi Jones' *Dutchman.*" *Studies in Black Literature* 1, no. 1 (Spring, 1970): 66-68.

Rowell, Charles H. "An Interview with Larry Neal." *Callaloo #23*, 8, no. 1 (1985): 11-35.

Savran, David. "Charles Fuller." In *In Their Own Words: Contemporary American Playwrights.* New York: Theatre Communications Group, 1988.

Scully, Vincent. *The Earth, The Temple, and the Gods: Greek Sacred Architecture.* New Haven: Yale University Press, 1962.

Seale, Bobby. *Seize the Time: The Story of the Black Panther Party and Huey P. Newton.* Baltimore, Md.: Black Classic Press, 1991.

Traylor. Eleanor W. "And the Resurrection, Let It Be Complete: The Achievement of Larry Neal (A Biobibliography of a Critical Imagination)." *Callaloo #23*, 8, no. 1 (1985): 36-70.

Walker, Alice. *In Search of Our Mother's Gardens: Womanist Prose.* San Diego, Calif.: Harcourt Brace Jovanovich, 1983.

Welsh-Asante, Kariamu. "The Aesthetic Conceptualization of Nzuri." In *The African Aesthetic: Keeper of the Traditions*, edited by Welsh-Asante. Westport, Conn.: Greenwood Press, 1993.

Williams, Mance. *Black Theater in the 1960s and 1970s: A Historical-Critical Analysis of the Movement.* Westport, Conn.: Greenwood Press, 1985.

Index